WORK AND FAMILY

Latin American and Caribbean Women
in Search of a New Balance

Laura Chioda

WORLD BANK GROUP

© 2016 International Bank for Reconstruction and Development / The World Bank
1818 H Street NW, Washington, DC 20433
Telephone: 202-473-1000; Internet: www.worldbank.org

Some rights reserved

1 2 3 4   18 17 16 15

This work is a product of the staff of The World Bank with external contributions. The findings, interpretations, and conclusions expressed in this work do not necessarily reflect the views of The World Bank, its Board of Executive Directors, or the governments they represent. The World Bank does not guarantee the accuracy of the data included in this work. The boundaries, colors, denominations, and other information shown on any map in this work do not imply any judgment on the part of The World Bank concerning the legal status of any territory or the endorsement or acceptance of such boundaries.

Nothing herein shall constitute or be considered to be a limitation upon or waiver of the privileges and immunities of The World Bank, all of which are specifically reserved.

ISBN (paper): 978-0-8213-8485-5
ISBN (electronic): 978-0-8213-9962-0
DOI: 10.1596/978-0-8213-8485-5

Cover image: © Florencia Micheltorena / World Bank. Further permission required for reuse.

Cover design: Bill Pragluski/Critical Stages

Library of Congress Cataloging-in-Publication Data

Names: Chioda, Laura, author.
Title: Work and family: Latin American & Caribbean women in search of a new balance / Laura Chioda, Office of the Chief Economist (LCRCE).
Description: Washington, D.C. : World Bank, 2016. | Includes bibliographical references and index.
Identifiers: LCCN 2015040500 (print) | LCCN 2015045964 (ebook) | ISBN 9780821384855 (alk. paper) | ISBN 9780821399620 (eISBN) | ISBN 9780821399620 ()
Subjects: LCSH: Women employees—Latin America. | Women—Employment—Latin America. | Women employees—Caribbean Area. | Women—Employment—Caribbean Area.
Classification: LCC HD5880.5.A6 C45 2016 (print) | LCC HD5880.5.A6 (ebook) | DDC 331.4098—dc23
LC record available at http://lccn.loc.gov/2015040500

Latin American Development Forum Series

This series was created in 2003 to promote debate, disseminate information and analysis, and convey the excitement and complexity of the most topical issues in economic and social development in Latin America and the Caribbean. It is sponsored by the Inter-American Development Bank, the United Nations Economic Commission for Latin America and the Caribbean, and the World Bank, and represents the highest quality in each institution's research and activity output. Titles in the series have been selected for their relevance to the academic community, policy makers, researchers, and interested readers, and have been subjected to rigorous anonymous peer review prior to publication.

Advisory Committee Members

Alicia Bárcena Ibarra, Executive Secretary, Economic Commission for Latin America and the Caribbean, United Nations

Inés Bustillo, Director, Washington Office, Economic Commission for Latin America and the Caribbean, United Nations

Augusto de la Torre, Chief Economist, Latin America and the Caribbean Region, World Bank

Daniel Lederman, Deputy Chief Economist, Latin America and the Caribbean Region, World Bank

Santiago Levy, Vice President for Sectors and Knowledge, Inter-American Development Bank

Roberto Rigobon, President, Latin American and Caribbean Economic Association

José Juan Ruiz, Chief Economist and Manager of the Research Department, Inter-American Development Bank

Ernesto Talvi, Director, Brookings Global-CERES Economic and Social Policy in Latin America Initiative

Andrés Velasco, Cieplan, Chile

Titles in the Latin American Development Forum Series

Work and Family: Latin American and Caribbean Women in Search of a New Balance (2015) by Laura Chioda

Great Teachers: How to Raise Student Learning in Latin America and the Caribbean (2014) by Barbara Bruns and Javier Luque

Entrepreneurship in Latin America: A Step Up the Social Ladder? (2013) by Eduardo Lora and Francesca Castellani, editors

Emerging Issues in Financial Development: Lessons from Latin America (2013) by Tatiana Didier and Sergio L. Schmukler, editors

New Century, Old Disparities: Gaps in Ethnic and Gender Earnings in Latin America and the Caribbean (2012) by Hugo Ñopo

Does What You Export Matter? In Search of Empirical Guidance for Industrial Policies (2012) by Daniel Lederman and William F. Maloney

From Right to Reality: Incentives, Labor Markets, and the Challenge of Achieving Universal Social Protection in Latin America and the Caribbean (2012) by Helena Ribe, David Robalino, and Ian Walker

Breeding Latin American Tigers: Operational Principles for Rehabilitating Industrial Policies (2011) by Robert Devlin and Graciela Moguillansky

New Policies for Mandatory Defined Contribution Pensions: Industrial Organization Models and Investment Products (2010) by Gregorio Impavido, Esperanza Lasagabaster, and Manuel García-Huitrón

The Quality of Life in Latin American Cities: Markets and Perception (2010) by Eduardo Lora, Andrew Powell, Bernard M. S. van Praag, and Pablo Sanguinetti, editors

Discrimination in Latin America: An Economic Perspective (2010) by Hugo Ñopo, Alberto Chong, and Andrea Moro, editors

The Promise of Early Childhood Development in Latin America and the Caribbean (2010) by Emiliana Vegas and Lucrecia Santibáñez

Job Creation in Latin America and the Caribbean: Trends and Policy Challenges (2009) by Carmen Pagés, Gaëlle Pierre, and Stefano Scarpetta

China's and India's Challenge to Latin America: Opportunity or Threat? (2009) by Daniel Lederman, Marcelo Olarreaga, and Guillermo E. Perry, editors

Does the Investment Climate Matter? Microeconomic Foundations of Growth in Latin America (2009) by Pablo Fajnzylber, José Luis Guasch, and J. Humberto López, editors

Measuring Inequality of Opportunities in Latin America and the Caribbean (2009) by Ricardo de Paes Barros, Francisco H. G. Ferreira, José R. Molinas Vega, and Jaime Saavedra Chanduvi

The Impact of Private Sector Participation in Infrastructure: Lights, Shadows, and the Road Ahead (2008) by Luis Andres, Jose Luis Guasch, Thomas Haven, and Vivien Foster

Remittances and Development: Lessons from Latin America (2008) by Pablo Fajnzylber and J. Humberto López, editors

Fiscal Policy, Stabilization, and Growth: Prudence or Abstinence? (2007) by Guillermo Perry, Luis Servén, and Rodrigo Suescún, editors

Raising Student Learning in Latin America: Challenges for the 21st Century (2007) by Emiliana Vegas and Jenny Petrow

Investor Protection and Corporate Governance: Firm-level Evidence Across Latin America (2007) by Alberto Chong and Florencio López-de-Silanes, editors

Natural Resources: Neither Curse nor Destiny (2007) by Daniel Lederman and William F. Maloney, editors

The State of State Reform in Latin America (2006) by Eduardo Lora, editor

Emerging Capital Markets and Globalization: The Latin American Experience (2006) by Augusto de la Torre and Sergio L. Schmukler

Beyond Survival: Protecting Households from Health Shocks in Latin America (2006) by Cristian C. Baeza and Truman G. Packard

Beyond Reforms: Structural Dynamics and Macroeconomic Vulnerability (2005) by José Antonio Ocampo, editor

Privatization in Latin America: Myths and Reality (2005) by Alberto Chong and Florencio López-de-Silanes, editors

Keeping the Promise of Social Security in Latin America (2004) by Indermit S. Gill, Truman G. Packard, and Juan Yermo

Lessons from NAFTA: For Latin America and the Caribbean (2004) by Daniel Lederman, William F. Maloney, and Luis Servén

The Limits of Stabilization: Infrastructure, Public Deficits, and Growth in Latin America (2003) by William Easterly and Luis Servén, editors

Globalization and Development: A Latin American and Caribbean Perspective (2003) by José Antonio Ocampo and Juan Martin, editors

Is Geography Destiny? Lessons from Latin America (2003) by John Luke Gallup, Alejandro Gaviria, and Eduardo Lora

Contents

PART III

Chapter 6: A Closer Look at Dynamics within the Household   179

Chapter 7: Concluding Remarks   217

Appendix: Background Papers   229

Index   231

Boxes

Figures

Tables

Foreword

Women are at the center of Latin American and Caribbean development today. Their impact on the creation of wealth, reduction of poverty, and improvement of opportunities for children is greater than at any time in history, placing them at the core of the region's hopes for progress.

Since 1980, nearly 80 million women have joined the labor market. More women in the region today work outside the home than not, narrowing the employment gap faster in LAC than in any other region in the developing world. We can expect these numbers to keep rising as young women enter and graduate from schools and universities in greater numbers than men.

These drastic reductions in gender disparities have grown out of and simultaneously feed into the region's efforts to broaden social equity, reduce poverty, and close social inequalities. Policies to eliminate discrimination, improve education of women, and increase access to services have paid off in ways not necessarily imagined.

Maternal mortality rates, for instance, have been declining continuously in the region since the 1980s, a direct consequence of better and improved access to services. In fact, those countries that previously had the highest rates of mortality have seen the most progress, with mortality dropping 40 percent in the Caribbean and 70 percent in the Andean region.

These advances don't mean differences between men and women in Latin America and the Caribbean have been overcome. Men and women continue to make decisions differently. The challenge for current and future leaders is to develop a more nuanced approach to gender issues that is better aware of this very different social environment.

In the twenty-first Century, more and more Latin American and Caribbean women will seek to fulfill the competing demands of work and family life. Understanding the conditions that affect their bargaining positions is therefore crucial to help them do so under less tension and pressures. Policies that help women find a better balance—through labor contracts that allow flexible leave and part-time arrangements, or regulations that better protect nonformal union—should be a rising priority for policy makers in the region.

Conditional cash transfer programs, pioneered in Latin America, are based on the assumption that money in the hands of women is spent differently and benefits children more. With the exception of these programs, however, household interactions are seldom exploited in policy design.

This latest regional study on gender comes, then, at a very important time, and will help shed light on how best to respond and support women as they attempt to reconcile their "new" roles and identities and better meet their aspirations.

Jorge Familiar
Vice President
Latin America and Caribbean Region
The World Bank

Acknowledgments

Work and Family: Latin American and Caribbean Women in Search of a New Balance is the product of a larger research project of the World Bank's Latin America and the Caribbean region on gender issues, intrahousehold dynamics, and labor market outcomes.

A product of the Office of the Chief Economist, the report was developed and prepared by Laura Chioda, under the patient direction of Augusto de la Torre. It builds on several background papers by economists in and outside the World Bank. It benefited from the support of Louise Cord. Outstanding and tireless research assistance was provided by Felipe Avilés Lucero, Florencia Paz Cazzaniga, and Eliana Rubiano Matulevich.

Background papers were prepared by Tami Aritomi, Orazio Attanasio, Gustavo Bobonis, Mariano Bosch, Mirela Carvalho, Roberto Castro, Laura Chioda, Gabriel Demombynes, Alejandro Hoyos, Valérie Lechene, Trine Lunde, William Maloney, José Montes, Hugo Ñopo, Analia Olgiati, Pedro Olinto, Maria Beatriz Orlando, Ricardo Paes de Barros, and Nistha Sinha. We are very grateful for their original and outstanding contributions, as well as many insightful discussions.

This report is the result of a long process set in motion by María Beatriz Orlando and Jaime Saavedra. It draws in part on draft paper, *Linking Labor Market Outcomes and Intra-Household Dynamics*, prepared by Laura Chioda, Rodrigo García-Verdú, and Ana Maria Muñoz Boudet (2010) for internal circulation.

The team is particularly indebted to William Maloney for his unwavering support and dedicated readings of early versions of the report and for his extensive and insightful suggestions, which contributed to shaping our thinking on the subject, and ultimately the final report.

The report also benefited from invaluable and insightful conversations with Tito Cordella, Tatiana Didier, Makhtar Diop, Francisco Ferreira, John Newman, Ana Revenga, and Sudhir Shetty. We also thank our peer reviewers, Suzanne Duryea, Alessandra Fogli, Andrew Mason, and Emmanuel Skoufias for their feedback on an early draft. Comments and advice of two anonymous referees are gratefully acknowledged.

Erika Bazan Lavanda, Ruth Delgado, Anne Pillay, and Ane Castro provided excellent production assistance. We are thankful to Joaquin Urrego, Magali Pinat and Liliana Lazo for preparation of the manuscript. We acknowledge the outstanding support and expert advice of the external communication regional team for the report's publication and dissemination, with particular thanks to Marcela Sanchez-Bender for her patient help. We would like to thank Pat Katayama and Kia Penso for their generous help and patience during the production process. Finally, the report was expertly edited by Bruce Ross-Larson and his team.

Abbreviations

CCT	conditional cash transfer
ECH	Encuesta Continua de Hogares
GDP	gross domestic product
IPUMS	Integrated Public Use Microdata Series
LAC	Latin America and the Caribbean
LFP	labor force participation
MBA	master of business administration
MDG	Millennium Development Goal
OECD	Organisation for Economic Co-operation and Development
PISA	Program for International Student Assessment
SEDLAC	Socio-Economic Database for Latin America and the Caribbean

Overview

Four decades of important achievements

As a region, Latin America and the Caribbean (LAC) has witnessed remarkable achievements toward gender parity over the past four decades. Women and girls have made important strides in several key areas, including but not limited to education and health.

By the early 1990s, girls had closed the gap and now outperform boys on a number of education indicators. Girls today are more likely than boys to be enrolled in secondary and tertiary schooling and are also more likely to complete both. A significant portion of these achievements is due to girls' increased attainment at the higher levels of education.

Nevertheless, the progress has not been homogeneous. Although school enrollment rates of young boys and girls (ages 6–11) are largely equal across the region, where present, gaps tend to favor girls. An important exception concerns the indigenous populations of Belize, Bolivia, and Guatemala, where boys' enrollment still exceeds that of girls by significant amounts. Despite the regional trend of girls outperforming boys in secondary enrollment, boys ages 12–14 still exceed girls on this measure in roughly half of the countries under study, with the gap being in excess of 6 percentage points in Guatemala and Bolivia.[1] The heterogeneity across countries in attainment, however, is less pronounced than for enrollment. Girls complete more years of schooling and progress through school more efficiently in most countries. Among the exceptions are Guatemala, Bolivia, Mexico, and Peru, where the years of schooling gap has not yet closed (Marshall and Calderón 2006).

Advances in gender parity in health have similarly been remarkable in LAC. Whereas other regions such as South Asia and Europe and Central Asia exhibit sex imbalances—wherein the proportion of males in the total population exceeds that of females by wide (and often unnatural) margins—the female share of the total population in LAC has been above 50 percent and has risen steadily since the 1960s.

1

This trend is indicative of girls' "wantedness" in the region, and stands in contrast with evidence of parental preferences for males in South Asia, for instance. It is also a reflection of increased investments in the health of girls and women as well as of better access to effective health care. These improvements have led to longer lives for both men and women, though life expectancy has risen faster for women than for men. Whereas men lived only four years less than women in 1960, women now outlive men by more than six years. Improvements in women's life expectancy in LAC are also the result of a continued decline in maternal mortality since the 1980s. The most dramatic declines have been in those subregions with the highest initial levels of maternal mortality, that is, Caribbean and Andean countries, where the incidence of maternal mortality fell by approximately 40 percent and 70 percent, respectively, since 1980.

Perhaps one of the most dramatic changes for women in LAC has been the rapid decline in fertility rates, which have converged to those of high-income OECD countries. In 1960, women in LAC had on average six births, compared to three in Organisation for Economic Co-operation and Development (OECD) countries. By 2012, births per woman had fallen to 1.66 in the OECD and to 2.18 in LAC. Although the downward trend in LAC was experienced regionwide, the degree and timing of the decline was heterogeneous. Two distinct patterns emerge. In one group of relatively higher income countries (including Brazil, Chile, Colombia, Costa Rica, and Panama), the fertility rate fell sharply in the early 1970s, declining at a slower pace thereafter. In contrast, a group of lower income countries (including Ecuador, El Salvador, Haiti, and Paraguay) experienced a more muted and gradual downward trend throughout.[2]

Accompanying the strides toward gender parity in education and health has been an unprecedented growth in female labor force participation (LFP), with nearly 80 million additional women entering the labor force since 1980. Three decades ago, only 36 percent of working-age women was in the labor force. Since then, female labor force participation in LAC has risen faster than in any other region of the world. Today, about 54 percent of working-age women are active in the labor market, and they represent roughly 40 percent of the entire labor force in the region. In most countries, the rate of female LFP has at least doubled since the 1960s, even tripling in Brazil. The expanded professional engagement of women in society has also translated into higher participation in politics, with the share of parliamentary seats held by women in LAC reaching nearly 25 percent, only marginally below that of high-income OECD countries (27 percent). Although female representation in parliaments is on the rise regionwide, it remains unevenly distributed across countries: it is less than 10 percent in Belize, Brazil, Haiti, and Panama, but exceeds 30 percent in Argentina, Costa Rica, Ecuador, Mexico, and Nicaragua.

The gains made by women in LAC have taken place in a context of important strides toward broader social equity, as reflected by significant reductions in poverty (about 68 million Latin Americans have risen above moderate poverty since 2003) and income inequality (12 out of the sample of 17 countries in the region experienced a decline in Gini coefficients), and a simultaneous rise in the share of people in the middle classes (from 20 to 30 percent, as measured by the proportion of people making more than $10 a day on a purchasing power-adjusted basis).[3]

New challenges for women and policy makers

In light of the region's remarkable achievements over the past four decades, one may be tempted to conclude that the gains in access mechanically translate into gains in labor market outcomes and that welfare can be unequivocally inferred from these trends. The findings in this study caution against such simplistic views and urge a more complete understanding of women's decision making to improve the design and efficacy of policy.

A number of patterns substantiate that point. The relationship between economic development and female economic participation is neither linear nor monotonic. Empirical evidence consistently points to a U-shaped relationship between female LFP and development, as measured by a country's income per capita. Female LFP initially declines as per capita income rises then eventually increases again (though not necessarily linearly) at higher levels of development. Different subgroups of women are drawn into the labor force at different times and in a heterogeneous fashion. In particular, single women enter the labor force at earlier stages of development than their married counterparts, with their behavior mimicking that of men; married women then follow—as social norms and adherence to traditional roles soften—in degrees that vary with their characteristics, including their level of education, cohort, and family structure.

The heterogeneity in labor market behaviors of women with different levels of education draws attention to the futility of simplistic mappings between the widening opportunities of women arising from gains in health and education and from economic development, on the one hand, and specific labor market outcomes, on the other. For example, marriage in LAC tends to be associated with a sizable drop in labor market participation. However, highly educated married women exhibit more attachment to the labor force than those with primary or secondary education, likely because they tend to view work as more of a career than just a source of income. At the other extreme, married women with less than primary education likewise have stronger ties to the labor force but for very different reasons, as they are likely compelled to work by need, rather than by choice. However, the presence of children in the household is associated with greater exits from the labor force among women with tertiary education—who are less likely to face budget constraints—than among women with less than primary education.

Likewise, the largest gender wage gaps appear at the bottom and top deciles of the earnings distribution, suggesting another nonmonotonic and possibly U-shaped relationship between human capital and labor market outcomes. Indeed, evidence from developed countries shows that among elite professionals, a wage gap emerges at the onset of fertility, with women's wages lagging behind those of men by substantial amounts. Moreover the wage penalties from shorter work hours and career interruptions that are related to motherhood are positively associated with their husband's level of income, suggesting that spousal income affords women the ability to reduce their labor supply.

Among those countries in LAC for which gender wage gaps can be constructed, three of the four that had not yet closed the education gap—Peru in the early 1990s and Mexico and Guatemala in 2007—exhibit a pattern of wage differentials that surprisingly favors women at the bottom of the income distribution. That is, among the lowest wage earners in these countries, women earn more than men. Despite this advantage over their male counterparts, arguing that such women are better off is difficult because their wage premium may act as a disincentive to pursuing further education, which may in turn explain part of the education gaps.

These and other findings documented in this report caution against a mechanical view of the relationship between equalization of access and labor market outcomes, and draw attention to how measures of participation offer only a partial view of welfare. The findings also point to the importance of understanding the role of mediating factors that enter the decision-making process underlying the economic behavior of women.

Expanded choice set, emergence of new identities, household dynamics, and new tensions

This study acknowledges the evidence discussed above and sheds light on the complex relationship between stages of economic development and female economic participation, and in line with recent research, it argues that female LFP cannot simply be described by an earnings-maximizing motive. Rather, it shows that the interactions of microeconomic and social factors such as human capital (for example, education, health, work experience, and skills), social norms, preferences, and household structure and dynamics are essential mediators that shape the economic opportunities and decisions of women regarding economic participation. By extension, these factors are likewise key determinants of women's well-being, weakening the validity of welfare assessments made exclusively on the basis of women's labor market outcomes. As development progresses and as advances are made in the equality of access agenda—by way of increased human capital accumulation, softening of social norms, or structural changes in the economy (for example, as the tertiary and public sectors gain more importance in the economy)—the set of options available to women expands.

The evidence and analysis in the report ties the historical process of female economic integration and widening choice sets to a fundamental change in paradigm in women's decision making (Goldin 2006). This paradigmatic transformation includes a shift in the horizon over which women's human capital investments yield returns and, consequently, in their attachment to the labor market. It also includes a contemporaneous shift in women's perceptions whereby they consider their work a fundamental part of their identity, which is related to the distinction between jobs and careers.

Careers that were once penalized by social norms or were unattainable because of the lack of education are now within reach for an increasing number of women in LAC. And, as elsewhere in the world, women's identities have ceased to be unequivocally tied to their families, as recounted by Goldin (2004, 21), on the U.S. experience:

It was about fifteen to twenty years ago that I first began to realize that college women as a group were talking about their futures in ways that would have been unimaginable to me when I was in college. They spoke, candidly and honestly, of "CAREERANDFAMILY" ... as if the words were not three but one.

In LAC in the 1960s, marital status—rather than the presence of children in the household—predicted women's status in the labor force almost perfectly, with married women withdrawing from the labor force and becoming homemakers. This dichotomy has softened somewhat since the 1970s, though the case remains that marriage is associated with significant exits of women from the labor force, and these effects are much larger than—nearly threefold—those associated with fertility. The major gains in labor force participation are concentrated among younger cohorts and more educated women, who increasingly remain in the labor force upon marriage. Social norms play an important role in explaining these trends. As illustrated in the report, discriminatory views regarding women in professional spheres have attenuated considerably, although beliefs about traditional gender roles within the household, which are less susceptible to change, have remained relatively stable. Women, who continue to value family and caring for their children, assign increasing importance to work. As a result, their struggle to negotiate a balance of family and career intensifies.

The challenge for research is, of course, to disentangle preferences from social norms, given that the latter are embedded in the former, though recent experiments suggest that preferences may also reflect more fundamental, biological differences independent of learned behaviors and early socialization (for example, difference in brain functioning).

Irrespective of the relative importance of norms and preferences, a central message of this study is the critical role played by family formation in shaping female LFP. Family structure and household dynamics affect a woman's valuation and perception of jobs as multidimensional bundles of characteristics, rather as a one-dimensional source of income. Household characteristics and dynamics shape her decision to enter the labor force, as well as the choice of occupation and whether it is in the formal or informal sector. It is mainly at the onset of family formation that gaps between men and women emerge and that preexisting ones accentuate.

Indeed, the relationship between female economic participation, economic development, and welfare is made more complex by the acknowledgment that individuals are part of larger economic units—families. Whatever the reasons for family formation—be they the result of evolution, or of Beckerian-type motives to take advantage of complementarities in consumption and economies of scale in the provision of household goods, or of Maslowian-type desires to achieve a sense of belonging that enhances intrinsic values and meets the aspirations of social relatedness—intrahousehold interactions play a central role in determining welfare and the efficiency and equity of outcomes. As a result, intrahousehold interactions define new margins for gender policy interventions and objectives that acknowledge the context of the household.

The importance of the family as a mediator of female economic participation and welfare results in large part from the recognition that men and women, while equal in dignity and fundamental rights, differ along important dimensions, beyond the obvious relative physical advantages in fertility.

Indeed, a mounting body of evidence rejects the hypothesis that men's and women's attitudes and preferences—and thus their choices—are identical. As a result, economic models that are appropriate for explaining male LFP have been adapted to accommodate gender differences in labor market decisions. This report documents evidence that risk-taking behavior and preferences over job attributes, for instance, are distinct across the sexes. Women are more risk averse than men and thus less inclined to seek positions that involve risk (physical or otherwise), or that involve a very competitive environment. These differences help explain certain disparities observed in the labor market, ranging from wage gaps to occupational choices. But the effects of gender differences in preferences are not limited to the labor market; they also manifest themselves within the household. Studies have shown that, among two-parent households, larger shares of resources controlled by women lead to larger budget shares spent on children's clothing, education, and health (Doepke and Tertilt 2011).

It is therefore inside the household that divergences of opinion, preferences, and comparative advantages are negotiated to reach decisions regarding the division of labor, child care responsibilities, home versus market production, and so on. In some cases, intrahousehold interactions can yield efficient specialization among spouses, such that both spouses do not have the same degrees of engagement in the labor force. In other instances, the resulting allocation of resources maybe inefficient, reflecting noncooperative behaviors.

Women in search of a balance

When I was at work ... I always felt I was shortchanging the girls. But when I was at home, I was worried that I was letting people at work down.

—*Michelle Obama*

Over the past four decades, social changes have increased the opportunities available to women. A standard economic framework would suggest that these expanded choice sets would unambiguously result in increased welfare. However, as women's goals and identities expand, so do the opportunities for trade-offs and tensions between potentially competing aspirations, some of which have received increasing attention in the literature.

Despite the extraordinary progress of women in the United States over recent decades, measures of subjective well-being indicate that women's happiness has declined both in absolute terms and relative to men, leading to the emergence of a new gender gap favoring men (Stevenson and Wolfers 2007). Recent research has also drawn attention to another form of trade-off, this time operating across generations (Bernal 2008; Morrill 2011). Under certain circumstances, maternal employment may be associated to lower child health and cognitive outcomes, suggesting that the additional income may not compensate fully for the reduction in time investments in children, particularly during the early and critical stages of human development.

This evidence illustrates a new set of tensions and challenges for women, which paradoxically have been made possible by four decades of steady gains. Understanding the nature and sources of tensions for women trying to balance work and family is thus crucial for policy. Today, married women in LAC still participate less in the labor market than their single counterparts, and although having children in the household is associated with comparatively smaller reductions in the likelihood of participation, it does influence sectoral occupations (for example, whether to work in the public or the private sectors or opt for informal work arrangements) and the intensity of labor supply (for example, whether to work full or part time).

Establishing whether adherence to traditional gender roles determines these behaviors, or whether they result instead from an efficient division of labor among spouses, is a difficult task empirically because social norms inform and shape preferences. Nevertheless, some insights can be gleaned from the fact that similar behaviors also surface in developed countries, including among those with gender-friendly labor market institutions (such as northern European countries). Even highly educated women appear to draw on their spouse's income to accommodate reductions in their labor supply when starting a family and to sort into sectors and occupations where experience premiums are forgone in exchange for greater flexibility.

Furthermore, the use of the relatively abundant resource (that is, time) when flexible arrangements are taken advantage of is akin to women's behavior in response to receipt of a conditional cash transfer. Giving women increased control over resources (in the form of income, education, or assets) leads to greater expenditures on their children's health, nutrition, education, and clothing. With low-income women spending additional resources on their children, it is by extension not surprising that women's time use (that is, their labor supply) is responsive to family formation and that women place a premium on flexible arrangements that are more forgiving of temporary work interruptions that result from child rearing.

The struggle to achieve work-life balance reflects the tension exerted by women's identities as mothers and workers, a phenomenon that has informally been given the name "mothers' guilt." In LAC, men and women, whose views about traditional gender roles have remained virtually unchanged since 1990, tend to believe that young children are likely to suffer if their mothers work. However, younger and more educated women often deem that a woman's identity extends beyond her role as a housewife and that working mothers can have just as healthy a relationship with their children as stay-at-home mothers. These seemingly contradictory beliefs among women are precisely an expression of the tension between the roles and identities they struggle to reconcile.

An interesting and discernible, yet lagged, parallel exists between the labor force experiences of women in LAC and those of women in the United States. Specifically, the evolution of labor force participation of single and married women in LAC has closely mimicked that of U.S. women, though with a 30-year lag. If the analogy to the U.S. experience is extended, the history of women's experiences in the United States could provide a glimpse into the future for LAC, a future that may come sooner than 30 years, given the region's current pace of change.

After a century of remarkable gains in economic engagement, female LFP started to level off in the United States in the late 1990s, despite continued advances in educational attainment. Given that the LFP of college-educated women had almost reached parity with that of men in the mid-1990s, this change in trend was particularly disappointing for the women's movement. The phenomenon was characterized in the popular press as one of "opting out" (Belkin 2003; Story 2005; Wallis 2004)—driven in part by a negative backlash from the workplace that made it difficult for women to reconcile their dual identities as homemaker and career woman. Among the professional and managerial ranks, where higher incomes afforded a wider range of choices, women became more reluctant to juggle their roles as executives and mothers and were more willing to forgo paychecks and prestige in favor of time with their families. It is conceivable that a similar phenomenon may occur in LAC in the coming decades.

This sentiment was well articulated by Regan Penaluna in Walravens's (2010, 159) account of "torn" women:

My parents raised us with the belief that we could be anything we wanted if we only put our mind to it and now my sister found herself of two minds: she wanted to be a mother raising her baby, but she also wanted to be a successful scientist. Like many modern mothers, myself included, she could not do one without feeling as though she was significantly short changing the other.

Striking the right balance between work and family is perhaps one of the most demanding tasks facing women in developed economies and a rising challenge in emerging economies. In the decades to come, any expansion of female labor force participation in the region will disproportionately be concentrated among married women. If LAC continues to follow in the footsteps of the United States, we might also expect these trends to level off (and perhaps even revert slightly). More important, the number of women attempting to balance career and family is destined to rise, such that a set of well-targeted, forward-looking policies may help alleviate the juggling act between professional and traditional identities.

Evidence discussed in the report surrounding the introduction of universal child care and labor market reforms illustrate women's quest to balance work and family. A recurrent finding across several studies in LAC and OECD countries is that the public provision of child care invariably results in high take-up rates but not in higher maternal LFP rates. The apparent demand for formal child care services seems driven largely by substitution out of existing arrangements, with women already in the labor force switching from informal child care arrangements (for example, agreements with extended family members) to the publicly provided (formal) alternative. Similarly, in response to Argentina's legalization of part-time work in 1995, a large fraction of married women with children rapidly transitioned from informal work to formal part-time jobs, without any appreciable effect on aggregate female participation.

Although some may view the absence of gains in participation as discouraging or disappointing, the results in this report lend themselves to a more optimistic interpretation. At least in the short run, access to child care and the lack of formal and flexible work options do not represent barriers to entry into the (formal or informal) labor force. These policies—introduction of universal child care and labor market reforms—nonetheless have the potential to raise female LFP in long run.[4]

Policy discussion

Today, the complex environment requires women to balance different roles, identities, and aspirations. Jobs, careers, and family place competing demands on women's time and attention, more so than at any other time, and pose new challenges for them and for policy makers. Gender policy in LAC is at a crucial juncture that calls for an expansion of the policy perspective.

This challenge is in large part the product of success, for substantial progress—amply documented in this study—has been made toward achieving gender parity in key dimensions relating to human dignity, particularly access to basic services (for example, health and education) and fundamental human rights. These achievements are welcome, as they implicate universal principles that should apply to all humans, independently of gender, race, and religion.

Nevertheless, the policy goal of gender parity with respect to basic rights and services has not been fully or uniformly reached across the region. Much room for improvement remains, particularly where chronic poverty is intertwined with precarious access and where certain institutional arrangements and social norms breed systematic barriers for women. But the improvements in the circumstances of women in

LAC over the past decades are undeniable and call for a reassessment and expansion of the policy focus.

The first generation of gender policies in LAC tended to set quantitative objectives for gender parity—focusing not only on equal access (for example, to health, education, and judicial services) but also on equality in certain outcomes (for example, equal pay for comparable experience and skills, or equal participation in the labor force, in electoral ballots, or in congressional seats). This focus is appropriate to the extent that societies are trapped in inefficient and inequitable equilibria characterized by discrimination and abuse of women. In such a context, quantitative gender parity targets established to monitor achievements can help societies break free from an unfair status quo.

But as the standing of women improves and their opportunities and choices widen—as is happening in LAC—new issues, tensions, and challenges arise. They point to the need for a second generation of gender policies, one that would still encompass certain (more focused) quantitative targets for gender parity but also would go well beyond them.

The evidence and analysis presented in this study indicate that women in LAC confront competing demands for their time and energy as, on the one hand, they join the labor force and increasingly see employment as part of a career (rather than a simple source of income) and on the other hand, they seek self-actualization through marriage, motherhood, and family. These complexities have to be brought to the center stage of policy design.

Of course no one-size-fits-all policy agenda exists that is well suited to these changing gender realities. Reform agendas have to be adapted to the contexts of individual countries. But the evidence examined in this study suggests at least three key directions for the new generation of policies.

> The highest equality is equity.
> —*Victor Hugo*

First and foremost is the need to revise gender policies' *goals and expectations*. This step follows naturally from the recognition that the equalization across genders of access to basic services and fundamental human rights translates neither mechanically nor monotonically into the equalization of outcomes, such as the extent and modality of female economic participation. Nor are outcomes a perfect reflection of well-being.

The ascribed role of preferences, household relationships, institutions, and social mores as mediating factors invites change in policy perspective from *gender parity* (which is akin to gender blindness) to *gender consciousness*. In turn, gender consciousness entails an emphasis on equity over equality. While equality implies sameness and, by definition, ignores differences, equity recognizes differences and engages them to facilitate the realization of each person's potential to the fullest extent possible—to which gender consciousness aspires.

The emphasis on equity sets the stage for policies that expand women's freedom, in particular the freedom to choose one's identity and to exercise that choice without facing discrimination or disadvantage. The ability of a person to choose, do, and be can be seen as an essential determinant of well-being. These principles are at the heart of Sen's notion of development as the process of enhancing substantive freedoms, and of an approach to development that:

...concentrates on the capabilities of people to do things—and the freedom to live lives— that they have reason to value.

—*Amartya Sen*

Second, acknowledging that men and women differ in substantive ways and that their differences are mediated through interactions within the household has important policy implications and yields an *expanded menu of policies* to address gender issues. These new policies have the potential not only to affect equity of allocations within the household, but also to increase effectiveness of policy instruments and ultimately elevate the discussion regarding their welfare implications. With the notable exception of conditional cash transfers, which are designed on the presumption that money in the hands of women is spent differently, household interactions are seldom exploited in the design of policy. The unexploited richness of (gender) policy instruments represents a missed opportunity that needs correction, by embedding in policy design certain insights on household dynamics.

As discussed in the report, in some cases, intrahousehold interactions can yield efficient allocations of resources, with both spouses gaining from cooperation. In such instances, policy interventions would be justified only on equity grounds. In noncooperative households, in turn, inefficient or destructive outcomes, or both, may arise, as in the extreme instance of domestic violence, justifying policy interventions on both equity and efficiency grounds. This discussion emphasizes the value of understanding the types of conditions that affect bargaining positions within the household and that have the potential to curb abusive and nonconsensual behaviors.

Whether directed at women by design or not, any government intervention that may influence women's control over fertility, their ability to choose a spouse with certain characteristics, their realized and potential labor market outcomes, and so on, can affect the bargaining positions of women within the household and thus the final allocation of resources. Bargaining positions of spouses and their subsequent interactions are affected not only by each spouse's direct control over resources (income, time, or otherwise), but also by their prospects outside of the union, should they leave marriage. Credible exit options raise the incentives for nonconflictual, respectful behavior within existing unions. These policies can thus contribute to reducing the risk of abusive relationships as well as to widening the scope for self-realization of women within the household. Hence, the expanded menu of policies could extend to reforms that include the provision of social insurance, the legal definition of informal unions (for example, unmarried cohabitation) and their corresponding parental obligations, the introduction of antidiscrimination laws, any regulation that directly or indirectly affects sectors or occupations dominated by one gender, the modernization of divorce laws, and the enhancement of property rights and even criminal laws.

Balancing work and family is one of the country's major challenges. The government wants to change labor laws that have companies help bear the cost of daycare, making women more expensive to hire.
—*Carolina Schmidt, Chile's Minister of National Women's Service*
(telephone interview)

Third, this study documents women's need for greater freedom to choose their identities, which manifests itself as an *unmet demand for flexibility*. This puts a premium on policies that help women find an equilibrium among competing demands. Women's ability to balance their new identities with traditional responsibilities is full of challenges. Whether it is with regard to child care choices or to part-time employment opportunities, an unmet demand for flexibility consistently emerges among women who are married with a family or who have children. Unfortunately, formal labor market institutions are still woefully insensitive to these realities. Although some (albeit limited) progress has been made in LAC in terms of regulations concerning maternity leave and the provision of child care services, for instance, formal labor contracts remain unduly rigid compared with women's needs. In the short run, these rigidities do not appear to prevent women from entering the labor force; however, all too often married women in LAC resort to informal employment and trade basic labor protections and career advancement for the job flexibility that facilitates balancing family responsibilities.

Legislation that acknowledges the pressures of motherhood, and of the day-to-day demands on households' time more generally, can generate important social returns by enabling women to fulfill their identities as mothers and workers, raising the quality of their economic participation, and thereby increasing their well-being as well as that of the entire household.

Notably, the welfare consequences of the aforementioned policies may not be limited to the short run. Interventions that alleviate the burden on working mothers and facilitate balancing work and life can afford parents the possibility of higher-quality parenting. Providing flexible alternatives that don't compromise working mothers' career objectives may attenuate the stress exerted by such trade-offs, which have been implicated in the recent emergence of a gap in subjective well-being that favors men in certain industrialized countries. Furthermore, invoking such institutions to foster a healthy equilibrium between work and family can mitigate some of the intergenerational costs that might arise from maternal employment in the event that the children's health and development benefit from time spent with their mothers.

Hence, a key policy message from this study concerns the need to revisit labor market institutions and regulations from the gender-conscious perspective, which focuses on welfare-enhancing flexibility. Any policy aimed at addressing the new set of issues facing women has to wrestle with (and ideally take advantage of) the fact that women's outcomes in the labor market—including whether or not to work, how much to work if so, and how to combine work and family—are the result of unobservable household negotiations that depend to a significant extent on individual preferences regarding work and family. Two women who are outside of the labor market may be so for very different reasons, which a gender-conscious policy should detect. One may have simply decided to invest more time and energy in her children while taking advantage of her spouse's income. The other may prefer to work but the lack of flexible contracts in the formal labor market renders it unfeasible for her to fulfill her desired roles in both motherhood and the professional realm. Labor market outcomes alone are not always informative about welfare, because they distinguish only imperfectly between unhindered decisions and institutional barriers (such as discrimination, rigidity in the labor market, social norms, and so on). In this context, policy can play a role by guaranteeing an environment that is devoid of discrimination and provide a richer menu of options in the labor market that recognizes the trade-offs that women face (as their choices widen) in the pursuit of self-realization.

Notes

[1] Among adolescents ages 15–19, wide gaps favor girls in some countries (for example, in Honduras, Nicaragua, Panama, and Uruguay, girls' school enrollment outpaces that of boys by more than 6.5 percentage points), whereas such gaps favor boys in others (for example, Bolivia, Guatemala, and Haiti).

[2] The decline in fertility rates among adolescents has also been heterogeneous across countries in the region. For example, adolescent fertility rates have declined sharply in El Salvador and Belize by about 33 and 35 percent, respectively, since 1998. By contrast, in Nicaragua, the Dominican Republic, and Guatemala, teenage pregnancy remains stubbornly high, with 1 out of every 10 teenage girls being a mother, matching the levels of Sub-Saharan Africa.

[3] Although the share of female-headed households in LAC has risen, contrary to popular understanding, these households do not appear to be at a higher risk of poverty.

[4] These policies can affect female LFP in the long run by increasing the quality of life of working mothers and, implicitly, by improving the quality of their children's care if the daughters of working mothers are themselves more likely to work and if their sons become more accepting of women in the workforce. Such a mechanism would thus operate across generations and yield an intergenerational multiplier effect (see Fernández, Fogli, and Olivetti 2004).

References

Belkin, Lisa. 2003. "The Opt-Out Revolution." *New York Times Magazine*, October 26.
Bernal, Raquel. 2008. "The Effect of Maternal Employment and Child Care on Children's Cognitive Development." *International Economic Review* 49: 1173–209.

Doepke, Matthias, and Michèle Tertilt. 2011. "Does Female Empowerment Promote Economic Development?" IZA Discussion Paper 5637, Institute for the Study of Labor, Bonn, Germany.

Fernández, Raquel, Alessandra Fogli, and Claudia Olivetti. 2004. "Preference Formation and the Rise of Women's Labor Force Participation: Evidence from WWII." NBER Working Paper 10589, National Bureau of Economic Research, Cambridge, MA.

Goldin, Claudia. 2004. "The Long Road to the Fast Track: Career and Family." *Annals of the American Academy of Political and Social Science* 596 (1): 20–35.

———. 2006. "Quiet Revolution That Transformed Women's Employment, Education, and Family." *American Economic Review Papers and Proceedings* 96 (2): 1–21.

Marshall, Jeffery H., and Valentina Calderón. 2006. "Social Exclusion in Education in Latin America and the Caribbean." Technical Papers Series, Inter-American Development Bank, Washington, DC.

Morrill, Melinda Sandler. 2011. "The Effects of Maternal Employment on the Health of School-Age Children." *Journal of Health Economics* 30 (2): 240–57.

Stevenson, Betsey, and Justin Wolfers. 2009. "The Paradox of Declining Female Happiness." *American Economic Journal: Economic Policy* 1 (2): 190–225.

Story, Louise. 2005. "Many Women at Elite Colleges Set Career Path to Motherhood." *New York Times*, September 20.

Wallis, Claudia. 2004. "The Case for Staying Home." *Time Magazine*, March 22.

Walravens, Samantha. 2010. *Torn: True Stories of Kids, Career, and the Conflict of Modern Motherhood*. Seattle, WA: Coffeetown Press.

Introduction: The Household Point of View

Background

Over recent decades the Latin America and the Caribbean (LAC) region has seen a dramatic and virtually uninterrupted rise in female labor force participation (LFP). Women in LAC have increased their participation faster than in any other region of the world, adding nearly 80 million women to the labor force. This evolution occurred in the context of more general progress in women's status. Female enrollment rates in primary through tertiary education have increased to the point of closing or even reversing the gender gap that traditionally favored boys. Family structures have changed markedly, and fertility rates have started to decline. And social norms have shifted toward gender equality.

This report argues that all of those changes are interrelated and need to be studied as such. Traditional explanations for low LFP, and for the patterns of employment once women join the workforce, have focused on discrimination or low human capital accumulation. In these views, the policies for generating more opportunities for women focus on labor market institutions or on the quantity and quality of human capital investments. However, the recent literature in developed countries has stressed the role and interaction of microsocial factors in determining economic opportunities available to women and, by extension, the evolution of female economic participation (such as LFP, sectoral choices, and family formation).[1] These microsocial factors include human capital[2] (education and health), social norms and preferences, and family formation and household structure (figure I.1).

FIGURE I.1: Key microsocial determinants of female economic participation

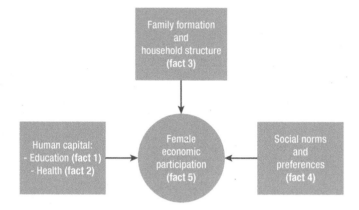

This report views the evolution of female participation through this microlens, drawing on the emerging literature on family formation (marriage and fertility) and household structure, including intrahousehold bargaining.[3] While not negating or dismissing the ongoing agenda of ensuring equal opportunity in the workplace, this approach shifts the focus to household dynamics and decisions about schooling, the allocation of work within the household, and the kinds of jobs each household member should seek.[4] It thus provides a powerful framework for interpreting the evolution of gender-related patterns.

The framework highlights the importance of understanding how household decisions are made, since different models of the household yield divergent implications for interactions between spouses, for the distribution of resources and its associated welfare, and for the relevant policy margins.[5]

The chapter begins by reviewing current thinking on household dynamics and on interactions between spouses. It then introduces changes in human capital investments, family formation and household characteristics, social norms, and economic participation.

Labor force participation: From an individual to a collective decision

The standard neoclassical view of the family and labor supply explains LFP in terms of the costs and benefits of participation in the labor market. It emphasizes the quantity and quality of human capital investments and considers how they translate into economic participation. In recent years, however, several authors have argued that female LFP cannot simply be captured by an earnings-maximizing rationale.

This newer literature relates the historical process of women's economic integration to three aspects of women's decision making:

- The horizon over which women's human capital investments yield returns, which depends on whether their involvement in the labor force is long and continuous or short and intermittent

- The extent to which women consider their work a fundamental part of their identity, which is related to the distinction between jobs and careers

- The way women's LFP decisions are made within the household: jointly (possibly through bargaining between spouses) or only after men have made their labor force decisions[6]

The interplay of these three considerations is thought to underlie one of the most widely recognized and uncontroversial stylized facts about female economic participation: the U-shaped relationship between women's LFP and economic development.[7] Similar considerations are not prominent in the economic literature on male LFP, which focuses mainly on the traditional trade-off between leisure and labor, the returns to education, and the potential for earnings.

The leading theory behind the U-shaped relationship starts with the observation that, in very poor countries, female economic participation is high, with women working mainly in farm or nonfarm family enterprises. The first stage of development is associated with a reduction in female LFP, partly because of the rise in men's market opportunities and partly because social barriers constrain women from entering the paid labor force. These barriers can take the form of social norms or even discrimination (Goldin 1995).

As countries continue growing, the development process is associated with investments in human capital, which increase women's education. These gains make staying at home more costly, not only through a traditionally positive return to education, but also as the increase in human capital makes available job opportunities that were previously socially unacceptable. As a result, later stages of development tend to be associated with increases in women's LFP.

This argument stresses the neoclassical income and substitution effects typical of labor supply decisions related to human capital investments. It also stresses culture, as embodied in the availability of socially acceptable forms of employment for women (Fernández 2007a, 2007b, 2010; Fernández and Fogli 2006; Goldin 2005).

Unitary and nonunitary models of the family and implications for women's welfare

An important lesson from the U-shape argument is the difficulty of mapping labor market indicators into women's well-being. Traditional economic models conclude that development unambiguously improves welfare (Lundberg and Pollak 1996), even when it results in fewer women in the labor force. In this view, increases in women's leisure as incomes rise are a benefit of development, and withdrawals from the labor market are largely voluntary (Mammen and Paxson 2000). So care must be taken when assuming that equality of outcomes is, in fact, the social goal to strive for.

Implicit in this view is that women are part of a larger economic unit—the household—and that families behave as unitary entities that make no distinctions between the well-being of different family members. Under this set of assumptions, a family acts as a single decision maker, such that individual welfare coincides with that of the household and is always maximized. Unitary models, also known as "common preference" models of the family, imply that the magnitude and composition of family expenditures are independent of which individuals in the household receive income or control resources (figure I.2).[8]

In this view, it follows that observed outcomes, such as decisions to participate in the labor market or to specialize in home production such as household chores or

---

FIGURE I.2: Characteristics of unitary and nonunitary models

Unitary *Household models*	Nonunitary *Household bargaining models* Necessary assumption: Different preferences occur across spouses.	
	Cooperative models	**Noncooperative models**
Family acts as a single decision maker. **Outcomes** depend on maximized common welfare function, which incorporates spouses' individual utilities. **Welfare** of the household and individuals coincide. Always maximized!	Spouses consult each other and explicitly negotiate to reach an agreement. Household has a pooled budget constraint. **Outcomes** depend on - Spouses' preferences - Differences in ability to assert preferences ("bargaining power") - Outside options: divorce threat or "nagging" threat Mutual gains from cooperation. Outcomes are always efficient.	Spouses do not consult each other. They try to maximize their own welfare given expectations about their spouse's behavior. **Outcomes** depend on - Spouses' preferences - Differences in ability to assert their preferences (bargaining power) - Agreements that may not be binding but are costly to enforce Possible breakdown in cooperation. Outcomes are not necessarily efficient.

child rearing, are always welfare maximizing and leave little space for policy intervention, other than to mitigate social barriers and discrimination in the labor market. This report, although not focusing on the institutional environment surrounding the gender dimension of labor demand, recognizes its relevance. Unfavorable attitudes toward women have, however, been shown to soften as more women enter the labor force, human capital accumulates, and countries' incomes rise (Fernández and Fogli 2009; Fernández, Fogli, and Olivetti 2004; Goldin 1995).[9]

Several empirical studies (some reviewed in chapters 5 and 6) have called into question the credibility of assumptions and the accuracy of predictions of the unitary model. These studies have shown that husbands' preferences differ systematically from those of wives, arguing that family decisions are more plausibly the product of the following:

- Divergent interests or preferences of husbands and wives

- Differences in the extent to which each spouse can assert his or her preferences ("bargaining power"), which emerge from differences in the distribution of resources across spouses and in their ability to negotiate, and from social norms and even biological dissimilarities

Heterogeneity in preferences and in ability to assert oneself implies, for instance, that the identity of the income recipient matters with respect to its use. In a rapid expansion of South Africa's pension program, school investments and nutritional outcomes of grandchildren were meaningfully influenced by whether they lived with a grandfather or a grandmother (Duflo 2003; Edmonds 2005). Among girls living with grandmothers who received the pension, anthropometric measures improved considerably. But no such effects were found when the pension was received by grandfathers. However, children were more likely to be in school when they lived with an eligible grandfather than with an eligible grandmother (Edmonds 2005). More generally, women's tastes and actions are more sensitive to context and cues, and women are more averse to competition and more reluctant than men to engage in interactions involving bargaining (Croson and Gneezy 2009).

In a nonunitary model these differences imply that households do not behave as a single decision maker and require acknowledgment of the possibility that spouses' interactions may lead to inefficient or inequitable outcomes, thereby providing opportunities for welfare-enhancing policy interventions. Such recognition implies that the efficacy of any policy directly or indirectly affecting women (and by extension, households) will be mediated by the household decision-making process. Spouses may cooperate and consult with each other to coordinate solutions that benefit them both—a cooperative bargaining model. Or they may withdraw from coordination and make unilateral decisions that maximize their own welfare, given their expectations about their spouse's (optimal) behavior. In the first case, household decision making follows a cooperative bargaining model, where collective household decisions are reached only if both spouses gain from cooperation. In the second case, family decisions follow a noncooperative bargaining model.

Consider a husband and wife who are deciding how to adjust their labor supply to manage the care of a newborn child. Because of preferences, social norms, comparative advantages (such as differences in wages, skills, and biological endowments), and the initial distribution of resources, women may opt to reduce their labor supply, if only temporarily (Bertrand, Goldin, and Katz 2010). With cooperative bargaining, the resulting division of labor between husband and wife is always efficient; that is, it would be impossible to improve the well-being of one spouse without making the other worse off. It is therefore possible that the cooperative allocation fails to maximize a wife's own utility (for example, she would like to work more than is possible given the demands on her time). In that event, she is compensated by some reallocation of other resources, including emotional or monetary resources.[10]

In cooperative models the alternative to coming to an agreement could be divorce (the divorce threat model of McElroy 1990) or, less radical, a situation in which the marriage is preserved but both parties stop consulting one another and each acts only in his or her own self-interest (the separate spheres model of Lundberg and Pollak 1993). These alternative states of the world, or "outside options" (divorce or cold shoulder), are always associated with lower utility than cooperation, and so are never chosen. They are, however, extremely important in determining the final allocation of resources within the household (such as time and consumption), because the strength of each spouse's bargaining position is directly influenced by the next best option.

In divorce threat models, for instance, changes in laws defining alimony payments and the division of property after divorce should affect the distribution of bargaining power among spouses. If new legislation assigned greater protection to women, it would increase a wife's bargaining position, and so could affect the allocation of labor within the household, even without higher divorce rates. These outside options, or "threat points," are likely to depend on environmental factors that do not directly affect the utility of a spouse while married, such as the conditions in the remarriage market, the income available to divorced men and women, and the social norms for dissolving a marriage.

Although household decisions in cooperative settings are efficient, they may not be equitable, which may suggest a role for policy.[11] For instance, if the ability to access credit factors into spouses' outside options, and in practice only men enjoy this right, the cooperative division of labor and consumption decisions are still efficient, but the distribution of bargaining power is inequitable, justifying policy intervention. Usually only policies that act on spouses' threat points can alter the outcomes of cooperative households' decisions, by redistributing bargaining power within the couple.

Spouses may agree to cooperate and reach agreement on the distribution of household chores, say, but one or both spouses may fail to follow through or later decide not to respect the pact. If such agreements and plans between spouses are not binding and cannot be enforced without cost (allowing for "cheap talk"), cooperation could break down. However, they are important because the majority of decisions for purchases, household chores, caregiving, and labor supply are made privately among household members. But many countries either have no institutions to enforce these decisions or have weak enforcement, leading to discordant or destructive unions.

In this noncooperative setting, spouses do not consult one another and simply decide what is best for them given their expectations about their partner's behavior. If both partners prefer to work and not do any household chores, an efficient outcome would be for both of them to work and to hire outside help—or for both to contribute a little to the housework. A situation in which both partners simply do not contribute to the upkeep of the household would be inefficient, because both spouses would be bothered by the disarray. Where both spouses value working, a solution in which one specializes in home production and the other in market production would be unsustainable and would lead one of the spouses to exercise the outside option by exiting the union or to make cohabitation unpleasant.[12] In noncooperative households (unlike cooperative households) allocations are not always economically efficient.

Households may appear similar in cooperative and noncooperative models with respect to observable characteristics such as income and education, but they may choose either an efficient or inefficient allocation of resources and division of labor between market and home production. Whether the ultimate equilibrium is vicious or virtuous is thought to depend on history and culture. Social norms, for instance, may prescribe codes of conduct and gender roles for home production, which favor an outcome that could be improved, from both spouses' perspectives (Lundberg and Pollak 1994). By allowing for the possibility of noncooperative bargaining, whether household decisions are efficient becomes an outcome in itself and depends not only on the distribution of resources between spouses and their preferences and characteristics (such as socioeconomic status and ability), but also on social norms and institutions for gender and marriage.

For example, evidence of inefficiency among West African households in their farming decisions arises from the fact that women and men retain separate property rights to land after marriage (Udry 1996). Within these unions, spouses tend to act independently and do not constitute a single economic unit. In fact, spouses often have their own individual budgets and make separate consumption and production decisions.

By contrast, evidence from LAC and developed countries is consistent with efficient household allocations, though the literature assigns an important role to cultural norms in understanding why some households function as cohesive and efficient unions while others are unions only in name (Bobonis 2009; Browning and others 1994; Browning and Chiappori 1998; Chiappori, Fortin, and Lacroix 2002). If households interact noncooperatively, policy intervention could be justified on grounds of efficiency as well as equity.

In sum, nonunitary models of the household, in which individuals' market and outside opportunities generate bargaining power within the household, can have qualitatively different implications from those of unitary models. For example, an increase in men's wages could in theory make women worse off, even as total household resources increase. If the additional resources tilt the balance of power toward men, that confers more say to the husband in household decisions and weakens the wife's ability to assert her preferences.

Assessing the effects of development on women's well-being thus requires a characterization of how resources are allocated within families, which affects whether welfare-enhancing policy margins can be identified to correct either inequities in the household (in the cooperative model) or inefficiencies (in the noncooperative model).

If women are part of a larger economic unit—the household—men's economic gains may benefit women to the extent that spouses share resources and interact. Studying gender issues—economic participation in particular—through a household lens provides a novel perspective for analysts to understand outcomes and see the margins that are amenable to policy intervention. Which family behaves according to which model will depend on the cultural context and on the characteristics of the spouses. Ultimately, this is an empirical question. But the fact is indisputable that the process of intrahousehold decision making matters and provides alternative policy angles depending on the nature of family interaction. (Chapter 6 provides a more detailed discussion of the different views of intrahousehold dynamics and their implications for resource allocation and welfare, with particular emphasis on consumption, LFP, and the division of labor among spouses.)

Structure of the report

The rest of the report is organized in three parts. Part I (chapter 1) presents the most relevant trends underlying women's economic participation through five sets of stylized facts, focusing in particular on changes in education, health, family structure, norms, and labor market outcomes. Following the organizing framework summarized in figure I.1, health, education, family structure, and social norms are discussed first, as they represent key inputs to and constraints on women's economic participation, which is considered the output and therefore is discussed second. In particular, part I presents an overview of the LAC region from a gender perspective and places it in historical and economic context, with specific comparisons with other regions. The empirical regularities presented in chapter 1 are building blocks for the rest of the report. Over the past four decades, LAC has made great strides in first-generation gender issues. Access to education has equalized, and it is now favoring girls. Health indicators, including life expectancy, have equalized. Women's participation in the labor force has expanded dramatically, particularly among married women. Changes in gender attitudes have accompanied these trends, with significant improvements in both sex's views regarding the role of women in professional spheres, but women's and men's views toward gender roles in the household have remained fairly stable. Although women value family and being involved in the care of their children, they assign increasing importance to work, requiring them to strike an appropriate balance between work and family.[13]

Building on the stylized facts in part I, part II (chapters 2–5) narrows the focus to LAC countries. It endeavors to further understand trends in women's economic participation, using a historical perspective to shed light on the dramatic trends in LAC and its determinants. Part II presents original and novel analyses characterizing the evolution of female LFP, focusing on progressively narrower features of women's economic activity, beginning with the decision to enter the labor force, moving to occupational choices, and finishing with earnings. Men's and women's views on gender roles within the household are reflected in their LFP decisions: for women, marital status, even more so than presence of children, remains the strongest predictor of their participation, with many fewer married women engaging in work than their single, divorced, or widowed counterparts, although this relationship has weakened over time. For married women, the presence of children, while not seeming to affect the decision whether to join the labor force, shapes the intensity and sectoral occupation of women's participation. Although single women appear to be overrepresented in the formal sector, their shift out of formal work and engagement in the corridor of self-employment and inactivity occurs as they form a family. Women with small children supply many fewer hours than their childless counterparts and appear to value the flexibility afforded them by the informal sector.

A woman's ability to juggle her dual roles in home production and in the labor market ultimately depends on her interactions with other household members, which shape division of labor within the household and between home and market production. This observation motivates the household perspective adopted in this report. In particular, the results that emerge from chapters 2–5 set the stage for part III (chapters 6 and 7). Chapter 6 considers causal relations—not just statistical relations. The chapter sheds light on intrahousehold dynamics and the decision-making processes underlying women's economic participation. It considers changes in women's bargaining positions relative to other household members and the consequences for female economic participation and the allocation of household resources. The lenses for studying these interventions are economic theories of interaction within the household, some of which explicitly allow stakeholders to have diverging interests and preferences. Chapter 7 concludes with policy recommendations and suggestions for future research.

Notes

[1] See Goldin (2006) and the citations therein.

[2] Human capital is typically defined as the set of skills, abilities, knowledge, and so on that increase individuals' productivity and can be accumulated through investments of time and resources.

[3] The household perspective includes not only the traditional two-spouse family structure, typical of bargaining models, but also more modern definitions of households, such as single-headed

households and cohabitation. Indeed, the rising proportion of female-headed households is explicitly documented in chapter 1 in the section titled "Family structure," along with changes in patterns of family formation and divorce rates.

[4] Individual and household decisions occur in the context of constraints. This study highlights the role of constraints imposed by income, time, and social norms in shaping women's economic participation.

[5] Policy margins indicate a dimension of behavior that may be sensitive to or call for policy intervention. The concept is fairly standard in policy and economics discussions.

[6] In other words, women may face a constrained optimization problem, which takes income and time allocations of other family members as givens.

[7] See Durand (1975), Goldin (1995), Horton (1996), Mammen and Paxson (2000), Psacharopoulos and Tzannatos (1989), and Sinha (1967), who document this relationship in a variety of settings.

[8] A family's common preferences may be the outcome of consensus among family members or of the dominance of a single family member, but all such models imply that family expenditures are independent of who has nominal control over resources. For a technical treatment of the concepts, see Samuelson's (1956) consensus model and Becker's (1974, 1991) altruism model.

[9] See also trends emerging in LAC as documented in stylized fact 4, in chapter 1.

[10] In cooperative households the alternative to reaching a consensus is a state of the world associated with a minimal level of utility, or reservation utility, that may be improved if the spouses agree to cooperate. This alternative plays the role of a threat, which could take the form of marital dissolution (the "divorce threat" model of McElroy 1990) or an unhappy spouse (the "separate spheres" models of Lundberg and Pollak 1993). As long as these threats of divorce or painful marital conditions exist, the outcomes will be a function of resources controlled by each spouse, the distribution of which will also affect the relative well-being of spouses within marriage.

[11] Simply changing the distribution of resources within the household may not suffice to alter outcomes if an intervention does not alter the value of the alternative, whether an outside option such as divorce (by, for example, improving the conditions of divorced women, or making divorce more accessible and socially acceptable) or an inside option such as the "cold shoulder."

[12] Any other outcome would be inefficient or unsustainable, since spouses may exercise their next-best outside option.

[13] This study adopts an equality of opportunity approach rather than an equality of outcome perspective. This emphasis is the major difference between the current study and the *World Development Report 2012*. Our choice was not made a priori but was a direct consequence of findings emerging from the study (this point is further elaborated in the closing remarks). The results documented in the study caution against a mechanical view of the relationship between equalization of access and labor market outcomes, and draw attention to how measures of economic participation offer only a partial view of welfare. The results also point to the importance of understanding the role of mediating factors that enter the decision-making process underlying the economic behavior of women. The study recognizes that the policy goal of gender parity in basic rights and services has not been fully or uniformly reached across the region. Much room for improvement remains, particularly where chronic poverty is intertwined with precarious access to basic services and where certain institutional arrangements and social norms breed systematic barriers for women. But the improvements in the circumstances of women in LAC over the past decades are undeniable and call for a reassessment and expansion of the policy focus.

References

Becker, Gary S. 1974. "A Theory of Social Interactions." *Journal of Political Economy* 82 (6): 1063–94.

———. 1991. *A Treatise on the Family*. Enlarged Edition. Cambridge, MA: Harvard University Press.

Bertrand, Marianne, Claudia Goldin, and Lawrence F. Katz. 2010. "Dynamics of the Gender Gap for Young Professionals in the Financial and Corporate Sectors." *American Economic Journal: Applied Economics* 2 (3): 228–55.

Bobonis, Gustavo J. 2009. "Is the Allocation of Resources within the Household Efficient? New Evidence from a Randomized Experiment." *Journal of Political Economy* 117 (3): 453–503.

Browning, Martin, François Bourguignon, Pierre-André Chiappori, and Valerie Lechene. 1994. "Income and Outcomes: A Structural Model of Intrahousehold Allocation." *Journal of Political Economy* 102 (6):1067–96.

Browning, Martin, and Pierre-André Chiappori. 1998. "Efficient Intra-household Allocations: A General Characterization and Empirical Tests." *Econometrica* 66 (6): 1241–78.

Chiappori, Pierre-André, Bernard Fortin, and Guy Lacroix. 2002. "Marriage Market, Divorce Legislation, and Household Labor Supply." *Journal of Political Economy* 110 (1): 37–72.

Croson, Rachel, and Uri Gneezy. 2009. "Gender Differences in Preferences." *Journal of Economic Literature* 47 (2): 448–74.

Duflo, Esther. 2003. "Grandmothers and Granddaughters: Old-Age Pensions and Intrahousehold Allocation in South Africa." *World Bank Economic Review* 17 (1): 1–25.

Durand, John D. 1975. *The Labor Force in Economic Development: A Comparison of International Census Data, 1946–1966*. Princeton, NJ: Princeton University Press.

Edmonds, Eric V. 2005. "Does Child Labor Decline with Improving Economic Status?" *Journal of Human Resources* 40 (1): 77–99.

Fernández, Raquel. 2007a. "Women, Work, and Culture." NBER Working Paper 12888, National Bureau of Economic Research, Cambridge, MA.

———. 2007b. "Culture as Learning: The Evolution of Female Labor Force Participation over a Century." NBER Working Paper 13373, National Bureau of Economic Research, Cambridge, MA.

———. 2010. "Does Culture Matter?" NBER Working Paper 16277, National Bureau of Economic Research, Cambridge, MA.

Fernández, Raquel, and Alessandra Fogli. 2006. "Fertility: The Role of Culture and Family Experience." *Journal of the European Economic Association* 4 (2–3): 552–61.

———. 2009. "Culture: An Empirical Investigation of Beliefs, Work, and Fertility." *American Economic Journal: Macroeconomics* 1 (1): 146–77.

Fernández, Raquel, Alessandra Fogli, and Claudia Olivetti. 2004. "Preference Formation and the Rise of Women's Labor Force Participation: Evidence from WWII." NBER Working Paper 10589, National Bureau of Economic Research, Cambridge, MA.

Goldin, Claudia. 1995. "The U-Shaped Female Labor Force Function in Economic Development and Economic History." In *Investment in Women's Human Capital*, edited by T. Paul Schultz, 61–90. Chicago: University of Chicago Press.

———. 2005. "From the Valley to the Summit: A Brief History of the Quiet Revolution That Transformed Women's Work." *Regional Review* 14 (3): 5–12.

———. 2006. "Quiet Revolution That Transformed Women's Employment, Education, and Family." *American Economic Review Papers and Proceedings* 96 (2): 1–21.

Horton, Susan, ed. 1996. *Women and Industrialization in Asia*. London: Routledge.

Lundberg, Shelly J., and Robert A. Pollak. 1993. "Separate Spheres Bargaining and the Marriage Market." *Journal of Political Economy* 101 (6): 988–1010.

———. 1994. "Noncooperative Bargaining Models of Marriage." *American Economic Review* 84 (2): 132–37.

———. 1996. "Bargaining and Distribution in Marriage." *Journal of Economic Perspectives* 10 (4): 139–58.

Mammen, Kristin, and Christina Paxson. 2000. "Women's Work and Economic Development." *Journal of Economic Perspectives* 14 (4): 141–64.

McElroy, Marjorie B. 1990. "The Empirical Content of Nash-Bargained Household Behavior." *Journal of Human Resources* 25 (4): 559–83.

Psacharopoulos, George, and Zafiris Tzannatos. 1989. "Female Labor Force Participation: An International Perspective." *World Bank Research Observer* 4 (2): 187–201.

Samuelson, Paul A. 1956. "Social Indifference Curves." *Quarterly Journal of Economics* 70 (1): 1–22.

Sinha, Jania N. 1967. "Dynamics of Female Participation in Economic Activity in a Developing Economy." In *Proceedings of the World Population Conference, Belgrade, 30 Aug.–10 Sep. 1965*, vol. 4., 336–37. New York: United Nations.

Udry, Christopher. 1996. "Gender, Agricultural Production, and the Theory of the Household." *Journal of Political Economy* 104 (5): 1010–46.

Part I

1
Trends in Human Capital, Family Formation, Norms, and Female Labor Force Participation

Introduction

Following the organizing framework described in the introduction (see figure I.1), this chapter presents five sets of stylized facts on gender in Latin America and the Caribbean (LAC), drawing comparisons with other regions and by country in the region where possible. It documents trends in the evolution of human capital, specifically education and health (stylized facts 1 and 2). Such investments are necessary for economic participation but are not sufficient, suggesting the need to characterize how preferences over family formation and household structure have changed, if at all (stylized fact 3), and to gain insight on social norms concerning gender blindness in the workplace and the role of women in the household (stylized fact 4). The chapter concludes with a discussion of the evolution of female labor force participation (LFP) and its relationship to economic development (stylized fact 5), postponing to chapters 2–5 a more thorough and novel analysis of female LFP in the region.

Education

Stylized fact 1: Gender gaps in enrollment, which have traditionally favored boys, have closed and, for the younger generation, switched. Changes in the gap in years of schooling are due largely to increased educational attainment of girls at the higher levels. In achievement, some gaps still favor boys, while others favor girls.

Education yields multiple returns. It improves earnings potential and opportunities in the labor market. It is associated with an improved intramarital share of the surplus one can extract in the marriage market—say, by tilting household allocations in one's favor through higher household income, better marriage prospects, and more desirable spousal roles within marriage. It influences intrahousehold shares by raising the prospects of marriage with an educated spouse, thus raising household income at marriage, and by affecting the competitive strength outside marriage and the spousal roles within marriage (Chiappori, Iyigun, and Weiss 2009). Finally, higher levels of education are symptomatic of, and can affect changes in, social norms surrounding women's economic role in and outside the household (Fernández 2007a, 2007b, 2010; Fernández and Fogli 2006).[1]

The interplay of these factors has implications for LFP. Until female education levels rise, it may not make economic or social sense for women to move into formal sector employment in large numbers. Several authors have argued that a deterrent to women's engagement in the formal labor market is that low-paying jobs and the stigma associated with them may not make the jobs attractive enough to compensate for the fixed costs of working away from home, though single women may accept them more readily than married women (Goldin 1995; Mammen and Paxson 2000; Schultz 1990).

Countries in LAC have made important progress in women's educational enrollment and achievement, to the point of closing and even overturning earlier gender gaps.

Enrollment

Most countries in LAC have virtually universal enrollment for girls in primary education (figure 1.1), and the gender gap that historically favored boys has disappeared.[2] LAC stands out as having both high female primary school net enrollment rates and a narrow gender gap, as reflected by its high ratio of female to male primary school net enrollment rates (figure 1.2).[3] Enrollment rates of 6- to 11-year-olds were lower among girls than among boys in only four Latin American countries: Bolivia, Guatemala, Mexico, and Peru (Marshall 2005).

At the secondary level, where enrollment rates in LAC for both girls and boys are lower, the increase in girls' rates has been greatest in LAC (figure 1.3). The ratio of female to male net enrollment rates shows that the gap in LAC favoring girls is even larger at the secondary level than primary level and far exceeds that of high-income Organisation for Economic Co-operation and Development (OECD) countries (figure 1.4).

The data suggest that the pattern of higher female enrollment at the primary and secondary levels also holds at the tertiary level in LAC. Recent studies also confirm that females outperform males in tertiary completion in most countries that record such data, a tendency that has also emerged in developed countries.[4]

FIGURE 1.1: Latin America and the Caribbean has virtually universal primary enrollment for girls

Female primary school net enrollment rates by region, 2000–11

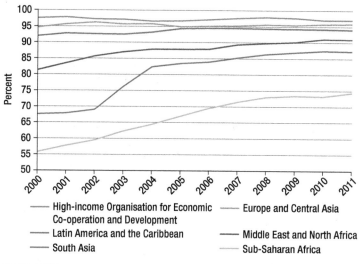

— High-income Organisation for Economic Co-operation and Development
— Latin America and the Caribbean
— South Asia
— Europe and Central Asia
— Middle East and North Africa
— Sub-Saharan Africa

Source: World Bank 2014.

FIGURE 1.2: Latin America and the Caribbean has the narrowest gender gap in primary enrollment

Ratio of female to male primary school net enrollment rates by region, 2000–11

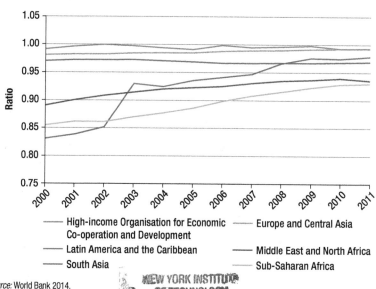

— High-income Organisation for Economic Co-operation and Development
— Latin America and the Caribbean
— South Asia
— Europe and Central Asia
— Middle East and North Africa
— Sub-Saharan Africa

Source: World Bank 2014.

FIGURE 1.3: The increase in girls' secondary enrollment rates has been greatest in Latin America and the Caribbean

Female secondary school net enrollment by region, 2000–11

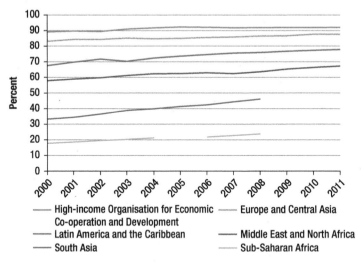

High-income Organisation for Economic Co-operation and Development ——
Latin America and the Caribbean ——
South Asia ——
Europe and Central Asia ——
Middle East and North Africa ——
Sub-Saharan Africa ——

Source: World Bank 2014.
Note: Data unavailable for the full period for South Asia and Sub-Saharan Africa.

FIGURE 1.4: Secondary school enrollment favors girls even more than primary enrollment

Ratio of female to male secondary school net enrollment by region, 2000–11

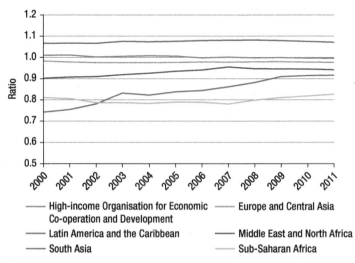

High-income Organisation for Economic Co-operation and Development ——
Latin America and the Caribbean ——
South Asia ——
Europe and Central Asia ——
Middle East and North Africa ——
Sub-Saharan Africa ——

Source: World Bank 2014.

Attainment

Girls today are, on average, achieving more years of education than boys, except for those in indigenous communities in Bolivia and Guatemala (Duryea and others 2007). For the most part, the gap in years of schooling closed over the past two decades. For all cohorts born at the end of the 1960s, the gap is closed. Since then, the gap has reversed such that for the cohort born in 1980, girls have an average of 0.25 more years of schooling than boys. For the four decades of birth cohorts in their analysis (1940–80), the gender gap in attainment has moved in favor of females at a pace of 0.27 years of schooling per decade (Duryea and others 2007). The changes in the schooling gap are explained mainly by the educational attainment of females at higher levels of education, rather than by improvements in the early years of education. Panels c and d of figure 1.5 provide some insight into this finding. In LAC, the gap in secondary completion rates (panel c) has closed since at least the 1950s and has favored girls ever since, with LAC outperforming the other regions. The ratio of female-to-male completion rates for tertiary education paints a different picture (panel d). In the 1960s, two women completed tertiary education for every 10 men; by 2010, the gap closed entirely, with only Europe and Central Asia keeping pace with LAC's gains. However, LAC's level of human capital for both boys and girls—measured by years of schooling (panel a)—still lags considerably behind that of other regions that have reached equality in educational outcomes, such as the developed economies of the OECD and the Europe and Central Asia region.

Achievement

All education indicators considered so far in this section refer to enrollment or attainment, rather than achievement. However, although the gender gaps in net enrollment and completion rates now favor girls, a gender gap in achievement still favors boys (though the higher completion rate for girls in primary school and their faster progression through school suggest that this is not the case). The evidence of gender gaps in performance in standardized achievement tests for LAC is scant. For the seven LAC countries taking part in the Program for International Student Assessment (PISA) of the OECD in 2012, the average test results show that boys perform better than girls in mathematics and, to a lesser extent, in science, and girls perform better in reading. This pattern is consistent with those in many other countries (figure 1.6).

Disparities in progress

LAC has progressed more than other regions in closing the gender gap in education. It is the developing region with the narrowest education gender gaps in the enrollment and achievement indicators, but the levels are unsatisfactory. Indeed, net secondary

FIGURE 1.5: Educational attainment and female-to-male completion rates, women ages 25 and older, across regions, 1950–2010

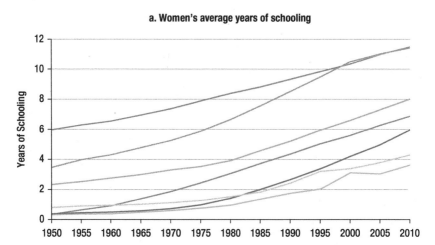

a. Women's average years of schooling

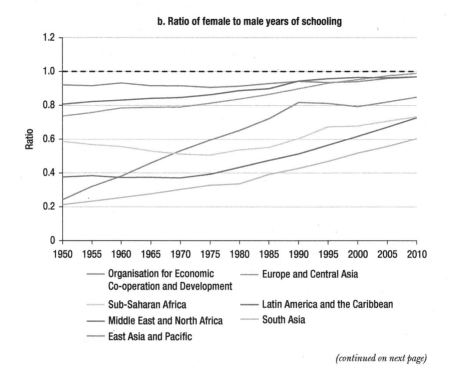

b. Ratio of female to male years of schooling

——— Organisation for Economic
Co-operation and Development

……… Sub-Saharan Africa

——— Middle East and North Africa

——— East Asia and Pacific

——— Europe and Central Asia

——— Latin America and the Caribbean

——— South Asia

(continued on next page)

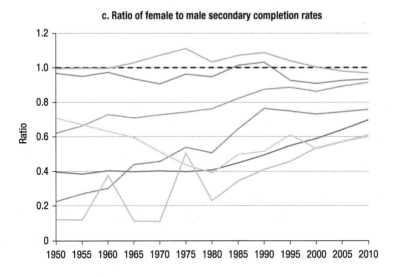

c. Ratio of female to male secondary completion rates

d. Ratio of female to male tertiary completion rates

———— Organisation for Economic Co-operation and Development

———— Sub-Saharan Africa

———— Middle East and North Africa

———— East Asia and Pacific

———— Europe and Central Asia

———— Latin America and the Caribbean

———— South Asia

Source: Based on Barro and Lee 2013.

Note: Only men and women ages 25 or older were considered in the construction of these charts, so that investment in tertiary education could plausibly be completed.

FIGURE 1.6: Girls perform better in reading—boys, in mathematics and science

Average scores on the 2012 Organisation for Economic Co-operation and Development PISA in selected countries, by gender

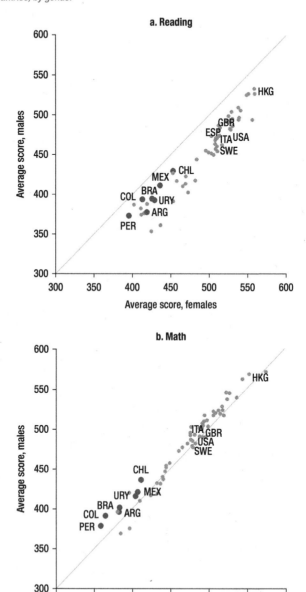

(continued on next page)

FIGURE 1.6: Girls perform better in reading—boys, in mathematics and science
(continued)

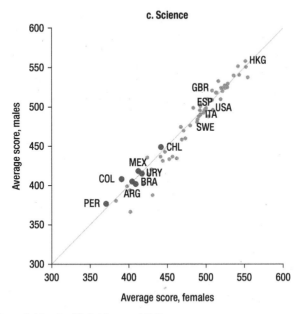

c. Science

Source: OECD Program for International Student Assessment 2012.
Note: The green line corresponds to the 45-degree line, or gender parity in test score performance. Latin America and Caribbean countries, in red, are Argentina, Brazil, Chile, Colombia, Mexico, Peru, and Uruguay. Additional benchmark countries are Hong Kong SAR, China; Italy; Spain; Sweden; the United Kingdom; and the United States.

enrollment rates in LAC are still well below universality (71 percent on average), even though most LAC countries have laws for compulsory secondary education.

Nor has progress been even across LAC countries or even within countries. Attendance and enrollment rates of girls and boys ages 6–18 in Bolivia, Guatemala, Mexico, and Peru—the only countries that have not closed the gap in adult schooling attainment—show several gender differences (Duryea and others 2007). The biggest difference in attendance is among those in the lowest income quintile. The differences are such that boys attend school in higher proportions than girls but still display lower attainment. In Bolivia, Guatemala, and Peru nonindigenous males and females have similar education outcomes. But unlike most LAC countries, where girls are less likely than boys to fail a grade and repeat, indigenous girls in these three countries appear to lag behind boys, though the gaps are much smaller than those for enrollment (Marshall and Calderón 2006). The quality of education in LAC also remains very low for both sexes, as evidenced by scores on standardized tests (PISA, for example). The gaps persist even after considering the region's lower GDP per capita.

Health

Stylized fact 2: The female share of the total population has risen in tandem with both female and male life expectancy at birth. The gap in life expectancy has widened in favor of women.

Gender gaps in health begin manifesting themselves early and continue over the life cycle. Health outcomes obviously have an intrinsic fundamental value, but also important repercussions for human capital investments and the ability to take part in economic activity (Becker 2007; Grossman 1972, 2000).

Sex imbalance

One of the earliest differences between the sexes is the imbalance in the ratio of male to female births (figure 1.7),[5] although LAC, like Europe and Central Asia and Sub-Saharan Africa, has no evidence of a sex imbalance in the total population.[6] In fact,

---

FIGURE 1.7: No unnatural male-female differences at birth in Latin America and the Caribbean

Sex ratio at birth (male births per 100 female births), selected countries, 2005–10

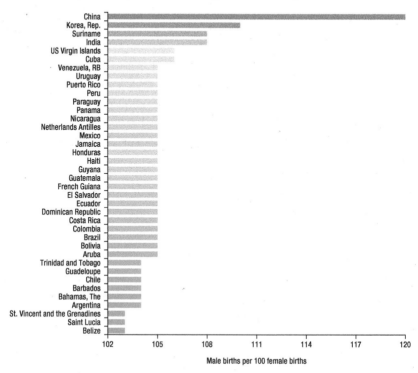

Male births per 100 female births

Source: United Nations Population Division, World Population Prospects, 2010 revision (international estimate).

FIGURE 1.8: Latin America and the Caribbean has the highest share of women in the population by region, 1960–2012

Women as a share of the total population by region, 1960–2012

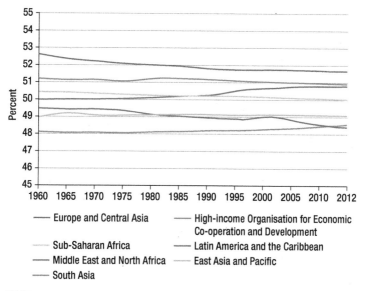

Europe and Central Asia — High-income Organisation for Economic Co-operation and Development
Sub-Saharan Africa — Latin America and the Caribbean
Middle East and North Africa — East Asia and Pacific
South Asia

Source: World Bank 2014.

LAC's share of women in the total population has been higher than that of men since 1960 and has been increasing since then, unlike other regions, such as South Asia and Europe and Central Asia, whose shares have declined. As a result, among developing regions, LAC has the highest share of women in the total population after Europe and Central Asia, on par with the group of high-income OECD countries (figure 1.8).

Life expectancy

The increase in the share of women in the total population might not be a good indicator of women's health status if it increases as a result of a decline in male life expectancy at birth. In LAC, the share of women in the total population has increased at the same time that both female and male life expectancies at birth have risen. This contrasts with other regions, such as Europe and Central Asia and Sub-Saharan Africa, where the share of women in the population has risen while male life expectancy at birth has simultaneously fallen or stagnated.

Life expectancy at birth is a measure of the overall health of a population. Along with the gap in life expectancy at birth between females and males, life expectancy is also a useful indicator of gender health disparities. After Europe and Central Asia, LAC stands out as the region with the highest gap in life expectancy, both in absolute terms (number of years) and in relative terms (as a proportion of male life expectancy; figure 1.9).

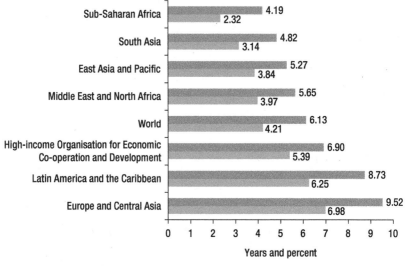

FIGURE 1.9: Women in Latin America and the Caribbean live longer than men
Differences in female and male life expectancy at birth, by region, 2012

Years and percent

▨ Gap in number of years ▨ Gap as a % of male life expectancy

Source: World Bank 2014.

Further, LAC consistently registered an elevated gap between female and male life expectancy at birth, in absolute and relative terms, during 1960–2012 (figure 1.10). In LAC, the variation in this gap in 2012, across countries, was similar to that across regions, again in absolute and relative terms. Notably, it ranged from a low of 3.71 years (or 6.1 percent) in Haiti and 4.01 years (or 5.2 percent) in Cuba, to a high of 9.34 years (or 13.8 percent) in El Salvador and 7.54 years (or 10.1 percent) in Puerto Rico. Argentina and Brazil had two of the five largest gaps: 7.32 years (or 10.1 percent) in Argentina and 7.22 years (or 10.1 percent) in Brazil.

Maternal mortality

The maternal mortality ratio is another important summary statistic of women's health. The death of women during pregnancy, childbirth, or in the 42 days after delivery, though not a gap in itself, is a main reason that mortality rates for women of childbearing age in many developing countries exceed those of males in the same age group. Recent estimates from a large sample of countries show significant reductions in the maternal mortality ratio throughout the past three decades (figures 1.11 and 1.12), albeit at different rates (Kassebaum and others 2014; Murray and others 2010).

FIGURE 1.10: The gap in life expectancy between women and men has narrowed slightly

Evolution of the gap in female and male life expectancy at birth in Latin America and the Caribbean, 1960–2012

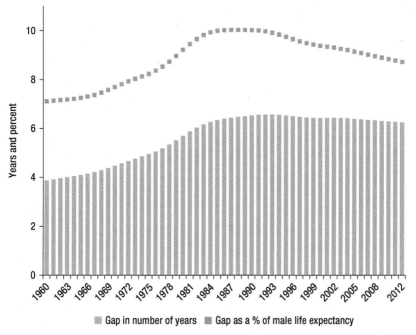

Gap in number of years   Gap as a % of male life expectancy

Source: World Bank 2014.

Some exceptions persist: certain Andean countries and Haiti exhibit ratios comparable to those of Sub-Saharan African countries.

Conclusion

Gaps in gender-specific health indicators in LAC are quite narrow relative to those in developed and developing countries in other regions. But, as with education, indicator levels are still too low. For example, even Chile and Uruguay—the countries with the lowest maternal mortality in 2013—had ratios almost twice as large as the average for developed countries. Moreover, if the rates of decline between 1990 and 2013 are extrapolated, most LAC countries (aside from Bolivia, Chile, Honduras, and Peru) will probably fail to meet the Millennium Development Goal (MDG) 3 on promoting gender equality and empowering women, which requires reductions to 75 percent of the 1990s maternal mortality ratio.

FIGURE 1.11: Maternal mortality in Latin America and the Caribbean has declined significantly

Maternal mortality ratios by region, 1980, 1990, 2003, and 2013

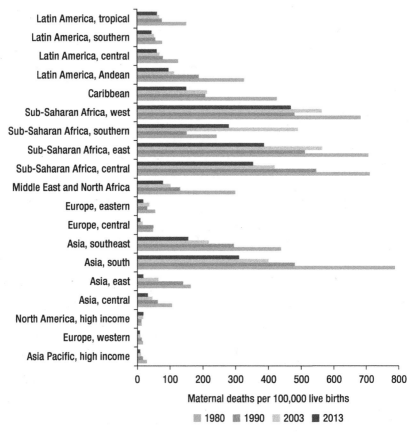

Source: Kassebaum and others 2014; Murray and others 2010.

Instead, these statistics should be interpreted as suggesting that there is no evidence of women in LAC being systematically worse off than those in other regions. But individual countries show significant heterogeneity in health gaps, similar to that across regions. And for subgroups within countries, the progress in closing gender health gaps may have stalled or even reversed.

Family formation and family structure

Investments in human capital and health are necessary, but perhaps not sufficient, for women engaging in economic activity, because preferences, social norms, and family

FIGURE 1.12: Maternal mortality has declined at different rates in different regions of Latin America and the Caribbean

Average annual change in maternal mortality ratios by region, 1980–90, 1990–2003, 2003–13

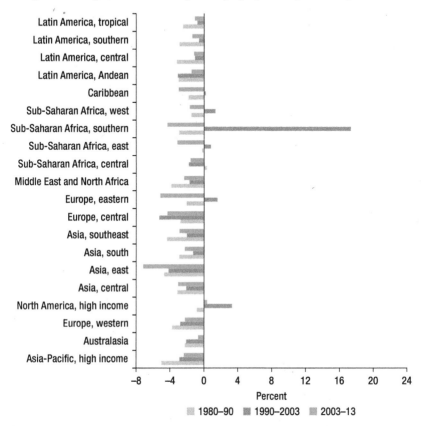

Source: Kassebaum and others 2014; Murray and others 2010.

structures also determine female participation. These latter factors shape women's family and professional aspirations and influence women's labor supply decisions and allocations of time between home and market.[7]

Fertility rates and age at first child and at marriage

Stylized fact 3a: Fertility rates in Latin America dropped dramatically over the past 50 years, converging to those of high-income OECD countries in recent years. A distinctive feature of this decline is that it took place without any major changes in the timing of family formation (of marriage and fertility).

Fertility rates

LAC fertility rates declined from 5.9 births per woman in 1960 to 2.2 in 2012 (World Bank data) unaccompanied by any delay in the onset of childbearing, the norm in Europe (Sobotka 2004). In many LAC countries in the early 1990s, lower fertility coexisted with traditional patterns of family formation—early nuptials and young motherhood.

The fertility decline in LAC started in the late 1960s and early 1970s, and the total number of births per woman fell from approximately 6.0 to 4.2 in the early 1980s. It then slowed until the 1990s, when it accelerated again, taking the regional fertility rate in 2012 (2.2 births per woman) to the rates in high-income OECD countries in the mid-1970s (figures 1.13 and 1.14). Although not as steep as the decline of birth rates in Middle Eastern and North African countries, LAC's decline has nevertheless been impressive.

For one group of countries (including Brazil, Chile, Colombia, Costa Rica, and Panama), the rate dropped rapidly in the early 1970s and then remained relatively

---

FIGURE 1.13: Fertility rate is declining in the Latin America and the Caribbean region
Births per woman by region, 1960–2012

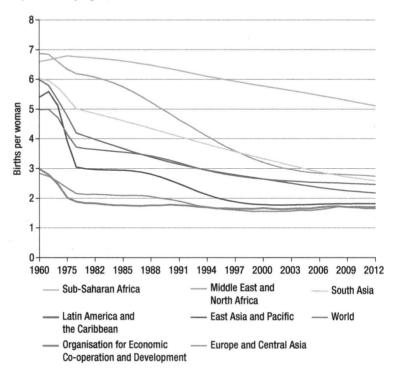

- Sub-Saharan Africa
- Middle East and North Africa
- South Asia
- Latin America and the Caribbean
- East Asia and Pacific
- World
- Organisation for Economic Co-operation and Development
- Europe and Central Asia

Source: World Bank 2014.

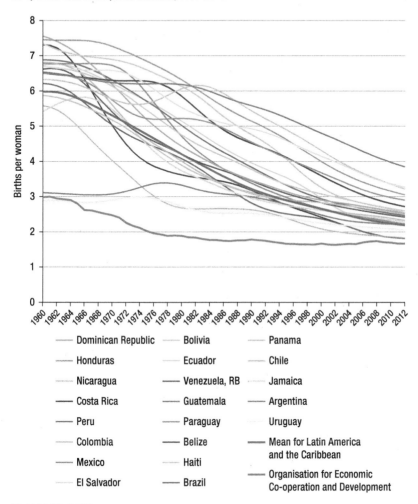

FIGURE 1.14: Fertility rates declining in countries of Latin America and Caribbean
Births per woman in Latin America and the Caribbean and in Organisation for Economic Co-operation and Development countries, 1960–2012

Legend (reads down, not across):

- Dominican Republic
- Honduras
- Nicaragua
- Costa Rica
- Peru
- Colombia
- Mexico
- El Salvador
- Bolivia
- Ecuador
- Venezuela, RB
- Guatemala
- Paraguay
- Belize
- Haiti
- Brazil
- Panama
- Chile
- Jamaica
- Argentina
- Uruguay
- Mean for Latin America and the Caribbean
- Organisation for Economic Co-operation and Development

Source: World Bank 2014.
Note: Legend reads down, not across.

stable until the beginning of the 1990s, when the decline again accelerated, mimicking trends in the rest of the world (see figure 1.13). For a second group (including Ecuador, El Salvador, Haiti, and Paraguay), the trend was more muted at the beginning of the sample period, proceeding to a slower and fairly constant pace over the decades. Both patterns substantially reduced the dispersion of fertility across the region.

Marriage and fertility

Fertility declined in LAC without major changes in family formation, as indicated by fairly stable rates and ages at first marriage and first birth (Mensch, Singh, and Casterline 2005; Rosero-Bixby 1996, 2004). Only two other regions have not experienced significant changes in age of first child. In South Asia, for instance, the mean age at first birth did not change between 1975 and the early 2000s, hovering around 19.8 years.

These magnitudes and dynamics are in line with those of several African nations and Sub-Saharan Africa in 2000. By contrast, Europe and Central Asia and OECD countries, which are more comparable to LAC in per capita income, have witnessed significant delays in family formation. Europe and Central Asia's age at first child was 22.8 years in the 1970s and reached 24.2 in the early 2000s. OECD countries have seen the largest increases, rising from 24.4 years in 1970 to 28.2 in 2000.

Within LAC, age at first child has been largely stable (figures 1.15 and 1.16). However, there are some notable exceptions. Although Caribbean nations like Jamaica, St. Lucia, and St. Vincent and the Grenadines experienced a 2.5-year delay in age at first birth over the period, Chile and Peru recorded opposite trends, with women having children almost a year younger in 2000 than in 1975.

FIGURE 1.15: Age at first child in selected Latin American and Caribbean countries (urban areas), 1985–2012

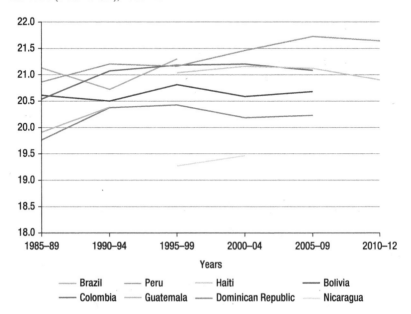

Source: Based on Demographic and Health Surveys, 2012.

FIGURE 1.16: Age at first child in selected Latin American and Caribbean countries (rural areas), 1985–2012

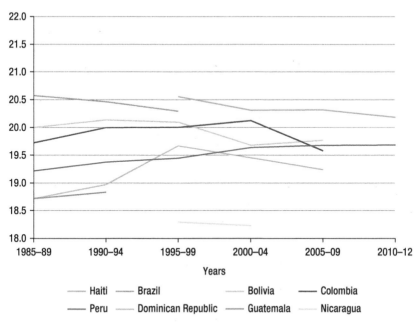

Source: Based on Demographic and Health Surveys, 2012.
Note: Data unavailable for the full period for some countries.

The age at first marriage has remained fairly constant, rising from 21 years on average for women in the 1970s to just over 23 in the early 2000s (figure 1.17). The increase in the average age at first marriage has been an important part of the fertility decline in most Asian countries (less so in Europe). But the age of first marriage has affected LAC's fertility decline little, if at all, because birth control has been adopted mainly by married women (Palloni 2009). The timing of marriage thus appears immune to LAC's demographic and socioeconomic transformations.

Still, among LAC countries the age of first marriage shows wide diversity. In some Caribbean countries (such as Barbados and Jamaica) women and men are currently marrying later than 30, but in Guatemala, Guyana, and Nicaragua women continue to marry at about 20. Among rural women, age at first marriage largely remains below age 20, showing no change since 1985.

For LAC the constancy of age at first marriage and first child lies in the value placed on family networks, the primary safety net guarding against economic and social instability (figure 1.18) (Fussell and Palloni 2004).

That would explain the persistence of nearly universal and early family formation, despite major changes in the economic, political, and social spheres (see figure 1.15).

FIGURE 1.17: The age at first marriage has been fairly stable for females in Latin America and the Caribbean

Age at first marriage and difference from 1970s to 2000s in selected Latin American and Caribbean countries

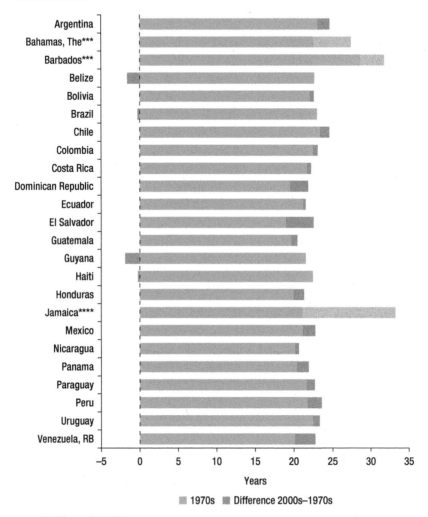

Source: World Marriage Data 2008.
Note: *** Survey methodology for the Bahamas, Barbados (only 1980s), and Jamaica changed across periods, so the change over time may be spurious.

FIGURE 1.18: Constancy in the mother's age at first child in Latin America and the Caribbean reflects the value of family networks

Distribution of mother's age at first child by region

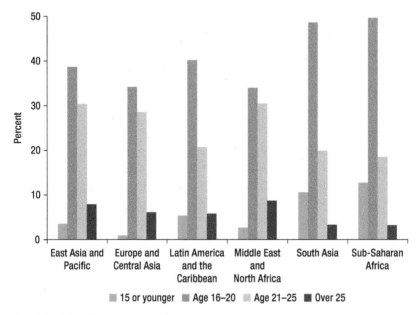

Source: United Nations 2010.

The rise in female education and employment, while reflecting a shift in tradition, might put further pressure on some of the region's typical family formation processes. LAC seems to have entered a new stage of the fertility decline in recent years. While the 1990s were characterized by a clear increase in the median age at first birth of almost three years, the proportion of women younger than 30 who have made the transition to motherhood has dropped in most Latin American countries in the past decade (Fussell and Palloni 2004).

Family structure

Stylized fact 3b: Family structure and the onset of family formation have remained largely constant. But over the last decades, there has been a moderate increase in divorce rates in urban areas and a sizable rise in female headship, especially at higher levels of education. These changes could reflect deeper changes in social norms and customs.

Marital status has also remained fairly stable since the 1970s, apart from Argentina, which experienced a 16.7-percentage-point drop in the incidence of married women, accompanied by a 12.6-percentage-point increase in the incidence of single and divorced women.[8] Although marital dissolution rates are below those in developed countries (Costa Rica and Uruguay are exceptions),[9] they nonetheless are high, and their trends may reflect changes in both institutions and, more fundamentally, social norms.

As dissolution of marriage becomes more common, the balance of bargaining powers between spouses shifts. For instance, this exit option may change the returns to specialization in household or market production by reducing the time women can expect to spend in marriage and by increasing the returns to investing in one's options outside marriage. Evidence from the United States suggests that women increase their LFP in the years prior to a divorce, and those who divorce engage in less household specialization (Johnson and Skinner 1986; Lundberg and Rose 2002). These studies do not suggest that female LFP causes divorce, but that the anticipation of a higher likelihood of divorce increases female economic participation in the labor market. And women seeking both insurance against divorce and greater bargaining power within marriage are more likely to enter and remain in the labor force (Stevenson 2008).

A related demographic shift that might put pressure on the traditional gender roles is the increase in the proportion of households headed by women in almost all LAC countries, closely mimicking that in developed countries (figure 1.19). The only exceptions are Colombia and Ecuador during the 1980s.

Female-headed households are often thought to be poorer than those headed by males, a perception arising in part from the preconception that female headship is related to unfavorable circumstances and life events such as family dissolution and adolescent parenthood. Such households are also thought to be marginalized as a result of and policies that target traditional nuclear family structures (Handa 1996; Whitehead 1978).

In LAC the increase in female-headed households is steepest among more educated women. Although female-headed households face a different set of vulnerabilities, they do not appear to be worse off than other households (Aritomi, Olgiati, and Orlando 2010). Because the financial burden falls on their shoulders, female heads of households should in principle make LFP decisions that resemble those of men, and one would expect an increase in female LFP to be related to the higher incidence of female-headed households. The changing prevalence of female headship could also signal changing norms that are manifested in the greater acceptance of women in the labor force.

Social norms

This chapter establishes that preferences (and thus decisions) are shaped by social norms, which influence household member preferences over home and market production and the division of labor between spouses. Norms can also present social barriers to female access to the labor market and to certain sectors—say, by influencing the availability of socially acceptable jobs for women (Fernández 2008; Goldin 1995).

FIGURE 1.19: The proportion of households headed by women is rising in almost all Latin American and Caribbean households

Changes in the percentage of female-headed households by region and by country and census year

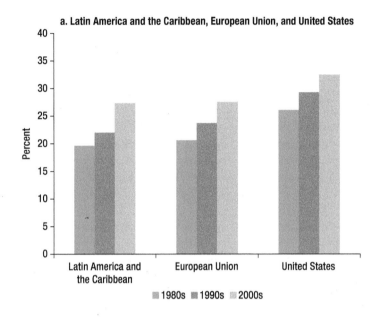

a. Latin America and the Caribbean, European Union, and United States

■ 1980s ■ 1990s ▒ 2000s

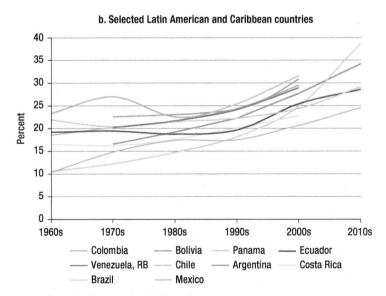

b. Selected Latin American and Caribbean countries

—— Colombia ——— Bolivia ········· Panama —— Ecuador
—— Venezuela, RB ·–·– Chile —— Argentina — Costa Rica
····· Brazil —— Mexico

Source: Integrated Public Use Microdata Series (IPUMS).

In recent years the economic literature has increasingly considered the role of culture in determining economic outcomes (Fernández 2010; Guiso, Sapienza, and Zingales 2006). *Culture* and *social norms* can be nebulous concepts, lending themselves to many alternative definitions. The most frequently cited definitions and the ones adopted in this report are, for culture, "the integrated pattern of human knowledge, belief, and behavior that depends upon one's capacity for learning and transmitting knowledge to succeeding generations" and, for social norms, "the customary beliefs, social forms, and material traits of a racial, religious, or social group."[10]

Traditional perceptions of gender roles and the family (where the man is the principal breadwinner and women tend to the home and care for children) and societal prescriptions on women's place in the labor market are likely to shape a woman's decisions about education, family formation, and participation in the labor market over her life cycle. This simple observation manifests itself through two relationships. The first is the impact of culture and norms on expectations and preferences; the second translates those expectations and preferences into economic outcomes (figure 1.20).[11]

Recent studies have considered the relationship between women's labor market behaviors across adjacent generations (Farré and Vella 2007; Fernández 2007b, 2010; Fernández and Fogli 2006; Fernández, Fogli, and Olivetti 2004; Fogli and Veldkamp 2011). They provide evidence of culture shaping a woman's labor supply by documenting its correlation with the economic participation of women in their country of ancestry. Women's labor market experiences correlate positively not only

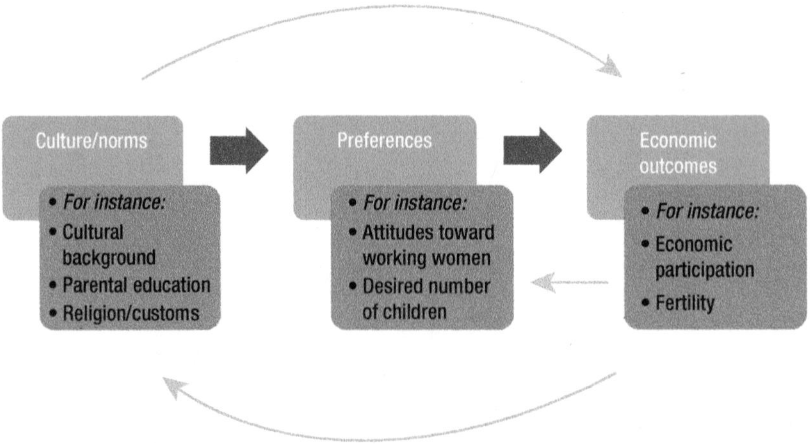

FIGURE 1.20: Cultural and social norms, preferences, and economic outcomes

with those of their daughters but also with those of their daughters-in-law. By assigning the direction of causality from the older to younger generations, the studies argue that women's roles in the labor market—and, by extension, in the family—are passed on from generation to generation.

This section turns to data from the World Values Survey[12] to present an overview of attitudes toward gender roles and work values in LAC and the rest of the world. It focuses on two sets of indicators:

- *The extent of egalitarian views toward women in the labor market and professional arena.* Among other questions, male and female respondents were asked to agree or disagree with the following statements: "When employment is scarce, men should have more right to a job than women"; "Men make better political leaders/executives than women"; and "A university education is more important for a boy than for a girl."

- *Perceptions of women's role in the household, likely formed in youth and related to cultural and religious ideology.* Questions capturing these types of norms— again, put to men and women—include "Being a housewife is just as fulfilling as working for pay"; "A working mother can establish just as warm and secure a relationship with her children as a mother who does not work"; and "A preschool-age child suffers with a working mother."

The paucity of data limits the ability to cover all LAC countries. Within LAC, the World Values Survey collects data only on Argentina, Brazil, Chile, Colombia, Ecuador, Guatemala, Mexico, Peru, and Uruguay, so comparisons with OECD countries and the rest of the world will be limited to these countries. The most recent wave of the survey (2011–13) shows systematic differences of opinion across sexes, ages, and levels of education, regardless of country or region (table 1.1):

- Women tend to have more egalitarian and progressive views of their role in the household, with a positive gradient in age and education. In addition, gender differences attenuate as education increases.

- Attitudes have changed greatly, as documented by several waves of the survey, the first covering 1989–93 and the latest covering 2011. Over the decade and a half, the views of both men and women in LAC have become more egalitarian and inclusive, a trend mirrored in OECD countries.

- Among the least educated (those with primary education or less), LAC's views are more similar to the rest of the world than to the OECD—that is, more conservative. But among the most educated (those with some tertiary education), LAC views mimic those of the OECD and are more progressive than those in the rest of the world.

LAC is an outlier in two respects. First, although men and women in LAC almost universally believe that both spouses should contribute to household income, they are

TABLE 1.1: Gender and education

Percentage in agreement

Gender and education level	Scarce jobs: Men should have more right to a job than women	University education is more important for boys than girls	Important in a job: good hours	Important in a job: personal goals	Men make better political leaders than women	Men make better executives than women	Approve of woman as a single parent	Relationship with working mother as good as stay at home	When a mother works for pay, the children suffer	Husband and wife should both contribute to income	Problems if wife earns more income than husband	Being a housewife is as fulfilling	Having a job is the best way for a woman to be independent
LAC, male													
Lower Education	40	28	42	34	46	39	47	60	58	86	49	70	65
Middle	25	20	37	32	34	24	56	63	47	88	42	60	62
Upper	14	14	28	30	29	15	65	70	38	91	37	57	61
LAC, female													
Lower	31	22	44	32	34	24	54	64	59	91	54	69	75
Middle	18	13	42	32	21	13	63	69	49	92	49	60	73
Upper	12	8	30	35	14	8	67	79	38	95	44	54	67
ROW, male													
Lower	53	38	57	34	66	61	20	59	65	81	49	67	50
Middle	39	29	51	36	59	52	28	70	50	83	39	66	49
Upper	33	23	50	37	53	46	30	69	48	79	33	66	48

(continued on next page)

TABLE 1.1: Gender and education *(continued)*

Gender and education level	Scarce jobs: Men should have more right to a job than women	University education is more important for boys than girls	Important in a job: good hours	Important in a job: personal goals	Men make better political leaders than women	Men make better executives than women	Approve of woman as a single parent	Relationship with working mother as good as stay at home	When a mother works for pay, the children suffer	Husband and wife should both contribute to income	Problems if wife earns more income than husband	Being a housewife is as fulfilling	Having a job is the best way for a woman to be independent
ROW, female													
Lower	49	30	59	32	58	51	21	66	60	87	44	66	61
Middle	34	19	57	36	45	36	34	77	43	86	35	64	62
Upper	25	12	56	39	36	26	38	79	38	84	30	60	64
OECD, male													
Lower	41	26	60	33	44	36	31	61	50	82	42	73	58
Middle	23	16	51	34	36	29	37	72	38	78	25	69	53
Upper	16	11	46	33	30	24	38	74	31	73	19	69	49
OECD, female													
Lower	38	22	65	30	40	29	32	66	51	87	45	73	67
Middle	18	10	57	32	24	17	41	81	31	77	28	66	66
Upper	10	5	52	36	16	10	45	81	26	74	22	60	63

Source: World Values Survey, 2012.

Note: LAC countries are Argentina, Brazil, Chile, Mexico, and Peru. Lower, middle, and upper education levels correspond to some primary, secondary, and tertiary education, respectively (completed or not). Each cell shows the percentage of respondents agreeing with the statements in the table's top row. LAC = Latin America and the Caribbean; OECD = Organisation for Economic Co-operation and Development; ROW = rest of the world.

significantly less concerned with job quality, as captured by good (that is, convenient) hours: only about 41 percent of respondents in LAC agreed that good hours were important, compared with 54 percent in the rest of the world and OECD. This may reflect the greater availability of help and of extended family in caregiving in LAC. The exception was less educated women, who likely face more binding budget and resource constraints and so value flexibility more.

Second, LAC appears more accepting of women as single parents, with about 56 percent approving compared with 29 percent for the rest of the world and 37 percent for the OECD. This statistic may reflect either a departure from traditional norms or the increasing prevalence of female-headed households documented in the previous section, thus supporting the notion that outcomes may influence opinions toward traditional household structures.

Egalitarian views

Stylized fact 4a: Proxies of social barriers to women's LFP and of acceptance of their role in professional environments have greatly improved in the region. Discriminatory views have significantly softened among younger cohorts and more educated individuals.

The term *egalitarian* is used here to describe attitudes that are not biased against women in the workforce or in positions of authority. Empirically, these sentiments across countries are most predictive of the prevalence of female LFP, though causality may go in both directions (Campa, Casarico, and Profeta 2009; Fortin 2005).

Older and less educated respondents have less egalitarian views on women in the workplace. Stated beliefs on the right to a job when employment is scarce remain unevenly distributed across men and women and across generations. In the early 1990s, between 25 percent (Argentina and Peru) and 40 percent (Brazil and Chile) of men thought that jobs were a male prerogative, though a younger generation in the 1990s already had more progressive views, roughly 10 percentage points lower (figures 1.21 and 1.22).

The response to this question might be interpreted either as a judgment about the presence of women in the workforce or, as hypothesized by Goldin (1995), as a reflection of a powerful social norm that "societies frown upon husbands who are unable to provide for their families, as if it were a sign of indolence and being negligent of his family." Across waves, regardless of sex, all countries but Argentina moved toward a more egalitarian view, especially the younger generation, with views catching up to those in developed countries.

In LAC, 44 percent of women with higher education consider it problematic if they earn more than their husbands (table 1.1), while men appear a bit less concerned about the source of income. (These figures are a little higher than those of less educated men and women in the OECD and in the rest of the world.) Among LAC women with lower and middle education, the rates are much higher—54 and 49 percent,

FIGURE 1.21: Views on "Men Have More Right to a Job" by sex, generation, and survey wave

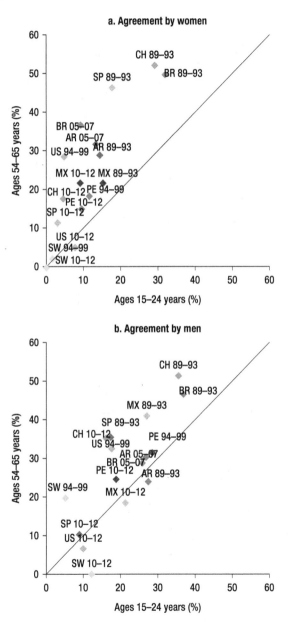

a. Agreement by women

Ages 54–65 years (%) vs. Ages 15–24 years (%)

CH 89–93
SP 89–93
BR 89–93
BR 05–07
AR 05–07
US 94–99 AR 89–93
MX 10–12 MX 89–93
CH 10–12 PE 94–99
PE 10–12
SP 10–12
US 10–12
SW 94–99
SW 10–12

b. Agreement by men

Ages 54–65 years (%) vs. Ages 15–24 years (%)

CH 89–93
BR 89–93
MX 89–93
SP 89–93
CH 10–12 PE 94–99
US 94–99
AR 05–07
BR 05–07
PE 10–12 AR 89–93
SW 94–99
MX 10–12
SP 10–12
US 10–12
SW 10–12

Source: World Values Survey, 1994–99, 2005–07, and 2010–12.
Note: Each data point corresponds to a country surveyed during the three waves: Argentina (ARG), Brazil (BR), Chile (CH), Mexico (MX), Peru (PE), Spain (SP), Sweden (SW), and United States (US).

FIGURE 1.22: Views on "Men Make Better Political Leaders" by sex, generation, and survey wave

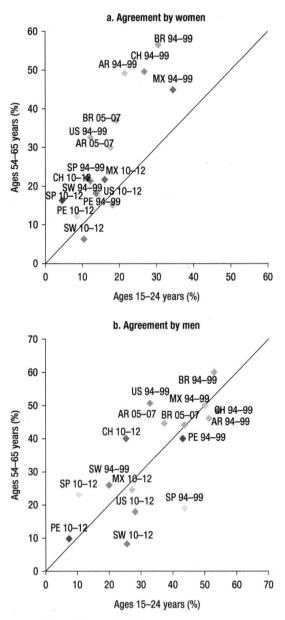

a. Agreement by women

b. Agreement by men

Source: World Values Survey, 1994–99, 2005–07, and 2010–12.
Note: Each data point corresponds to a country surveyed during the three waves: Argentina (ARG), Brazil (BR), Chile (CH), Mexico (MX), Peru (PE), Spain (SP), Sweden (SW), and United States (US).

respectively. The conservative pattern in LAC is consistent with the expectation that husbands should provide for their families, and with the perception that the distribution of resources among household members matters for the dynamics of their relationship and affects how they interact, possibly in a noncooperative fashion (as discussed in the introduction in reference to intrahousehold bargaining).

Concerns about the gender distribution of earnings in the household do not, however, translate into unfavorable attitudes toward women contributing to family income. In fact, almost universal in LAC is the expectation that both spouses should contribute to household income (roughly 90 percent for men and women, regardless of education), considerably higher than in the OECD (80 percent) and the rest of the world (85 percent).

Another dimension of egalitarian opinion relates to beliefs about differences in the abilities of men and women, particularly for holding positions of authority (figures 1.23 and 1.24). Respondents in LAC are more skeptical about women's abilities as political leaders and business leaders, although these concerns attenuate with education and for younger cohorts.

FIGURE 1.23: Share of parliamentary seats held by women

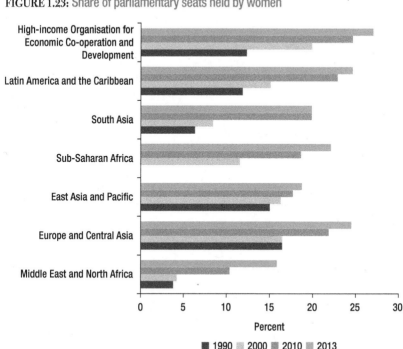

Source: World Bank 2014.

At lower levels of education, men in LAC are almost as likely as their OECD counterparts to believe that men make better political (around 46 percent) and business (39 percent) leaders than do women. Among the more educated this gap closes completely. The views of women in LAC more closely mimic those of their OECD counterparts at all levels of education (see table 1.1). These attitudes

FIGURE 1.24: Views on "Men Make Better Executives Than Women Do" in selected countries, by sex, educational level, and age

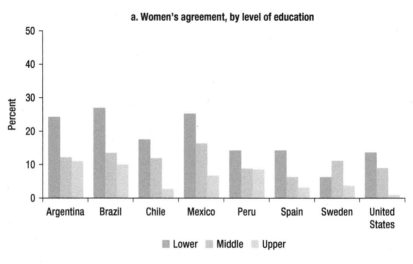

a. Women's agreement, by level of education

■ Lower ■ Middle ■ Upper

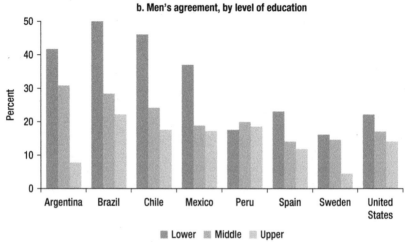

b. Men's agreement, by level of education

■ Lower ■ Middle ■ Upper

(continued on next page)

FIGURE 1.24: Views on "Men Make Better Executives Than Women Do" in selected countries, by sex, educational level, and age *(continued)*

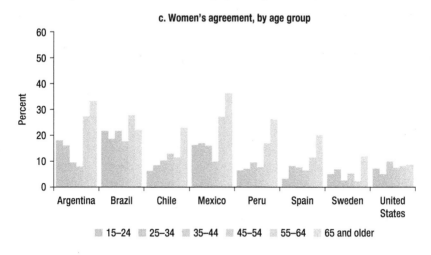

c. Women's agreement, by age group

15–24   25–34   35–44   45–54   55–64   65 and older

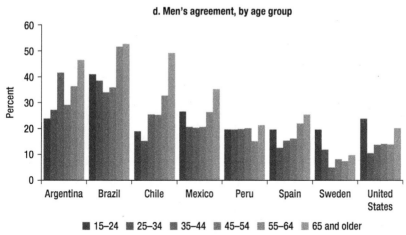

d. Men's agreement, by age group

15–24   25–34   35–44   45–54   55–64   65 and older

Source: World Values Survey.
Note: Lower, middle, and upper denote primary, secondary, and tertiary levels of education (whether completed or not). Argentina and Brazil are from the survey wave 2005–07. Chile, Mexico, Peru, Spain, Sweden, and the United States are from the wave 2010–12.

could either explain or be a byproduct of the past decade's successes at the ballot box among LAC women. Indeed, women's participation in politics in LAC has grown steadily in the past 20 years. Their share of parliamentary seats has risen from an average of 12 percent in 1990 to almost 25 percent in 2010 (Htun and Piscopo 2010) (see figure 1.23).[13]

In all regions with data, women's share of parliamentary seats rose in the two decades since 1990, with particularly dramatic changes in Europe and Central Asia, LAC, and South Asia. Besides high-income OECD countries, LAC is the region with the highest present-day female political representation, despite its higher resistance to women in positions of authority, particularly among less educated men.

The changes in sentiment over time and between generations are dramatic in LAC, even among women. In the early 1990s LAC was quite conservative on women's aptitude for leadership (except Peru): 40–60 percent of women ages 55–64 and of men of all ages agreed that men make better political leaders than women.

By the 2005–07 and 2010–12 waves, however, the proportion of older women with unfavorable opinions of female politicians declined by an average of 20 percentage points in Argentina, Brazil, and Mexico. Among men the changes were much more varied, perhaps owing to divergent experiences with female politicians. In Argentina older men in 2005–07 remained as skeptical as those in 1989–93, while younger men became 10 percent less unfavorable. The opposite was true in Brazil, with only small changes in younger men's opinions and a 10-percentage-point decline among older men. In Mexico and Peru, the proportion agreeing that men make better politicians declined between 25 and 30 percentage points among both younger and older men. In Chile, older men barely changed opinions from the early 1990s, while the proportion of younger men agreeing with the statement decreased about 25 percentage points (see panel b in figure 1.22).

Although more muted than sentiments toward female politicians, opinions about female executives in LAC are more conservative than in the OECD (Peru is again something of an exception, resembling Spain; see figure 1.24). Among the least educated in the last waves, 20–40 percent of men and 10–20 percent of women believe that men make better executives than women. Although this group is unlikely to influence managerial hiring decisions, these figures reveal their views about women in the professional arena. Nevertheless, there is a sizable gradient in education across countries and among both sexes, with those having at least some secondary education often 20 percentage points less conservative than those with primary education or less. In summary, although both men and women welcome the idea of a dual-earner household, women express a greater concern surrounding the scenario in which they would be earning more than their spouse. These concerns could be linked to the departure from traditional gender roles within households and consequent tensions generated by the social expectation that a suitable husband should be able to provide for his family.

Disparities across countries in LAC are also wide: antiegalitarian views on female executives remain sizable among the most educated in Chile (about 30 percent) and Brazil (about 20 percent), but in Argentina, Mexico, and Peru the corresponding rates are all below 10 percent (much lower than 20 percent in the United States). Differences across generations are pronounced, too: older generations (men and women) are often twice as likely to believe that men make better executives, with the notable exceptions of Brazil and Peru, where the age profile is close to flat.

Similar gradients in education and age are found in response to other questions on egalitarian views (such as those on the right to a job and women as political leaders). Because of generational shifts in norms, increased investments in education, and the higher incidence of women in the labor force, younger cohorts tend to be more gender-blind. This trend is likely to continue if, as documented in the literature, these attitudes are carried forward to future generations.[14] This optimism is partially corroborated by the trend toward egalitarian views across survey waves.

In sum, LAC men and women have the expectation that both spouses should contribute to household income, more so than in any other region, including high-income OECD countries. They thus hold fairly liberal views toward women's participation in the labor force, with the caveat that roughly a third of less educated individuals, both male and female, feel that men should be granted the priority for employment when it is scarce. Whereas two-thirds of LAC men see no problem with earning less than their wives, roughly half of women see earning more than their husbands as problematic.

On women's employment, LAC men and women remain somewhat more conservative than their OECD counterparts in that they deem men better suited for positions of authority in business and politics. Yet, despite this sentiment, LAC currently enjoys the highest share of female parliamentary representation than any other region, suggesting that this stated preference may be weak.

Opinions about gender differences in professional roles have been interpreted as measures of social barriers and even, in some instances, of discrimination against women in the labor market (see Fortin 2005). In this light, the encouraging trends documented here indicate a softening of these social barriers, with the education and cohort gradients providing evidence that norms are not immutable. They can evolve over time, and cultural differences may attenuate with individual characteristics.[15]

Perceptions of women's role in the household

Stylized fact 4b: Men's and women's views about traditional roles remain fairly stable, less susceptible to change. Women value family and caring for their children; they assign increasing importance to work, requiring them to negotiate a balance between work and family.

As documented earlier, the prevalence of discriminatory views continues to weaken with time and higher education. But a second dimension of social norms is relevant for women's economic participation: their role in the household.

The literature assigns key roles to two interrelated shifts in women's attitudes as drivers of their greater integration in the labor force (Akerlof and Kranton 2010; Fortin 2009). The first is women's inclination to view their economic participation as including a career, rather than merely a transition until marriage and family formation ("changed identities," in Goldin's [2006] terminology). This change lengthens the horizon for women to tailor their human capital investments to prepare for longer working lives and greater attachment to the labor force ("expanded horizons," according to Goldin).

In a similar vein, some commentators interpret agreement with statements like "Being a housewife is as fulfilling as working for pay" and "Women want a house and children" as markers of women's aspirations and identities. For example, the greater the rate of agreement with such statements, the greater the adherence to traditional gender roles and identities (Fernández 2007b; Fortin 2005). Illustrating the importance of these attitudes, the gap between men and women in agreeing with such statements predicts gender wage gaps in OECD countries (Fortin 2005). Because the upward-trending gap is driven largely by changes in men's attitudes, men's increasing support for housewifery represents a societal countercurrent for women, who continue to "swim upstream" in the sense of Blau and Kahn (1997).

The upper panels of figure 1.25 report the rate, by age group and gender, at which respondents in the 1990s agree that housewifery is as fulfilling as paid employment, as well as its change since the 1990s. The lower panels provide a disaggregation by educational attainment.

In the 2005–07 or 2010–12 waves of the World Values Survey, 60 percent of 15- to 24-year-olds in LAC agreed with the statement that housewifery is as fulfilling as paid employment, compared with 70 percent among those older than 55 (see figure 1.25). Younger cohorts are more inclined to assign intrinsic value to women's attachment to the labor force, consistent with the view that a career contributes to one's identity (Akerlof and Kranton 2010). By this measure, LAC countries remain more traditional in their gender attitudes than the European countries used as benchmarks (Spain and Sweden).[16] Though modest, gradients in age were more pronounced in the early 1990s than in the 2000s, and young and old respondents are now more likely to share the same opinion.

Perceptions of women as homemakers are remarkably similar between the sexes, with changes in men's attitudes over the past 15 years largely mirroring those of women. For most countries these movements are only modest, in contrast to the rapid changes in antiegalitarian views seen earlier. This pattern is consistent with Fortin (2005), who also notes that perceptions of women's role as homemaker are more persistent over time than antiegalitarian views in OECD countries. With her finding that such perceptions are associated with labor market outcomes, she speculates that the perceptions could be implicated in the recent slowdown of the convergence in pay across genders.

By further contrast to antiegalitarian views, which have uniformly improved across countries, age ranges, and education levels, changes in attitudes toward homemakers are far less monotonic and systematic. Brazil, Chile, and Mexico have progressed toward further acknowledging the importance of careers to women, but

FIGURE 1.25: Views on "Being a Housewife Is Just as Fulfilling as Working for Pay" in selected countries, by sex, age group, and education level

a. Women's agreement, by age group

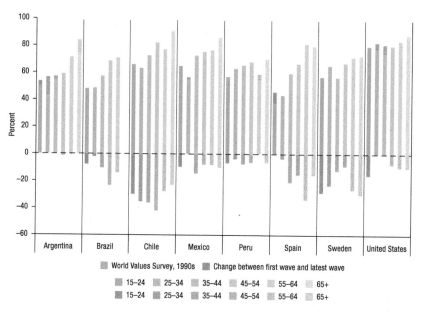

b. Men's agreement, by age group

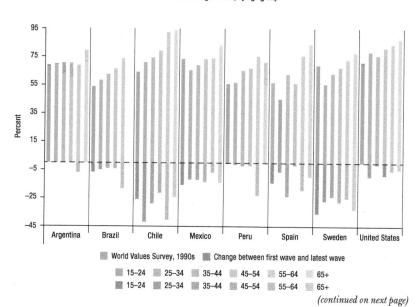

(continued on next page)

FIGURE 1.25: Views on "Being a Housewife Is Just as Fulfilling as Working for Pay" in selected countries, by sex, age group, and education level *(continued)*

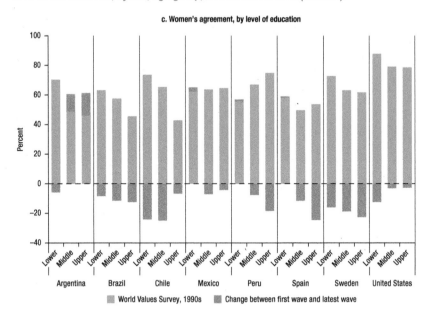

c. Women's agreement, by level of education

World Values Survey, 1990s   Change between first wave and latest wave

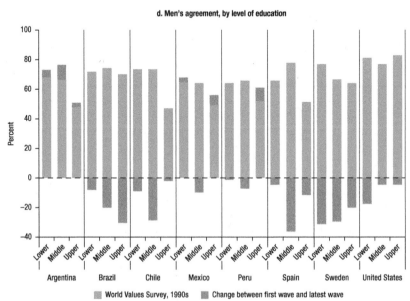

d. Men's agreement, by level of education

World Values Survey, 1990s   Change between first wave and latest wave

Source: World Values Survey, latest available waves.

Argentina has moved in the opposite direction, with both younger and older cohorts and highly educated women more frequently affirming traditional gender roles and identities in the 2000s than in the 1990s. Countries with views toward traditional gender roles attenuated most over the past 15 years. Brazil and Chile also experienced the steepest ascent in female LFP over the same period, as will be documented in the following chapters, but this is of course far from definitive evidence that changing attitudes caused greater female LFP.

The country with the strongest traditional values in LAC at baseline, Chile, saw the largest declines in those views among women and men over the past 15 years. Young and middle-aged women, more than 60 percent and 80 percent of whom supported housewifery, respectively, in the 1990s, have since both experienced declines of almost 40 percentage points in those views.

The belief that a woman's identity extends beyond her role as a housewife exhibits greater—though still modest—variability with age than with education. Although their signs remain consistent with the notion that more highly educated individuals adhere less to traditional gender roles, the education gradients are remarkably flat. This finding is surprising in that education is viewed as a long-term investment in human capital directed at building future competencies for the labor market.

One possible reason for support for housewifery to remain high in LAC is that women believe children are harmed by their mother's participation in the labor force, or that the bond between mother and child is somehow weakened. In that event, one would expect women in LAC to disagree with statements such as, "A working mother can establish just as warm and secure a relationship with her children as a mother who does not work" and "A preschool child is likely to suffer if his or her mother works." This is not the case, however (figure 1.26).

In LAC, both women and men agree—at rates of 55 percent and 85 percent, respectively—that the relationship between a mother and her child can be just as secure if she works, with a moderate gradient in education, which is relatively uniform across countries. Since the early 1990s this sentiment has only strengthened, with many countries experiencing at least a 10-percentage-point rise in agreeing with such statements across all education levels. Relative to the mid-1990s, women and men in Mexico both agree, by almost 20 percentage points more, that working mothers can establish equally warm and secure relationships with their children. This timing coincides precisely with the steep acceleration in married Mexican women's participation in the labor market.

A large majority of both women and men believe that young children are likely to suffer if their mother participates in the labor force, but they agree that working mothers have relationships just as healthy as stay-at-home mothers. Are there insights to be gained from this apparent contradiction? Growing inner conflict for women, termed by some as "mothers' guilt," may well be the answer (Buttrose and Adams 2005). This conflict has real implications for women's LFP and the gender wage gap among OECD countries (Fortin 2005).

Contrary to the case of egalitarian norms, men's and women's views of women's role in the household are remarkably similar. Differences of opinion on women's roles are on average less than 7 percentage points, contrasting with the previous section, where discrepancies across sexes could reach 30 percentage points. Furthermore, for LAC countries in the sample, gradients for age and education are less pronounced—and nearly flat in some instances—implying some stability of these values. Variation over time is also more muted, confirming the higher persistence of the set of values

FIGURE 1.26: Views on "A Child's Relationship with a Working Mother Is Just as Good as with a Stay-at-Home Mother" in selected countries, by sex, education level, and age

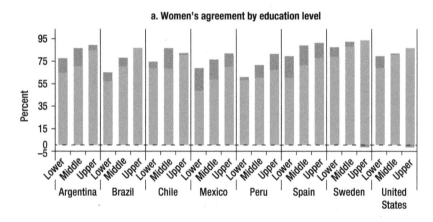

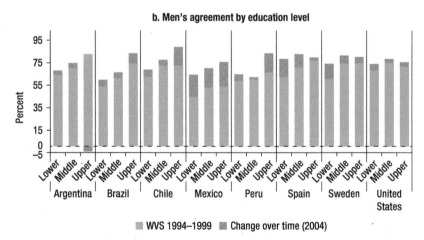

(continued on next page)

FIGURE 1.26: Views on "A Child's Relationship with a Working Mother Is Just as Good as with a Stay-at-Home Mother" in selected countries, by sex, education level, and age *(continued)*

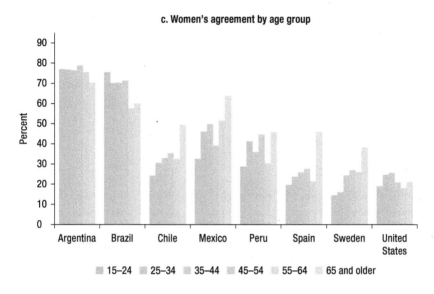

c. Women's agreement by age group

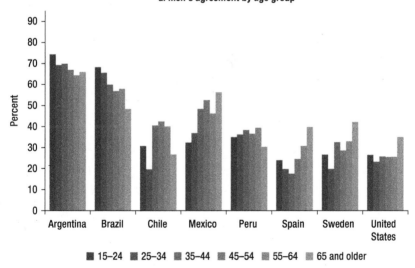

d. Men's agreement by age group

Source: World Values Survey, 1994–99, 1999–2004, 2000–13.

relating to women's role in the household compared with egalitarian views (Alesina, Giuliano, and Nunn 2011; Fortin 2005; Pande and Ford 2011; Piscopo 2006).

The growing "inner conflict" in women, whereby their continued support for housewifery and family values clashes with increasingly egalitarian views, is consistent with shifting identities, as careers become more important to women beyond wages earned, with implications for women's LFP and the gender wage gap in OECD countries (Fortin 2005). As participation becomes less economic and more related to identity, women's labor supply (hours worked) is expected to become much less responsive to wages, as in the United States, where the elasticity of married women's labor supply declined 50–56 percent from 1980 to 2000 (Blau and Kahn 2007).

Female economic participation

Labor force participation

Stylized fact 5a: Female LFP rates have climbed sharply in almost all LAC countries over the past few decades, more so than in any other developing region. The average rate in LAC is slightly above what its level of development would predict.

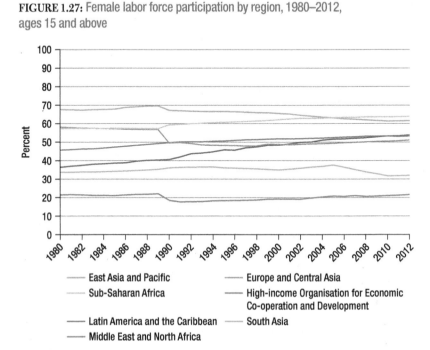

FIGURE 1.27: Female labor force participation by region, 1980–2012, ages 15 and above

——— East Asia and Pacific ——— Europe and Central Asia
——— Sub-Saharan Africa ——— High-income Organisation for Economic Co-operation and Development
——— Latin America and the Caribbean ——— South Asia
——— Middle East and North Africa

Source: World Bank 2014.

Female LFP in LAC over the past three decades has risen faster than in any other region, jumping from roughly 36 percent in 1980 to more than 53 percent in 2012 (figure 1.27). This increase is equivalent to nearly 80 million additional women in the region's labor force.

Only two other regions registered sizable gains in female LFP: Sub-Saharan Africa and high-income OECD countries. The drivers behind high-income OECD countries' rise, from 45 percent to 53 percent over the same period, are very different, given their more mature stage of development.

Female LFP in Sub-Saharan Africa rose only moderately (from 57 percent to 63.5 percent in 2012). It fell slightly in South Asia and East Asia and the Pacific (from 33 percent to 31 percent and from 67 percent to 61 percent, respectively), and significantly in Europe and Central Asia (from 58 percent to 50 percent).

Male LFP declined moderately in most regions except Europe and Central Asia, where it tumbled from 77 percent in 1980 to 67 percent in 2009 (largely reflecting the structural changes following the breakup of the former Soviet Union). In LAC male LFP fell marginally, from 81 percent to 80 percent (figure 1.28).

FIGURE 1.28: Male labor force participation by region, 1980–2012, ages 15 and above

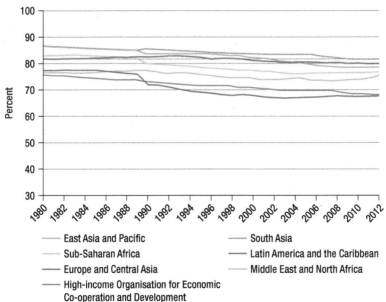

East Asia and Pacific
Sub-Saharan Africa
Europe and Central Asia
High-income Organisation for Economic Co-operation and Development

South Asia
Latin America and the Caribbean
Middle East and North Africa

Source: World Bank 2014.

As shown in figures 1.27 and 1.28, regional trends in LFP reveal large differences between men and women. Male LFP exhibits a slight downward trend, distributed narrowly around 80 percent, and the dispersion appears related to the level of regional development, human capital investments, and regional economic cycles and fluctuations. Female LFP rates, trending upward in almost all regions, are characterized by a more pronounced and steady dispersion. The exception of LAC's steeper rise and Europe and Central Asia's postcommunist transition (linked to changes in ideological prescriptions, which informed female economic participation) stand out. The observed gender-specific variation is consistent with the notion that the differences in social norms for female participation are larger than those for men's labor market decisions.

Gender gap in participation

Stylized fact 5b: Largely as a result of the fast-paced growth of female LFP, the gender gap in LFP has narrowed faster in LAC than in any other developing region.

FIGURE 1.29: Ratio of female to male labor force participation rates by region, 1980–2012, ages 15 and above

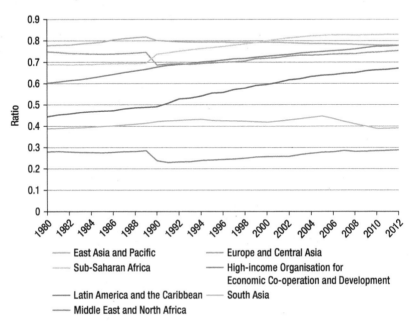

Source: World Bank 2014.

FIGURE 1.30: Female labor force participation rates in selected Latin America and the Caribbean countries, 1980–2012, ages 15 and above

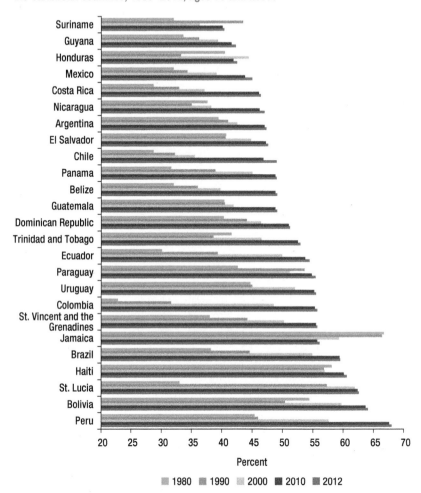

Source: World Bank 2014.

Given the main trends in LAC—the sharp increase in female LFP and the near constancy in the male rate—the gender gap has narrowed considerably (figure 1.29). Similar, if less dramatic, patterns are also observed in the Middle East and North Africa region and in high-income OECD countries. In other regions the ratio of female to male LFP stayed roughly constant.

LAC has significant variation in the ratio of female to male LFP, mainly because of differences across countries in female rates (figure 1.30). In fact in 2012, average

FIGURE 1.31: Relationship between female labor force participation and GDP per capita in Latin America and the Caribbean and the world

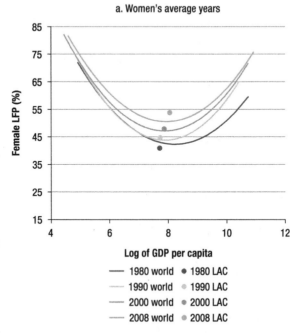

a. Women's average years

Female LFP (%)

Log of GDP per capita

— 1980 world   ● 1980 LAC
— 1990 world   ● 1990 LAC
— 2000 world   ● 2000 LAC
— 2008 world   ● 2008 LAC

Source: World Bank data; International Labour Organization data (female labor force participation).
Note: LAC = Latin America and the Caribbean; LFP = labor force participation. Each colored dot represents the position of Latin America and the Caribbean in a given decade, with the log of per capita income (2000 US$) measured on the horizontal axis and the rate of female LFP on the vertical axis. Each U-shaped curve corresponds to a separate decade's estimated relationship between (log per capita) income and female LFP, based on that decade's cross-section of all countries in the world.

male LFP rates were tightly concentrated around 79 percent, while the female LFP rate averaged about 52 percent, with dispersion across countries twice that of males.

LAC has been on the move. In 1980 its female LFP resembled that of the Middle East and North Africa and South Asia, the regions with the lowest LFP. But the past decades have witnessed rapid convergence toward the regions with the highest female LFP. For every 100 men in the labor force in 2012, 83 women were working in Sub-Saharan Africa, 78 in East Asia and the Pacific and in high-income OECD countries, 75 in Europe and Central Asia, and 67 in LAC.

The observed trend and the position of LAC relative to other regions may in part be explained by differences in the rate and level of development, proxied by per capita income. Indeed, the economic literature has extensively documented a robust U-shaped relationship between the level of economic development and adult women's LFP (figure 1.31).[17] When income is extremely low and agriculture dominates the economy, women are to a large extent in the labor force. They are traditionally unpaid

FIGURE 1.32: Evolution of the relationship between female labor force participation and GDP per capita (constant 2000 US dollars), by region

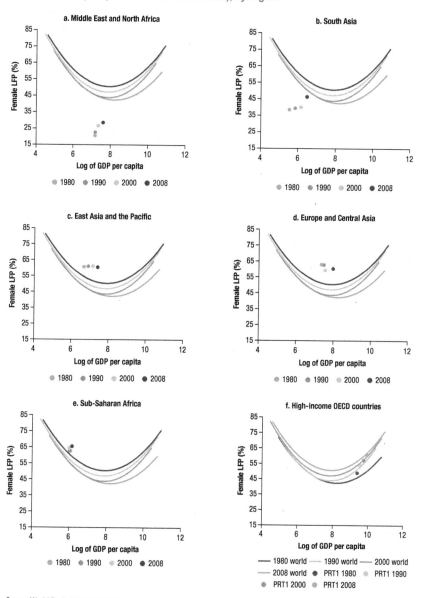

Source: World Bank data; International Labour Organization data (female labor force participation).
Note: OECD = Organisation for Economic Co-operation and Development. Each colored dot represents the particular region's position in a given decade, with the log of per capita income measured along the horizontal axis and the rate of female LFP on the vertical axis. Each U-shaped curve corresponds to a separate decade's estimated relationship between (log per capita) income and female LFP, based on that decade's cross-section of all countries in the world.

workers on family farms and in household businesses and are almost completely in charge of home production such as child rearing or household chores.

Development initially moves women out of the labor force, partly because of the rise in men's market opportunities and wages, and partly because of social barriers against women entering the paid labor force. As countries develop and women become more educated, the opportunity cost of their staying out of the labor force rises, such that they eventually move back in.[18] Figures 1.31 and 1.32 illustrate the evolution of female LFP in LAC over time, relative to the predicted U-shaped relationship between per capita income and female LFP, which is estimated from a panel of countries over four decades. In figure 1.32, LAC's regional experience is compared with that of other developing regions and high-income OECD countries.

Figure 1.31 illustrates the sense in which LAC has been on the move over the past decades. At the beginning of the sample in the 1980s, LAC located itself below the level of female LFP predicted by its average per capita income and to the left of the lowest point on the corresponding decade's estimated curve. Female LFP then grew so rapidly in LAC as to rise above the curves corresponding to each subsequent decade, while output grew at a more moderate pace. Nevertheless, income growth was sufficient to exceed the curve's minimum by 2000, which places LAC in the segment of the horizontal axis where income growth is related to growth in female LFP.

Figure 1.32 demonstrates that similar rates of female LFP are consistent with very different levels of income. For instance, the more rural economies of Sub-Saharan Africa exhibit female LFP comparable to that of industrialized economies. In turn, with LAC's income falling between these two regions, its women are engaged in the labor force at a lower rate.

The observation that very different levels of national income are related to similar levels of female LFP highlights the nonlinear relationship between development and female LFP rates. The relationship is further corroborated by the consideration that welfare assessments based on participation rates would be somewhat incomplete and misleading. As will be discussed later in the report, the ability to choose is what matters.

Although seemingly robust, the U-shaped relationship between female LFP and income is only approximate and does not perfectly predict female LFP. Much of the variation in female LFP remains unexplained by income, in all likelihood because of cultural and institutional characteristics that differ across regions and that are unaccounted for in the relationship. The Middle East and North Africa, for instance, has per capita incomes comparable to LAC, but its female LFP rates are half those of LAC.

Notes

[1] In addition to labor market returns, women's education has strong social externalities beyond social norms. A large body of literature shows that higher levels of education of women contribute to reducing fertility (Cochrane 1979; Schultz 1973), which in turn decreases infant mortality and

increases life expectancy (Behrman and Deolalikar 1988). The literature has also documented the intergenerational effects of maternal education on the education, health, well-being, and adult productivity of their children (Behrman 1997; Schultz 1988, 1993; Strauss and Thomas 1995). Studies of rates of return have also documented the economic benefits of investing in girls' education (Psacharopoulos 1994).

[2] Net enrollment rates compare students enrolled in each grade with individuals in the corresponding age cohort. Gross enrollment rates are sometimes higher for boys than for girls owing to the higher repetition rates for boys in several LAC countries. See, for example, Behrman, Sengupta, and Todd (2005), for rural Mexico. See also Grant and Behrman (2010), who find that gender gaps in schooling increasingly favor females, on the basis of data from Demographic and Health Surveys in 38 developing countries.

[3] Although similar in trend, differences appear among LAC countries in net enrollment rates at all three levels. In primary schooling, the gap ranged from 0.94 in St. Vincent and the Grenadines and 0.97 in Guatemala, to above parity in 17 countries, including the three most populous. At the secondary level, the average ratio was 1.09. In tertiary education, it was 1.39.

[4] Becker, Hubbard, and Murphy (2009) present evidence from a sample of 120 developed and developing countries, which shows that in 67 countries a larger fraction of women than men ages 30–34 years had completed college in the late 2000s, whereas in 1970 women in only five countries in the same sample did, and all five countries had above-average levels of GDP per capita. So the worldwide boom in higher education has been driven by women.

[5] The biological norm of male to female births is about 105 newborn boys for every 100 newborn girls. Thus, male bias, or sex imbalance, refers to a ratio above this biological norm. The literature has attempted to link these imbalances to parental preference for sons, which manifests itself in greater household time and resources allocated to boys, which increases their chances of surviving and results in excess mortality of girls (Das Gupta 2005, 2006, 2008; Lin and Luoh 2008; Lin, Liu, and Qian 2008; Oster 2005, 2006, 2009; Oster, Chen, and Yu 2010; Sen 1990, 1992). The bias may arise prenatally through selective abortion, particularly among cohorts born during the diffusion of sex determination technologies.

[6] These figures refer to sex ratios among the total population, not just among newborns.

[7] See, for example, Fogli and Fernández (2009) and relevant literature on social norms.

[8] Integrated Public Use Microdata Series (IPUMS), Minnesota Population Center, University of Minnesota. https://usa.ipums.org/usa/index.shtml.

[9] According to IPUMS data, Costa Rica has a crude divorce rate of 2.1, in line with that of Canada and France; the divorce rate in Uruguay (4.4) is greater than that of the United States (3.7).

[10] Fogli and Fernández 2009; Merriam-Webster's Collegiate Dictionary, 10th edition, 2002. A similar definition was also employed by Guiso, Sapienza, and Zingales (2006), who identify culture as "those customary beliefs and values that ethnic, religious, and social groups transmit unchanged from generation to generation."

[11] In much of the literature, culture is assumed to be roughly constant within a given generation, allowing for feedback between outcomes and culture and preferences only across generations (Guiso, Sapienza, and Zingales 2006).

[12] The World Values Survey is a worldwide network of social scientists studying changing values and their impacts on social and political life. In collaboration with the European Values Study, it carried out representative national surveys in 97 societies containing almost 90 percent of the world's people. These surveys show pervasive changes in what people want out of life and what they believe. To monitor these changes, the World Values Survey and European Values Survey have executed six waves of surveys, from 1981 to 2013.

[13] In Latin America, quota schemes have been on the rise since the early 1990s and have mainly taken the form of legislated candidate quotas: parties are required by law to reserve a certain number of candidacies for women. First adopted by Argentina in 1991, this type of quota has since been implemented in 11 other Latin American countries: Bolivia, Brazil, Costa Rica, the Dominican Republic, Ecuador, Guyana, Honduras, Mexico, Panama, Paraguay, and Peru. Countries with voluntary party quotas (parties committing voluntarily to nominate a certain percentage of female candidates for electoral lists) include Chile, El Salvador, Guatemala, and Nicaragua. The quota adoption process was facilitated by the consolidation of democracy in the 1980s, which fostered the emergence of women's associations and other civil rights groups (Pande and Ford 2011; Piscopo 2006). The 12 adopting countries have improved their worldwide ranking for female parliamentary representation: eight rank in the top 50 percent of parliaments worldwide, and two—Argentina and Costa Rica—rank within the top 10 percent (Piscopo 2006).

[14] See Fernández (2010) and the works cited therein.

[15] See, for example, Farré and Vella (2007); Fernández, Fogli, and Olivetti (2004); and Vella (1994), who discuss mechanisms underlying the intergenerational transmission of attitudes.

[16] The United States is an exception among OECD countries, with women of many age and education categories revealing themselves to be more conservative than American men as well as women and men in Western Europe and many LAC countries. By this measure both young men and women in the United States have become more conservative in the past 15 years.

[17] See Goldin (1995) and Mammen and Paxson (2000), who present evidence from a cross-section of countries that female LFP first declines and then increases as income rises. See also Horton (1996), Psacharopoulos and Tzannatos (1989), and Sinha (1967).

[18] Several factors underlie female LFP, notably the opportunity cost of a woman's time and unearned income, which can include her spouse's income (if she is married) as well as safety net transfers and transfers from other family members. If men's wages rise with their increasing productivity, such that a spouse's income rises, for instance, then a woman may be less likely to participate in the labor force. If rising male productivity is accompanied by more elevated female productivity, however, such that the opportunity cost of the woman's time also rises, her increased wages in the labor market may induce her to enter the labor force if the substitution effect from her own rising wages outstrips the income effect from her spouse's higher income.

References

Akerlof, George A., and Rachel E. Kranton. 2010. *Identity Economics: How Our Identities Shape Our Work, Wages, and Well-Being*. Princeton, NJ: Princeton University Press.

Alesina, Alberto F., Paola Giuliano, and Nathan Nunn. 2011. "On the Origins of Gender Roles: Women and the Plough." NBER Working Paper 17098, National Bureau of Economic Research, Cambridge, MA.

Aritomi, Tami, Analia Olgiati, and Maria Beatriz Orlando. 2010. "Female Headed Households and Poverty in LAC: What Are We Measuring?" Background paper to this report, World Bank, Washington, DC.

Barro, Robert, and Jong Wha Lee. 2013. "A New Data Set of Educational Attainment in the World, 1950–2010." *Journal of Development Economics* 104: 184–98.

Becker, Gary S. 2007. "Health as Human Capital: Synthesis and Extensions." *Oxford Economic Papers* 59 (3): 379–410.

Becker, Gary S., William H. J. Hubbard, and Kevin M. Murphy. 2009. "Explaining the Worldwide Boom in Higher Education of Women." Working paper, University of Chicago.

Behrman, Jere R. 1997. "Women's Schooling and Child Education: A Survey." Working paper, University of Pennsylvania.

Behrman, Jere R., and Anil B. Deolalikar. 1988. "Health and Nutrition." In *Handbook of Development Economics*, edited by Hollis Chenery and T. N. Srinivasan, 631–711. Amsterdam: Elsevier.

Behrman, Jere R., Piyali Sengupta, and Petra Todd. 2005. "Progressing through PROGRESA: An Impact Assessment of a School Subsidy Experiment in Rural Mexico." *Economic Development and Cultural Change* 54 (1): 237–75.

Blau, Francine D., and Lawrence M. Kahn. 1997. "Swimming Upstream: Trends in the Gender Wage Differential in the 1980s." *Journal of Labor Economics* 15 (1, pt. 1): 1–42.

———. 2007. "The Gender Pay Gap: Have Women Gone as Far as They Can?" *Academy of Management Perspectives*, February, 1–23.

Buttrose, Ita, and Penny Adams. 2005. *Motherguilt: Australian Women Reveal Their True Feelings about Motherhood*. Camberwell, Victoria: Viking.

Campa, Pamela, Alessandra Casarico, and Paola Profeta. 2009. "Gender Culture and Gender Gap in Employment." Working Paper 2738, CESifo Group, Munich.

Chiappori, Pierre-André, Murat Iyigun, and Yoram Weiss. 2009. "Investment in Schooling and the Marriage Market." *American Economic Review* 99 (5): 1689–1713.

Cochrane, Susan H. 1979. "Fertility and Education: What Do We Really Know?" Baltimore, MD: Johns Hopkins University, for World Bank.

Das Gupta, Monica. 2005. "Explaining Asia's Missing Women: A New Look at the Data." *Population and Development Review* 31 (3): 529–35.

———. 2006. "Cultural versus Biological Factors in Explaining Asia's 'Missing Women': Response to Oster." *Population and Development Review* 32 (2): 328–32.

———. 2008. "Can Biological Factors Like Hepatitis B Explain the Bulk of Gender Imbalance in China? A Review of the Evidence." *World Bank Research Observer* 23 (2): 201–17.

Duryea, Suzanne, Sebastian Galiani, Hugo Ñopo, and Claudia Piras. 2007. "The Educational Gender Gap in Latin America and the Caribbean." Working Paper 4510, Inter-American Development Bank, Washington, DC.

Farré, Lídia, and Francis Vella. 2007. "The Intergenerational Transmission of Gender Role Attitudes and Its Implications for Female Labor Force Participation." IZA Discussion Paper 2802, Institute for the Study of Labor, Bonn, Germany.

Fernández, Raquel. 2007a. "Culture as Learning: The Evolution of Female Labor Force Participation over a Century." NBER Working Paper 13373, National Bureau of Economic Research, Cambridge, MA.

———. 2007b. "Women, Work, and Culture." NBER Working Paper 12888, National Bureau of Economic Research, Cambridge, MA.

———. 2008. "Culture and Economics." In *New Palgrave Dictionary of Economics*, edited by Steven N. Durlauf and Lawrence E. Blume (2nd ed.). [Online edition] Palgrave Macmillan. http://www.dictionaryofeconomics.com/dictionary.

———. 2010. "Does Culture Matter?" NBER Working Paper 16277, National Bureau of Economic Research, Cambridge, MA.

Fernández, Raquel, and Alessandra Fogli. 2006. "Fertility: The Role of Culture and Family Experience." *Journal of the European Economic Association* 4 (2–3): 552–61.

Fernández, Raquel, Alessandra Fogli, and Claudia Olivetti. 2004. "Preference Formation and the Rise of Women's Labor Force Participation: Evidence from WWII." NBER Working Paper 10589, National Bureau of Economic Research, Cambridge, MA.

Fogli, Alessandra, and Raquel Fernández. 2009. "Culture: An Empirical Investigation of Beliefs, Work, and Fertility." *American Economic Journal: Macroeconomics* 1 (1): 146–77.

Fogli, Alessandra, and Laura Veldkamp. 2011. "Nature or Nurture? Learning and the Geography of Female Labor Force Participation." *Econometrica* 79 (4): 1103–38.

Fortin, Nicole M. 2005. "Gender Role Attitudes and the Labour-Market Outcomes of Women across OECD Countries." *Oxford Review of Economic Policy* 21 (3): 416–38.

———. 2009. "Gender Role Attitudes and Women's Labor Market Participation: Opting-Out, AIDS, and the Persistent Appeal of Housewifery." Working paper, Department of Economics, University of British Columbia.

Fussell, Elizabeth, and Alberto Palloni. 2004. "Persistent Marriage Regimes in Changing Times." *Journal of Marriage and the Family* 66 (5): 1201–13.

Goldin, Claudia. 1995. "The U-Shaped Female Labor Force Function in Economic Development and Economic History." In *Investment in Women's Human Capital*, edited by T. Paul Schultz, 61–90. Chicago: University of Chicago Press.

———. 2006. "Quiet Revolution That Transformed Women's Employment, Education, and Family." *American Economic Review Papers and Proceedings* 96 (2): 1–21.

Grant, Monica J., and Jere R. Behrman. 2010. "Gender Gaps in Educational Attainment in Less Developed Countries." *Population and Development Review* 36 (1): 71–89.

Grossman, Michael. 1972. "On the Concept of Health Capital and the Demand for Health." *Journal of Political Economy* 80 (2): 223–55.

———. 2000. "The Human Capital Model." In *Handbook of Health Economics* (Vol. 1), edited by A. J. Culyer and J. P. Newhouse, 347–408. Amsterdam: Elsevier.

Guiso, Luigi, Paola Sapienza, and Luigi Zingales. 2006. "Does Culture Affect Economic Outcomes?" *Journal of Economic Perspectives* 20 (2): 23–48.

Handa, Sudhanshu. 1996. "Expenditure Behavior and Children's Welfare: An Analysis of Female Headed Households in Jamaica." *Journal of Development Economics* 50 (1): 165–87.

Horton, Susan, ed. 1996. *Women and Industrialization in Asia.* London: Routledge.

Htun, Mala, and Jennifer Piscopo. 2010. "Presence without Empowerment? Women and Politics in Latin America and the Caribbean." Paper prepared for the Conflict Prevention and Peace Forum, December.

Johnson, William R., and Jonathan Skinner. 1986. "Labor Supply and Marital Separation." *American Economic Review* 76 (3): 455–69.

Kassebaum, Nicholas J., Amelia Bertozzi-Villa, Megan S. Coggeshall, Katya A. Shackelford, Caitlyn Steiner, Kyle R. Heuton, and others. 2014. "Global, Regional, and National Levels and Causes of Maternal Mortality During 1990–2013: A Systematic Analysis for the Global Burden of Disease Study 2013." *Lancet* 384 (9947): 980–1004.

Lin, Ming-Jen, Jin-Tan Liu, and Nancy Qian. 2008. "More Women Missing, Fewer Girls Dying: The Impact of Abortion on Sex Ratios at Birth and Excess Female Mortality in Taiwan." CEPR Discussion Paper 6667, Centre for Economic Policy Research, London.

Lin, Ming-Jen, and Ming-Ching Luoh. 2008. "Can Hepatitis B Mothers Account for the Number of Missing Women? Evidence from Three Million Newborns in Taiwan." *American Economic Review* 98 (5): 2259–73.

Lundberg, Shelly J., and Elaina Rose. 2002. "The Effects of Sons and Daughters on Men's Labor Supply and Wages." *Review of Economics and Statistics* 84 (2): 251–68.

Mammen, Kristin, and Christina Paxson. 2000. "Women's Work and Economic Development." *Journal of Economic Perspectives* 14 (4): 141–64.

Marshall, Jeffery H. 2005. "Social Exclusion in Education in Latin America and the Caribbean." Paper presented to the Social Inclusion Trust Fund, Inter-American Development Bank, Washington, DC.

Marshall, Jeffery H., and Valentina Calderón. 2006. "Social Exclusion in Education in Latin America and the Caribbean." Technical Papers Series, Inter-American Development Bank, Washington, DC.

Mensch, Barbara S., Susheela Singh, and John B. Casterline. 2005. "Trends in the Timing of First Marriage among Men and Women in the Developing World 2005." Working Paper 202, Population Center, New York.

Murray, Christopher J. L., Margaret C. Hogan, Kyle J. Foreman, Mohsen Naghavi, Stephanie Y. Ahn, Mengru Wang, Susanna M. Makela, Alan D. Lopez, and Rafael Lozano. 2010. "Maternal Mortality for 181 Countries, 1980–2008: A Systematic Analysis of Progress Towards Millennium Development Goal 5." *Lancet* 375 (9726): 1609–23.

OECD Program for International Student Assessment. 2012 PISA 2012 results. http://nces.ed.gov /surveys/pisa/pisa2012/.

Oster, Emily. 2005. "Hepatitis B and the Case of the Missing Women." *Journal of Political Economy* 113 (6): 1163–1216.

———. 2006. "Explaining Asia's Missing Women: A New Look at the Data—Comments." *Population and Development Review* 32 (2): 323–27.

———. 2009. "Proximate Sources of Population Sex Imbalance in India." *Demography* 46 (2): 325–40.

Oster, Emily, Gang Chen, and Xinsen Yu. 2010. "Hepatitis B Does Not Explain Male-Biased Sex Ratios in China." *Economics Letters* 107 (2): 142–44.

Pande, Rohini, and Deanna Ford. 2011. "Gender Quotas and Female Leadership: A Review." Background paper for the *World Development Report 2012*, World Bank, Washington, DC.

Palloni, Alberto. 2009. "Is Marriage Here to Stay? Educational Attainment, Labor Force Participation, and the Transition to First Marriage among Mexican and Costa Rican Women." Paper presented at the Annual Meeting of the Population Association of America, Detroit, MI, April 30–May 2.

Piscopo, Jennifer. 2006. "Engineering Quotas in Latin America." CILAS Working Paper 23, Center for Iberian and Latin American Studies, University of California, San Diego, CA.

Psacharopoulos, George. 1994. "Returns to Investment in Education: A Global Update." *World Development* 22 (9): 1325–43.

Psacharopoulos, George, and Zafiris Tzannatos. 1989. "Female Labor Force Participation: An International Perspective." *World Bank Research Observer* 4 (2): 187–201.

Rosero-Bixby, Luis. 1996. "Nuptiality Trends and Fertility Transition in Latin America." In *The Fertility Transition in Latin America*, edited by José. M. Guzmán, Susheela Singh, Germán Rodríguez, and Edith A. Pantelides, 135–150. Oxford, UK: Oxford University Press.

———. 2004. "La fecundidad en áreas metropolitanas de América Latina: La fecundidad de reemplazo y más allá." *Notas de Población* 37 (78): 35–63.

Schultz, T. Paul. 1973. "A Preliminary Survey of Economic Analysis of Fertility." *American Economic Review* 63 (2): 77–78.

———. 1988. "Education Investments and Returns." In *Handbook of Development Economics*, edited by Hollis Chenery and T. N. Srinivasan, 543–630. Amsterdam: Elsevier.

———. 1990. "Testing the Neoclassical Model of Family Labor Supply and Fertility." *Journal of Human Resources* 25 (4): 599–634.

———. 1993. "Investments in the Schooling and Health of Women and Men: Quantities and Returns." *Journal of Human Resources* 28 (4): 694–734.

Sen, Amartya. 1990. "More Than 100 Million Women Are Missing." *New York Review of Books*, December 20.

———. 1992. "Missing Women." *British Medical Journal* 304 (6827): 587–88.

Sinha, Jania N. 1967. "Dynamics of Female Participation in Economic Activity in a Developing Economy." In *Proceedings of the World Population Conference, Belgrade, 30 Aug.–10 Sep. 1965*, vol. 4., 336–37. New York: United Nations.

Sobotka, Tomáš. 2004. *Postponement of Childbearing and Low Fertility in Europe*. Amsterdam: Dutch University Press.

Stevenson, Betsey. 2008. "Divorce Law and Women's Labor Supply." NBER Working Paper 14346, National Bureau of Economic Research, Cambridge, MA.

Strauss, John, and Duncan Thomas. 1995. "Empirical Modeling of Household and Family Decisions," RAND Reprint Series, Paper 95–12, RP-454. Santa Monica, CA: RAND.

United Nations. 2010. "World Fertility Report 2007." Department of Economic and Social Affairs, United Nations, New York.

Vella, Francis. 1994. "Gender Roles and Human Capital Investment: The Relationship between Traditional Attitudes and Female Labor Market Performance." *Economica* 61 (242): 191–211.

Whitehead, Tony. 1978. "Residence, Kinship, and Mating as Survival Strategies: A West Indian Example." *Journal of Marriage and the Family* 40 (4): 817–28.

World Bank. 2014. *World Development Indicators* 2014. Washington DC: World Bank.

Part II

2
The Regional Trend: Two Paths to the Labor Market

Introduction

Building on the set of stylized facts presented in chapter 1, this chapter aims to further the understanding of women's economic participation. The first chapter's historical perspective sheds new light on the dramatic trends that have seen Latin America and the Caribbean (LAC) transition from a region with one of the lowest rates of female economic participation to one whose growth in participation is outpacing that of all the other developing regions.

The most striking characteristic of the region's transition is the segregated nature of the trajectories of single and married women. Just as in the United States at the beginning of the 20th century, marital status virtually defined the economic role of women in LAC in the 1960s, with wives dominating the domestic realm and their husbands being the breadwinners. As both single and married women's participation grew over the past four decades, the gender specialization broke down progressively, with married women joining the labor force at unprecedented rates.

This feature of the evolution of female labor force participation (LFP) rates further supports the household perspective adopted in this study, buttressed by other findings in chapters 3–5. These consider narrower features of women's economic activity: the decision to join the labor force, the choice of occupation, and the level of earnings.

- Of the several factors the literature identifies as key determinants of women's decisions to enter (and stay in) the labor force, education and family formation decisions explain nearly two-thirds of the region's evolution since the 1960s.

- Participation in the labor market can take different forms and transitions across occupational states (formal employment, informal employment, unemployment, and out of the labor force) and can shed light on additional aspects of female LFP. This issue is considered in the fourth chapter and identifies a particular relationship between fertility and marital status and the choice of occupation.

- The evolution of the gender earnings differentials and the principal drivers are interpreted in light of the earlier findings in the report and other research, which both question the notion that maximizing earnings adequately describes the labor supply decisions of women, as illustrated in the introduction of the report.

A historical account of women's economic participation

The second half of the 20th century witnessed a dramatic transformation in the economic role of women in LAC, which is clearest in the sharp increase in the prevalence of women in the labor force. Since the 1960s, the rise in female LFP has been steep and nearly uninterrupted (figure 2.1), outpacing all other regions of the world and resulting in nearly 80 million additional women in the labor force (Chioda and Demombynes 2014). The female LFP rate rose from roughly 36 percent in 1980 to more than 51 percent in 2008 (53 percent in 2007), a nearly 34 percent increase. Although a social and economic revolution for women in the United States, Europe, and other developed countries has spawned a vast literature, corresponding shifts in LAC have not. The main reason has been limited data: lacking repeated cross-sectional household surveys over long stretches of time, studies of the economic role of women have largely relied on snapshots at a single point or on analyses of short-term changes.[1] Chioda and Demombynes (2014) begin to fill this gap by analyzing the rise in female LFP in LAC and its determinants.[2] Their analysis relies on newly available microdata from 43 censuses in 10 Latin American countries over 1960–2010. The countries covered in their sample account for about 80 percent of the region's population.[3]

In the typical LAC country, the percentage of women in the labor force doubled between the early 1960s and the early 2000s (table 2.1; see also figure 2.2). The increase has ranged from 15 percentage points in Costa Rica to a staggering 50 percentage points in Brazil, where the presence of women in the workforce more than tripled. And it occurred in both upper-middle-income and low-income countries.

The countries experiencing the largest changes are at opposite ends of the per capita income spectrum: Bolivia, which is relatively poor, and Argentina and Brazil, which are relatively rich. But considerable heterogeneity exists across countries in both the magnitude and the timing of the changes. The peak rate of change in women's work rates was in the 1970s for Colombia and República Bolivariana de Venezuela; the 1980s for Argentina and Bolivia; the 1990s for Brazil, Chile, Costa

FIGURE 2.1: The rise in female labor force participation has been steep and uninterrupted

Evolution of female labor force participation in Latin America and the Caribbean, women ages 25–55, 1960–2010

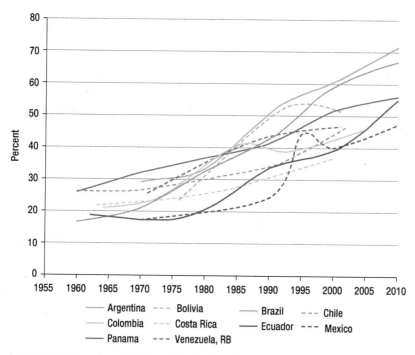

Sources: Chioda and Demombynes 2014; Minnesota Population Center, Integrated Public Use Microdata Series (IPUMS), https://www.ipums.org/ (hereafter cited as IPUMS).

TABLE 2.1: Labor force participation rates in selected Latin American and Caribbean countries, women ages 25–55, 1960–2010

Country	Year	Women in labor force (%)	Implied annual growth rate (%)
Argentina	1970	29	
	1980	33	0.4
	1991	52	1.7
	2001	61	0.9
	2010	71	1.1
	Total change over entire period	42	1.1

(continued on next page)

Country	Year	Women in labor force (%)	Implied annual growth rate (%)
Bolivia	1976	23	
	1992	52	1.8
	2001	51	–0.1
	Total change over entire period	28	1.1
Brazil	1960	17	
	1970	21	0.4
	1980	32	1.2
	1991	44	1.0
	2000	60	1.7
	2010	67	0.7
	Total change over entire period	50	1.0
Chile	1960	26	
	1970	26	0.0
	1982	31	0.4
	1992	35	0.5
	2002	47	1.1
	Total change over entire period	21	0.5
Colombia	1964	21	
	1973	24	0.4
	1985	41	1.4
	1993	39	–0.2
	2005	46	0.6
	Total change over entire period	25	0.6
Costa Rica	1963	22	
	1973	23	0.2
	1984	27	0.3
	2000	37	0.6
	Total change over entire period	15	0.4
Ecuador	1962	19	
	1974	17	–0.1
	1982	23	0.7

(continued on next page)

TABLE 2.1: Labor force participation rates in selected Latin American and Caribbean countries, women ages 25–55, 1960–2010 *(continued)*

Country	Year	Women in labor force (%)	Implied annual growth rate (%)
	1990	33	1.4
	2001	40	0.6
	2010	55	1.7
	Total change over entire period	36	0.8
Mexico	1970	17	
	1990	24	0.4
	1995	44	4.0
	2000	40	−0.8
	2010	47	0.7
	Total change over entire period	30	0.8
Panama	1960	26	
	1970	32	0.6
	1980	36	0.5
	1990	41	0.5
	2000	51	1.0
	2010	56	0.4
	Total change over entire period	30	0.6
Venezuela, RB	1971	25	
	1981	36	1.1
	1990	43	0.8
	2001	47	0.3
	Total change over entire period	21	0.7

Sources: Chioda and Demombynes 2014; IPUMS 2014.

Rica, and Mexico; and the 2000s for Ecuador (see table 2.1). These heterogeneous rates of change result in an increased end-of-sample dispersion in LFP relative to the beginning of the sample.

For LAC countries with available data, the female employment rate rose from about 20.5 percent in the 1960s to about 67 percent in the 2010s. To put this in perspective, the LAC region as a whole experienced a rise in female LFP since the 1960s that was comparable to that of the United States between 1890 and 1990. In 1890, U.S. female LFP hovered around 19 percent, in line with the levels of all LAC

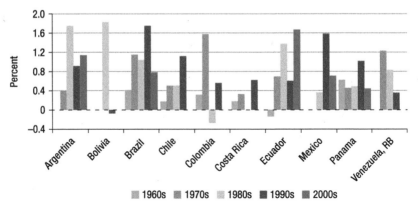

Sources: Chioda and Demombynes 2014; IPUMS 2014.

countries in table 2.1 in the first available decade. Nearly a century later, in 1980, the U.S. LFP rate reached 51 percent (Goldin 1990). Since the 1960s, certain countries even outpaced the United States' 1890–1980 gains. For instance, Brazil's female LFP grew from 17 percent to 67 percent.

The pattern of entry into the labor market by women in LAC has been similar to that of women in the United States, with a lag of roughly 30 years. The remarkable gains in female LFP over the last half-century were achieved by both married and unmarried women, as illustrated in figure 2.3, which contrasts the average LAC regional trends with those of the United States. To showcase the regional heterogeneity, panel b of figure 2.3 portrays participation rates for married women and single women by country, starting in the early 1960s. In both panels, as benchmarks, the regional average LFP rates of married and unmarried men in LAC are also reported, along with the rates for U.S. women starting in 1890. The historical trends appear to segregate along the lines of marital status. Although both married and unmarried women achieved large gains in LFP, they began the sample at very different baseline participation rates, with single women on average more than four times more likely to be in the labor force as their married counterparts in 1960.

Single women's LFP has risen steadily since the 1960s—a trend that likely started in previous decades—with a slight acceleration in the late 1990s. Although single women's economic participation exhibits very low dispersion around 45 percent in the 1960s, the subsequent rise is accompanied by greater variability across countries. Thus, considerable heterogeneity is seen around the upward trend across countries and over time within a country, the latter correlated with nation-specific economic fluctuations and resembling the idiosyncrasies of their male counterparts' LFP.

FIGURE 2.3: The four-decade rise in female labor force participation in Latin America and the Caribbean is comparable to the U.S. rise between 1980 and 1990

Female labor force participation in selected Latin America and the Caribbean countries and the United States, by marital status

a. Historic regional trends in female labor force participation, married versus single

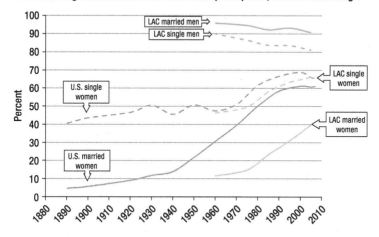

b. Historic country trends in female labor force participation: married versus single

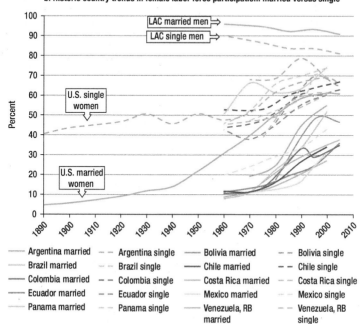

Sources: Chioda 2014; IPUMS 2014; U.S. Census Bureau Current Population Survey and U.S. Census data for United States.

The region's average annual percentage-point increase in single women's participation over the past four decades is 0.94. Argentina registered annual growth of nearly 0.1 percent over the entire period, with the very high 1.31 percent a year among single women in the 1980s balanced by a symmetrical decline during the economic contractions of the early 2000s (Chioda and Demombynes 2014). At the other extreme, República Bolivariana de Venezuela, Mexico, and Brazil enjoyed yearly growth over the period of 1.48 percent, 1.08 percent and 1.23 percent, respectively. Despite the heterogeneous growth rates in the 1990s and early 2000s, single women in those countries participated in the labor force at similar rates in 2005: 68 percent in Argentina, 69 percent in Mexico, 62 percent in República Bolivariana de Venezuela, and a staggering 70 percent in Brazil.

During the early 1970s to the mid-1980s, Colombia enjoyed an impressive annual growth rate of 5.2 percent in female LFP (7.9 percent for married women and 2.1 percent for single women), though the country falls short of the LFP predicted by its per capita income (that is, the LFP on the estimated U-shaped relationship between female LFP and log per capita income; see box 2.1).[4]

Similarly, although Mexico ranks among the highest in single women's LFP rate in the early 2000s (69 percent), it also falls well short of the level predicted by its GDP per capita, owing largely to the low participation among married women (31 percent), in which it ranks second to the last in the Chioda and Demombynes (2014) sample.

This finding again confirms that development alone fails to explain a large part of the evolution of women's economic participation. The substantial amount of noise around the GDP–LFP relationship can thus be interpreted as evidence of the importance of additional omitted factors in explaining the evolution of female LFP. It is worth noting that the Andean region has a sizable agriculture sector.

BOX 2.1: *Economic development and female labor force participation in Latin America and the Caribbean*

Development, as measured by per capita GDP, can only partially explain the dynamics of labor force participation over the past decades. Figure B2.1.1, analogous to figure 1.31 in chapter 1, illustrates the evolution of the relationship between female labor force participation (LFP) and (log) per capita GDP in the region. As documented in chapter 1, LFP rates in Latin America and the Caribbean have been higher than would be predicted by per capita GDP. This also holds true for all the subregions, except Central America, which in 2008 appears in line with or slightly below the female LFP rates predicted by its level of development.

(continued on next page)

FIGURE B2.1.1: Development and female labor force participation in Latin America and the Caribbean

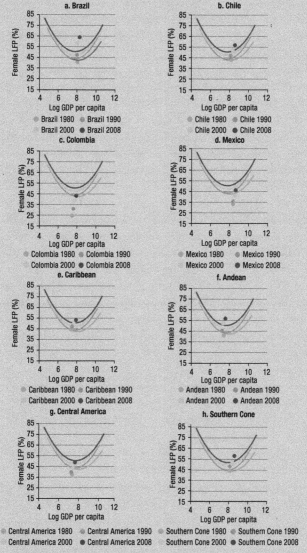

Sources: World Bank (GDP data); ILO (female LFP data).

Note: Each U-shaped curve corresponds to a separate decade's estimated relationship between (log per capita) income and female labor force participation, based on that decade's cross-section of all countries in the world.

Female participation since 2000 has exceeded that predicted by the Andean region's GDP, a fact that has caught the attention of researchers and led them to wonder whether a feminization of the agricultural sector is taking place in this subregion.

Over the same period, men's LFP declined slightly. Since 1960 married and unmarried men's LFP fell by 6 and 8 percentage points, respectively. These declines have been observed elsewhere and are not uncommon in the development process. But their magnitudes are dwarfed by the concomitant advances by women, such that women cannot merely be replacing men one-for-one in the labor force. Changes in the value of education to LFP across sexes are largely responsible for this shrinking gap (Chioda and Demombynes 2014).

Understanding trends is intrinsically more involved for married women than for single women. In addition to spouses making household labor supply decisions jointly, the distinction between home and market production in the early stages of economic development can be blurred, because of farm work and family enterprises, for instance. As a result, the measurement of economic participation among married women is complicated—and is plausibly underestimated. Even so, marital status more than any other characteristic defined women's economic roles in the 1960s and 1970s. Only 11.5 percent of married women were active in the labor market. Except for Panama (where married women's LFP was 19.5 percent in 1960), all countries in the sample were tightly clustered around 9 percent in the 1960s, with little regional dispersion. Early stages of development and urbanization tend to be associated with high degrees of specialization, not only in the economy but also in the household (Goldin 1995; Mammen and Paxson 2000). As younger men and unmarried women are drawn into the paid workforce and away from sharing household chores, the work and home spheres become more separate. Starting in the 1960s and 1970s, participation rates among married women grew with every subsequent decade, both in absolute terms and relative to single women (figure 2.4).[5] Indeed, for the region married women joined the labor force at a staggering annual rate of 3.2 percent, compared with 0.95 percent for single women.

Differences in growth rates of LFP between single and married women are sizable, so much so that the gap between their LFP rates is visibly shrinking over time, reflecting both the natural diminishing returns to the growth process at higher LFP rates, as the pool of single women who can become employed diminishes, and the extraordinarily fast-paced changes experienced by married women over the last four decades. However, as panel a in figure 2.4 illustrates, considerable heterogeneity exists in the growth rate of married women's LFP across countries, owing in particular to heterogeneity in the *timing* of the acceleration of their entry into the labor force, such that they are staggered across decades. For Colombia and República Bolivariana de Venezuela, the decade of steepest growth in married women's LFP is the 1970s, for Argentina, Bolivia, Brazil, and Ecuador the 1980s, and for Chile and Mexico the 1990s.

FIGURE 2.4: Labor force participation rates grew rapidly for married women

Annual growth rates in female labor force participation, women ages 25–55, by country and decade

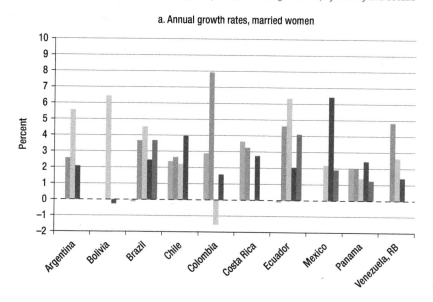

a. Annual growth rates, married women

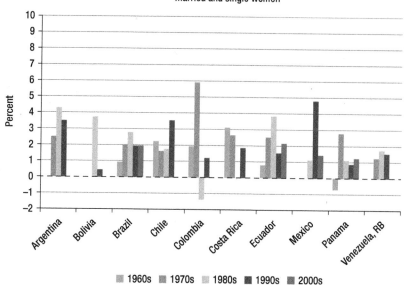

b. Difference in annual growth rates between married and single women

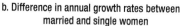

■ 1960s ■ 1970s ■ 1980s ■ 1990s ■ 2000s

Sources: Chioda 2014; IPUMS 2014.

Note: The exact period defined for each decade varies with the census year for each country. See table 2.1.

The relationship between trends in female labor force participation and social norms

As described previously, the pace of this change has been uneven. Female LFP increased at a moderate pace in the 1960s, then more rapidly during the 1970s, and accelerated dramatically between 1980 and the 1990s. Although married women's participation rates are still growing, those of single women appear to have slowed down during the 2000s. The interplay of these components has contributed to an S-shaped trend in total female LFP in LAC (Chioda and Demombynes 2014) (see panels a and b of figure 2.3) and in the United States (Goldin 1995).

The S-shaped trend in female LFP has reminded some authors of the S-shaped pattern commonly observed in models of technological diffusion[6] and led Fernández (2008) to conjecture that similar learning mechanisms to those of information diffusion could also underlie the path of women's economic decisions. The egalitarian views documented in chapter 1 indicate that women's (market) work has historically been contentious. The decision to enter the formal labor force requires carefully balanced economic, household, and societal considerations, rather than a simple trade-off between earnings and leisure. Fernández (2008) posits that women possess private valuations of the costs associated with entering the labor market, which are related to their human capital investment and their beliefs about the costs of working (such as marital stability and their children's well-being). However, as illustrated in figure I.1 in the introduction, their decision is also influenced by cultural factors, including societal beliefs and norms regarding female economic participation, of which women observe only a noisy signal. It is not implausible to imagine that the public signal is a function of the proportion of women who participated in the labor force in the previous generation. This information is used by women to update their prior beliefs and help them decide whether to work (Fernández 2008). In this manner, beliefs evolve endogenously through intergenerational learning. Alternatively, women learn about the effects of their participation in the labor force on children by observing employed women around them. So when few women are in the labor force, information is scarce and participation rises only slowly at first. As information accumulates, the effects of maternal employment become known with more certainty, and more women enter the labor force (Fogli and Veldkamp 2011).

Rural and urban trends

The introduction and chapter 1 presented the U-shaped relationship between development and married women's LFP, which was documented empirically by exploiting cross-sectional income variation *across* countries. Alternatively, this shape might approximate the relationship between married women's economic participation and income *within* a country as it progresses through different stages of development. The same reasoning underlying the U shape can help explain differences between urban and rural married women's LFP within a given country at a given point in time.

Urban married women's LFP rate is significantly higher than that of their rural counterparts, reflecting not only greater opportunity but also more progressive norms and traditionally higher human capital (figure 2.5). The evolution of LFP rates among single women in urban areas is much less steep than the national figures, beginning the sample just short of 60 percent in the 1960s and ending near 70 percent in the 2000s. By contrast, the trend in urban married women's LFP is steeper than the national trend, accelerating in recent decades, thereby tracing the beginning of an S-shaped profile consistent with learning about social norms—norms thought of as less conservative in urban centers.

In accordance with the U-shaped theory relating female LFP and growth, rural female participation is lower for both single and married women, and the dynamics are much more nuanced, possibly reflecting more conservative norms, lower human capital, and fewer economic opportunities. In addition, in (typically poorer) rural areas, the distinction between labor for home and market production is often blurred. Even so, the relative rankings of countries in the participation of single and married women are

---

FIGURE 2.5: Urban labor force participation rates are higher than rural

Urban and rural female labor force participation rates among women ages 25–55, 1960–2010

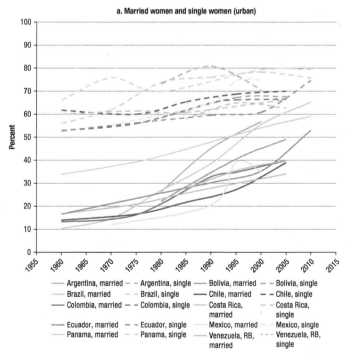

a. Married women and single women (urban)

—— Argentina, married	– – Argentina, single	—— Bolivia, married
—— Brazil, married	---- Brazil, single	—— Chile, married
—— Colombia, married	– – Colombia, single	—— Costa Rica, married
—— Ecuador, married	– – Ecuador, single	Mexico, married
—— Panama, married	– – Panama, single	—— Venezuela, RB, married

– – Bolivia, single
– – Chile, single
---- Costa Rica, single
Mexico, single
--- Venezuela, RB, single

(continued on next page)

FIGURE 2.5: Urban labor force participation rates are higher than rural *(continued)*

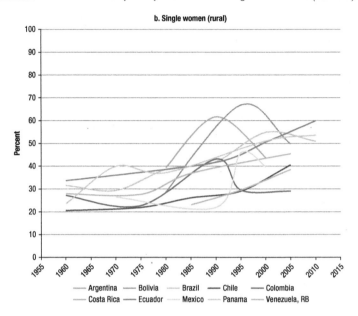

b. Single women (rural)

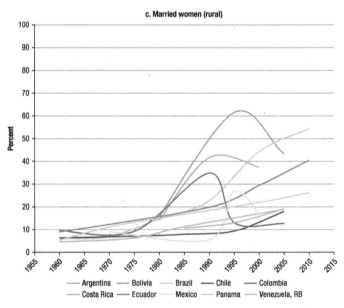

c. Married women (rural)

Sources: Chioda 2014; IPUMS 2014.

preserved, despite the higher variability in single female LFP across countries. Married rural women's LFP rates are more muted than in urban areas, the "married women revolution" appearing to have started almost a decade later than in urban areas and to have proceeded at a significantly slower pace. Instead, the LFP of rural married women remains fairly flat until the 1990s, starting from a regional average of 6.8 percent in the 1960s and moving to only 22 percent in 2005. When Argentina, Brazil, and Bolivia are excluded, the 2005 average drops to 17.2 percent.

Another interesting pattern is the relationship between the gaps in participation between married and single women in urban and rural settings (see figure 2.5). Not only do rural women lag their urban counterparts in the timing of the revolution in female LFP, but also the differences in participation according to marital status are much milder. Whereas single urban women participated in the labor force at a rate that exceeded that of married women by upward of 40 percentage points in the 1960s, this gap narrowed to 20–25 percentage points by 2010. In rural areas, the single-married gap began near 20 percentage points in the 1960s and was roughly halved by 2010.

But in contrasting outcomes across urban and rural women, one must acknowledge that differences in female LFP are likely also to reflect compositional changes over time given that migration to urban areas tends to accompany development. Selective emigration from rural areas may result from greater economic opportunities in urban centers or from women who place a high value on attachment to the labor force selectively migrating to where female participation and careers fall within the norm. Either mechanism—as well as others—complicates and confounds urban-rural comparisons.

Cohort and age profiles

Thus far, the analysis has considered the entire population of adult women over time. An alternative approach is to consider changes across censuses by birth cohorts, which has several advantages. First, one can observe the average changes in working patterns over the life cycle of particular generations of women, which cannot be understood from cross-sectional changes. Second, one can study the timing of changes in female LFP—for the cohorts with the most dramatic changes. Because increases in female LFP are likely to be enduring—once women start working, they tend to be in the labor force at later ages—the generational shifts for cohorts may be more important than the shifts for the entire adult female population.

Contrasting the age profiles of single and married women shows that single women have entered the labor market at a fairly constant rate across ages, without much of a gradient until retirement age (figures 2.6 and 2.7). Although the process has been fairly uniform over time, it is very smooth when increasing, as in Brazil and Colombia. The rise in LFP in Argentina, Brazil, and Panama has been such that the rates of participation among single women between 25 and 34 reached 80 percent during the 1990s and early 2000s.

FIGURE 2.6: Evolution of age profiles of single female labor force participation in selected Latin American and Caribbean countries

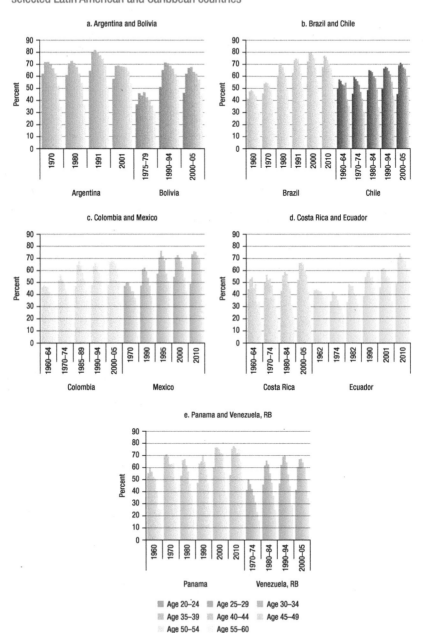

Sources: Chioda 2014; IPUMS 2014.
Note: For each country, the darkest bar represents the youngest age cohort (20–24) and the lightest bar the oldest age cohort (55–60).

FIGURE 2.7: Evolution of age profiles of married female labor force participation in selected Latin American and Caribbean countries, from 1960

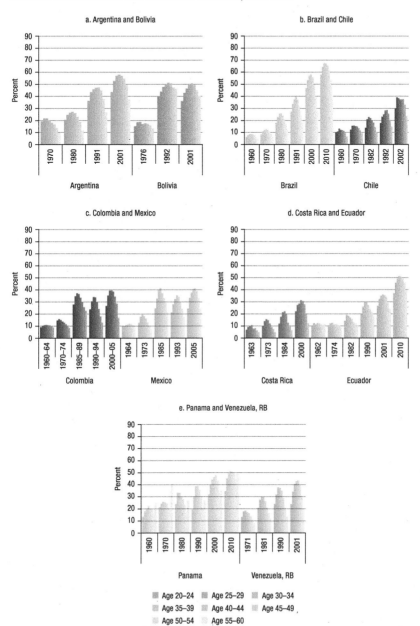

a. Argentina and Bolivia

b. Brazil and Chile

c. Colombia and Mexico

d. Costa Rica and Ecuador

e. Panama and Venezuela, RB

Legend:
■ Age 20–24 ■ Age 25–29 ■ Age 30–34
■ Age 35–39 ■ Age 40–44 ■ Age 45–49
■ Age 50–54 ■ Age 55–60

Sources: Chioda 2014; IPUMS 2014.
Note: For each country, the darkest bar represents the youngest age cohort (20–25) and the lightest bar the oldest cohort (55–60).

The picture for married women is very different. The level of their participation, as discussed earlier, is significantly lower than for single women, but the rates at which married women have joined the labor force across years has been rapid across all age ranges. Married women's participation rates nearly doubled in two decades, irrespective of age. But for women ages 30–44, their participation tripled and even quintupled in Argentina, Brazil, Chile, Colombia and Ecuador. In these countries LFP rates for this age range rose 10 to 20 percent—to nearly 60 percent. The rapid increase emerges as a regional feature, especially following the mid-1980s. Costa Rica looks like the only exception, with more muted gains in female LFP.

The differences for single and married women in the age when LFP is at its peak are instructive. For single women, the age of maximum participation is consistently in the late 20s or early 30s. For married women it is 5–10 years later, perhaps following childbearing.

Countries in the region can roughly be grouped into two categories of cohort profiles. The first group exhibits uniform cohort effects irrespective of age range. Graphically, these are countries for which the series are equally spaced for the different cohorts, making them appear as if one cohort is on top of the other. This group includes Argentina, Bolivia, Chile, Costa Rica, and República Bolivariana de Venezuela. They appear to experience a uniform upward shift in female LFP in every generation born after 1929, so the LFP of successive cohorts always rises.

The second set of countries is characterized by heterogeneous cohort effects over the life cycle, a widening of age effects, and the emergence of convex profiles as time progresses for certain age ranges, with more recent generations of women joining the labor force at accelerating rates. Cohort effects for married women are larger than those for single women. Age effects are negligible for the majority of these and, when present, they are small but suggest increases in their labor force attachment through the life cycle (Chioda 2014).

The age effects between women ages 25 and 35 are relatively small; in some instances, the two adjacent cohorts' lines remain approximately equally distanced over time such that they are parallel between censuses, especially for the most recent years (figure 2.8). The two exceptions are Panama and República Bolivariana de Venezuela, where greater heterogeneity exists, particularly at the end of the sample period. In many of the countries considered here, participation among the youngest cohorts (while 20–24 years of age) appears systematically lower in the 2000s, possibly a mechanical result of young women increasingly raising their level of education, which has the effect of delaying entry into the labor force until their later 20s.

Overall, the LFP of married women has risen, with successive cohorts entering the labor market at higher rates but tending to remain fairly constant over the life cycle within the cohort. Single women's LFP dynamics are almost entirely dominated by age effects, with discrepancies in the rate of LFP between young (25–34) and old (46–60) age groups nearing 20 percentage points, thus confirming the intuition that the motives for LFP by single women differ substantially across the two age groups.

FIGURE 2.8: Cohort profiles of female labor force participation in selected Latin American and Caribbean countries

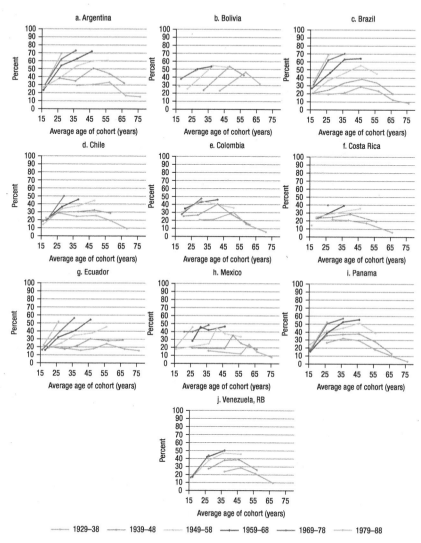

Sources: Chioda 2014; IPUMS 2014.

Note: The figure presents female LFP rates by cohort and census year for selected age ranges. Each line represents mean LFP rates for individuals within a given cohort, with each data point corresponding to the LFP rate of that specific cohort in a given census year. Movements along a given line capture the age effects (age effects can be read from the charts as vertical differences between consecutive points on a given line). In turn, the vertical distance between two different lines in a given census year provides a measure of cohort effects: it embodies the difference in participation rates between two distinct cohorts at a given time.

The remarkable differences in the labor market behavior of married and single women documented here provide a compelling case for the perspective adopted in this study: that of the household. These stylized facts imply that any future increase in women's participation will disproportionately be concentrated among married women. Policies intended to increase women's LFP will therefore need to target this group. This recognition requires acknowledging that labor market policies will be mediated by interactions among household members and must therefore take household dynamics specifically into account.

The next chapters shed light on the determinants of these historic trends and gain further insight on dimensions of economic participation other than the dichotomous decision to be active in the labor force (extensive margins), considering gender-specific transitions in and out of formality and gender wage gaps. A consistent message emerging is that families matter and that married women's decisions do not simply conform to an objective of maximizing earnings.

Notes

[1] See, for example, León (2000) and Duryea, Edwards, and Ureta (2001), which focus on the 1980s and 1990s.

[2] Employment, as used by Chioda and Demombynes (2014), is measured by the Integrated Public Use Microdata Series variable, EMPSTAT, which indicates whether the respondent was part of the labor force—working or seeking work—over a specified period. Depending on the sample, EMPSTAT can convey additional information. The combination of employed and unemployed yields the total labor force. *Employment status* is sometimes referred to in other sources as *activity status*.

[3] Chioda and Demombynes (2014) restrict the sample to women and men ages 25–55 to minimize biases induced by workers transitioning in and out of the labor force, either because their schooling is not complete or because they are retiring.

[4] The Colombian figures for female LFP computed based on the Integrated Public Use Microdata Series differ from those based on the household survey (Encuesta Continua de Hogares [ECH] of SEDLAC [Socio-Economic Database for Latin America and the Caribbean]), in which they appear systematically higher. The two surveys classify individuals as unemployed if they were not employed in the last week, but the census definition requires the individual to have searched for employment over the four previous weeks. The discrepancy in definitions can generate substantial gaps in the measurement of female LFP amounting to between 6 and 10 percentage points.

[5] The exception is Colombia, where LFP declined for married women in the late 1980s and early 1990s. Some authors attribute this fact to the same events that led to these years being known as the "Age of Narco-Terrorism."

[6] For a review of the literature on learning and technology adoption, see Chamley (2004).

References

Chamley, Christophe. 2004. "Delays and Equilibria with Large and Small Information in Social Learning." *European Economic Review* 48 (3): 477–501.

Chioda, Laura. 2014. "How Family Formation Has Shaped Labor Force Participation in LAC." Background paper for this report, World Bank, Washington, DC.

Chioda, Laura, and Gabriel Demombynes. 2014. "The Rise of Female Labor Force Participation Rate in LAC, 1960–2000." Background paper for this report, World Bank, Washington, DC.

Duryea, Suzanne, Alejandra Cox Edwards, and Manuelita Ureta. 2001. "Women in the LAC Labor Market: The Remarkable 1990's." William Davidson Institute Working Paper 500, University of Michigan, Ann Arbor.

Fernández, Raquel. 2008. "Culture and Economics." *New Palgrave Dictionary of Economics*, edited by Steven N. Durlauf and Lawrence E. Blume (2nd ed.). [Online edition] Palgrave Macmillan. http://www.dictionaryofeconomics.com/dictionary.

Fogli, Alessandra, and Laura Veldkamp. 2011. "Nature or Nurture? Learning and the Geography of Female Labor Force Participation." *Econometrica* 79 (4): 1103–38.

Goldin, Claudia. 1990. "Understanding the Gender Gap: An Economic History of American Women." New York: Oxford University Press.

———. 1995. "The U-Shaped Female Labor Force Function in Economic Development and Economic History." In *Investment in Women's Human Capital*, edited by T. Paul Schultz, 61–90. Chicago: University of Chicago Press.

IPUMS (Integrated Public Use Microdata Series, International). 2015. Version 6.4 [Machine-readable database]. Minneapolis: University of Minnesota, Minnesota Population Center.

León, Francisco. 2000. "Mujer y trabajo en las reformas estructurales latinoamericanas durante las décadas de 1980 y 1990." Economic Commission for Latin America and the Caribbean, Santiago.

Mammen, Kristin, and Christina Paxson. 2000. "Women's Work and Economic Development." *Journal of Economic Perspectives* 14 (4): 141–64.

3
Determinants of Historical Trends: Hints of a "Quiet Revolution"

Introduction

What underlies the dramatic increase in female labor force participation (LFP)? The literature that considers the rise of female economic activity in developed countries describes *evolutionary* and *revolutionary* phases (see Fernández 2007; Fogli and Veldkamp 2011; Goldin 1990, 1995, 2004, 2006). As with the narrative of the previous chapter, the literature argues that much of the growth in female LFP has resulted from long-run changes in economic opportunities (urbanization and the greater availability of acceptable jobs for women) as well as from advances in education, changing norms, and the diffusion of time-saving household technologies. The evidence presented in this chapter suggests that Latin America and the Caribbean (LAC) has been experiencing a transformation analogous to that of the United States, which Goldin (2006) characterizes as a "quiet revolution." That is, over time, women entering the labor market underwent significant changes stemming from shifts in the horizon over which women's human capital investments yield returns. This horizon depended on whether their involvement in the labor force is long and continuous or short and intermittent and on a redefinition of women's identities whereby women consider their work a fundamental part of their persona, which is related to the distinction between *jobs* and *careers*. These factors reinforced the ongoing changes in women's bargaining power and ultimately contributed to altering the decision-making process within the household.

As Goldin (2006) remarks, explanations for the rise in women's participation generally fall into two categories. The first emphasizes the labor supply function, including changes in preferences, family responsibilities, and shifts in fertility. The second emphasizes the time cost of producing household goods (food, clothing), as well as income and the resources of other family members. Factors operating on the demand side of the labor market may involve sectoral changes, advances in technology that increase the substitutability between male and female labor, and shifts in employers' tastes toward married women's employment. Those on the supply side include increases in formal education and family formation.

For female economic participation, the distinctions between demand and supply factors, respectively, map into distinctions between constraints and choices, and the interplay between those factors may shed light on whether the constraints facing women changed or whether instead women modified their behavior (Goldin 2006). In some instances, the distinction between demand and supply constraints and choices is blurred. For example, a decrease in fertility can be viewed either as a shift in preferences or as a result of constraints lifted—say, if access to family planning and contraceptives is frowned upon or unavailable. Ultimately, the evolution of women's participation results from the interplay of these forces, as constraints and choices change concomitantly.

The literature implicates five sets of factors in the rise of female LFP rates: rising education levels, changes in marriage patterns and declining fertility, urbanization, increases in the use of labor-saving household technology, and changes in the sectoral structure of the economy. The interplay of these factors is believed to shape the evolution of female LFP. Implicit in the choice of these factors is a transformation at a more primitive level that involves fundamental changes in household technology and changes in the sectoral structure of the economy. Also implicit in the choice of these factors is a transformation at a more primitive level that involves fundamental changes in perceptions about women's participation, for instance the shift in women's attitudes toward employment from *jobs* to *careers* (Goldin 2006)—ranging from individuals who work out of necessity to those who are employed because their occupation in part defines their identity (Akerlof and Kranton 2010).

This change in perspective has important implications both for the horizon over which human capital investment decisions are made and for household choices concerning home or market production. Careers extend the horizon over which educational investments reap dividends. They also weaken the concept of a working wife merely as an additional source of income with weak attachment to the labor force by endowing her not only with long-term earnings but also, importantly, with broader options outside her marriage. Thanks to more credible outside options, she gains bargaining power within the household and greater control over the allocation of resources.

The revolution in women's roles has been documented and studied in rich bodies of research in the United States and Europe (see Cardia 2009; Fernández, Fogli, and Olivetti 2004; Goldin 2006; Greenwood, Seshadri, and Yörükoğlu 2005; Mammen and Paxson 2000). But despite the salient trends documented in the earlier chapters, relatively little analysis of the LAC region exists.[1]

Using the Integrated Public Use Microdata Series (IPUMS), Chioda and Demombynes (2014) explain the changes in female LFP in terms of the five categories of drivers between the 1960s and the early 2000s.[2] Their figures should be interpreted as informed correlations and do not pretend to identify the exact magnitude of the causal effects of each factor.

A marked pattern emerges from the sample of countries considered by Chioda and Demombynes (2014).[3] As illustrated in figure 3.1, their (nonlinear) Oaxaca-type decompositions indicate that approximately two-thirds of the changes in female LFP are explained solely by changes either in women's education and household characteristics or in their returns over time. Here, household characteristics encompass variables such as marital status, fertility, and the presence of young children. In figure 3.1 the sum of positive bars less negative bars represents the total change in female participation rates (in percentage points) experienced by each country since the 1960s. Solid bars embody the fraction of the total change that is explained by changes in the characteristics of women (say, if they become more educated over time), whereas shaded bars denote the portion of the change that results from changes in the returns to the corresponding characteristic over four decades (say, changes in the returns to education in terms of likelihood of entering the labor force).[4]

FIGURE 3.1: Decomposition of changes in female labor force participation, women ages 25–55, since the 1960s

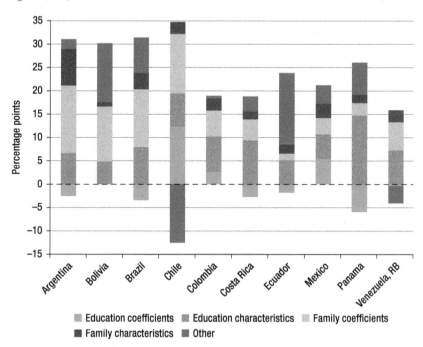

Sources: Chioda and Demombynes 2014; 2014 Minnesota Population Center, Integrated Public Use Microdata Series, https://www.ipums.org/ (IPUMS).

Education

Changes in women's education consistently account for large shares of changes over the four decades in female LFP across countries—between 18 and 81 percent.[5] Human capital accumulation not only increases the opportunity cost of home production but also is associated with more progressive views toward the roles of women and may ultimately reflect the joint decision to pursue family and career as part of women's changing identity (Akerlof and Kranton 2010; Goldin 1995).

In addition to presenting the contributions of human capital and family characteristics to explaining the total gap, figure 3.1 further disentangles the explanatory power of these two sets of variables into shifts in endowments (that is, shifts in the characteristics of the population) and shifts in their marginal returns in terms of LFP. The decomposition thus addresses whether the increase in economic participation occurred mainly because the pool of women is more educated, say, or because the marginal value of education in terms of labor supply has changed. For instance, in Argentina the increasing *level* of female education explains roughly 7 percentage points of the total change of about 27 percent (30–3), while changes in the *value* of education to LFP between the 2000s and the 1960s predict a widening gap. This occurs, for instance, if more education predicts a greater likelihood of participating in the labor force in both time periods, but the coefficient on education declines over time, such that a woman in 2000 is *less* likely to work than an equally educated woman in 1960, all else being equal.

As documented in chapter 2, women in LAC have made sustained gains in education along several dimensions of achievement.[6] The changes in women's educational attainment have translated into higher LFP for all 10 countries in the sample, with some heterogeneity in the magnitude (between 5 and 10 percentage points).

Changes in the marginal contribution of an additional year of education to LFP are more subtle. For Chile, Colombia, and Mexico, changes in the returns to education have widened the gap between women's LFP in the two time periods. The implication is that, in contrast to the Argentina example, the returns to education in participation terms have increased in these countries. In Chile the growth in the returns to an additional year of education dominates the contribution of higher average educational attainment, such that the blue bar is (positive and) taller than the light grey bar. As with Argentina, however, in the remaining countries, the marginal effects of education have declined over time, such that they would predict narrower changes in female LFP than was actually observed. Interestingly, declines in returns to education tend to be recorded in countries with the largest gains in female participation and where their levels in the 2000s are highest, such as Argentina and Brazil. This observation suggests the possibility of diminishing returns to education whereby the larger the female workforce, the less the returns in LFP to an additional year of schooling. We revisit this hypothesis later in the context of a theory in which women overinvest in education to compensate for discrimination they may face in the labor market as a signal of ability and productivity to prospective employers. We also consider the possibility that human capital investments not only pay off for women in the labor market but also reap benefits in the marriage market, where more education secures a "higher-quality" husband.

To further investigate the role of education in economic participation, Chioda and Demombynes (2014) undertake a synthetic cohort analysis and compute the LFP returns to various factors across cohorts, including to education. Whereas the decomposition exercise describes how changes in female LFP over time have been achieved as a function of changes in the factors considered, the synthetic cohort analysis sheds light on an alternative form of heterogeneity, disentangling aggregate changes over time into differences across cohorts in women's baseline propensity to work and in the shape of that propensity over their life cycle.

A noteworthy result is the relative stability of the participation returns to an additional year of schooling: the effect hovers around 2 to 4 percentage points per year for all countries in the sample (the exception being Bolivia, for which education is weakly correlated with economic participation) (figure 3.2, panel a). This is the case even across cohorts, with only moderate differences in the likelihood of entering the labor

FIGURE 3.2: Returns of an additional year of education in terms of likelihood of economic participation, by cohort

a. Marginal effect of an additional year of education

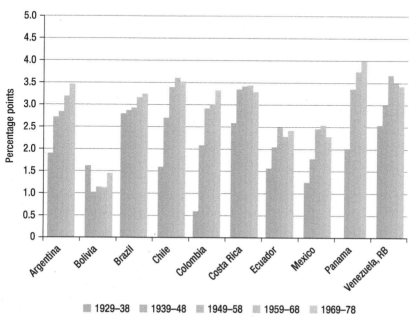

(continued on next page)

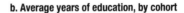

FIGURE 3.2: Returns of an additional year of education in terms of likelihood of economic participation, by cohort *(continued)*

b. Average years of education, by cohort

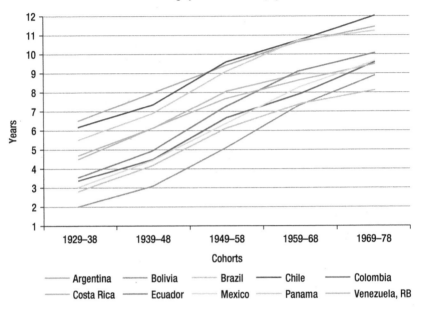

Sources: Chioda and Demombynes 2014; IPUMS 2014.

force for a given level of education: the oldest cohort (born between 1929 and 1938) is, for instance, 2.8 and 0.5 percentage points, respectively, more likely to enter the labor force with each additional year of schooling in Brazil and Colombia (where the cohort gradient is steepest), while the corresponding figure is 3.0 percentage points for younger cohorts.[7] The relatively stable effect of education across countries and cohorts is at first glance puzzling, particularly in light of the heterogeneous group of countries and trends presented in chapters 1 and 2.

This heterogeneity extends to the average level of education across countries, which represents an important complementary piece of information for understanding the role of education and its correlation with the likelihood of entering the labor force. Staggering differences emerge across countries and cohorts (see figure 3.2, panel b). In Bolivia, Brazil, Colombia, Costa Rica, Ecuador, Mexico, and the República Bolivariana de Venezuela, women born between 1969 and 1978 had twice the level of education as those of the earliest generation, born between 1929 and 1938. In turn, women in the oldest Argentine cohort are more than twice as educated as their contemporaries in Brazil and Bolivia. These observations provide intuition for the results of the decomposition exercise that a sizable portion of the gains in female LFP over the last four decades was driven by large increases in the average level of education, with only minor contributions from the marginal effects of an additional year of education, which remained fairly constant over this period.

Higher investments in education do not translate mechanically into higher economic participation. Brazil has among the lowest levels of education, yet it ranks among the top performers in the region in terms of growth and female participation. Chile, by contrast, which leads the region in educational attainment and cohort-specific returns to education, has had middling female LFP rates, on par with or slightly below the levels predicted by its degree of development, as discussed in box 2.1 in chapter 2. Thus, education is only an imperfect predictor of female LFP and cannot alone account for all of its variation.

Human capital investments are cumulative, implying that the gains from an additional year of education depend on the accumulated stock of human capital. For example, the benefits of participation for an individual who acquires an extra year of schooling after completing her 4th year will plausibly differ from those of an individual who decides to complete her 10th year of schooling, having just completed the 9th. In other words, the cumulative nature of human capital investments suggests that the relationship between education and LFP is nonlinear.

These conjectures find support in figure 3.3, which presents the probability of being in the labor force as a function of primary, secondary, and higher education.[8] Differences across levels of education are sizable. Tertiary education (completed or not) is associated with an increase in the probability of LFP ranging between approximately 15 and 55 percentage points, while the average return to (any) primary education is only approximately 5 percentage points. Of course, remembering that the process that induces different individuals to select into various levels of education is driven by differences in their unobservable or intangible characteristics is important. Women who decide to invest in tertiary education tend to differ along such dimensions as ability and aspiration and thus in employability, which results in their higher labor force attachment rates. Indeed, differences in (implied yearly) returns across education levels may capture heterogeneity reflecting progressively stronger motivation that leads women to view economic participation less as merely a job and more as a career (Goldin 2006). These women necessarily have a stronger attachment to the labor force not just because of the quality of their job or because of weaker social stigma attached to their occupation, but also because attachment to the workforce forms part of their identity. This conjecture receives some support from the evidence on norms in chapter 1. For instance, substantial proportions of women, particularly in Brazil and Chile and among highly educated women, disagree that being a housewife is as satisfying as being in the labor force, suggesting that they assign intrinsic value to employment.

Consider cohort differences in the returns to educational attainment. Many exhibit an inverted-U pattern or are decreasing across cohorts such that the participation returns to education are declining in more recent cohorts (see figures 3.3 and 3.4).

FIGURE 3.3: Returns to educational attainment (whether completed or not) in terms of the likelihood of economic participation, women ages 25–55

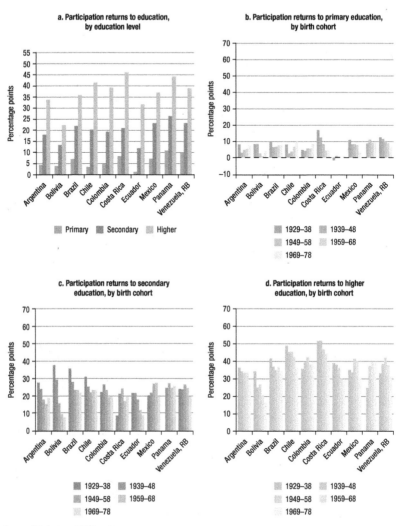

a. Participation returns to education, by education level

b. Participation returns to primary education, by birth cohort

c. Participation returns to secondary education, by birth cohort

d. Participation returns to higher education, by birth cohort

Sources: Chioda 2014; IPUMS 2014.

Note: Charts provide the coefficients associated with each level of education in linear probability models of labor force participation, expressed in percentage points. For each country, we plot the return to education in terms of the likelihood of entering the labor market for five different cohorts to capture the cohort effects. *Level of education* is defined as the highest level attended (regardless of whether it was completed).

FIGURE 3.4: Returns to educational attainment (completed) in terms of the likelihood of economic participation, women ages 25–55

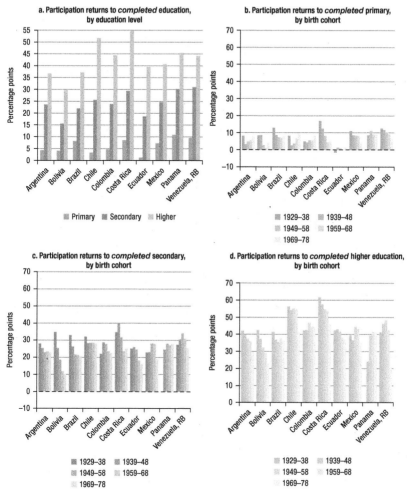

a. Participation returns to *completed* education, by education level

b. Participation returns to *completed* primary, by birth cohort

c. Participation returns to *completed* secondary, by birth cohort

d. Participation returns to *completed* higher education, by birth cohort

Sources: Chioda 2014; IPUMS 2014.
Note: Charts provide the coefficients associated with each level of education in linear probability models of labor force participation, expressed in percentage points. For each country, we plot the return to education in terms of the likelihood of entering the labor market for five different cohorts, to capture the cohort effects. *Level of education* is defined as the highest education level *completed*.

This is an alternative illustration of the results from the decompositions carried out by Chioda and Demombynes (2014), which indicate that the changing returns to education narrowed the gap in female LFP between the early 1960s and the 2000s—that the returns to education in the early decade exceeded those of the later decade. This drop in returns is plausibly related to the rapidly increasing levels of education in LAC. The opposite phenomenon has been documented in the United States, where the rising wage returns to education among young males is owing to the increasing scarcity of highly educated young men (Card and Lemieux 2001).

Further, an additional year of schooling plausibly has a stronger effect on earnings, and consequently the likelihood of participation, if it corresponds to the completion of a diploma or degree. The argument is that employers may use the information embodied in a degree as a positive signal of a worker's unobserved productivity relative to those who do not obtain a degree. Degree completion may be informative if it indicates, for example, a worker's perseverance, motivation, and discipline, all of which enhance productivity (Weiss 1995). As a result, diploma effects also imply a nonlinear and discontinuous relationship between education and labor outcomes (participation and earnings)—the so-called sheepskin effect.[9]

The conjecture is corroborated by figure 3.4, where the returns to completed education are even larger and the size of the differences appears to be increasing in the level of education. On average, the sheepskin effects for younger cohorts become smaller, especially for those countries with higher (average) levels of education. This evidence is consistent with a rising supply of more educated workers in the labor force, thus diluting the importance of a higher degree as a signal of higher productivity. Indeed, between 1982 and 2004 the sheepskin effect for Brazilian workers effectively disappeared for primary school and fell for secondary school and college degrees (Crespo and Cortez Reis 2009). A fading sheepskin effect does not invalidate the value of education, since the estimated earnings gains associated with the completion of these degrees remained elevated in 2004.

As documented in chapter 1, one of the most salient trends in recent decades is the increased investment in education by women and the closing and reversal of the education gender gap, not only in LAC but also among several developed countries.

With positive market returns to schooling, women's demand for education, not surprisingly, has risen. Puzzling, however, is the differential response of men and women to changes in the returns to schooling. Women's investments in education have outpaced those of men even though women receive lower wages in the labor market and spend more time at home than men, although these gaps have narrowed over time, as is discussed in the next chapters. In light of the existing wage gap and of the reductions in participation associated with marriage (see figures 3.5 and 3.6 and the

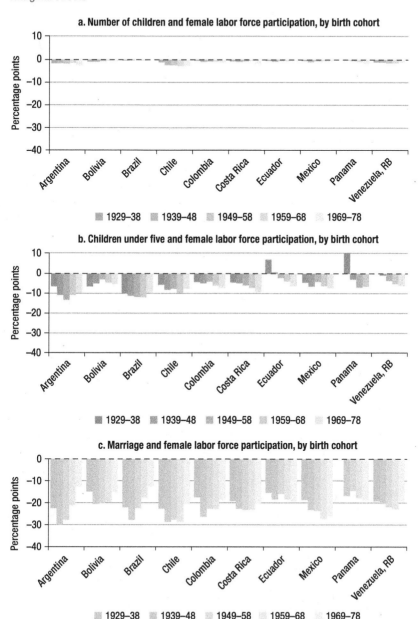

FIGURE 3.5: Family formation and labor force participation, women ages 25–55, marginal effects

a. Number of children and female labor force participation, by birth cohort

■ 1929–38 ■ 1939–48 ■ 1949–58 ■ 1959–68 ■ 1969–78

b. Children under five and female labor force participation, by birth cohort

■ 1929–38 ■ 1939–48 ■ 1949–58 ■ 1959–68 ■ 1969–78

c. Marriage and female labor force participation, by birth cohort

■ 1929–38 ■ 1939–48 ■ 1949–58 ■ 1959–68 ■ 1969–78

Sources: Chioda and Demombynes 2014; IPUMS 2014.

FIGURE 3.6: Family formation and labor force participation, by education level, women ages 25–55, marginal effects

a. Marginal effects: Number of children and female labor force participation

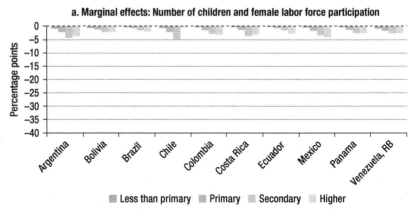

Less than primary   Primary   Secondary   Higher

b. Marginal effects: Children under five and female labor force participation

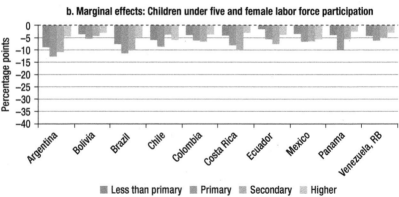

Less than primary   Primary   Secondary   Higher

c. Marginal effects: Marriage and female labor force participation

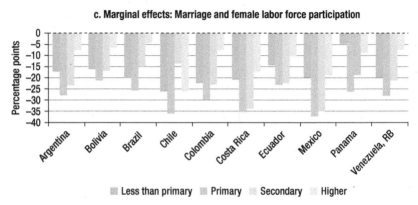

Less than primary   Primary   Secondary   Higher

Sources: Chioda and Demombynes 2014; IPUMS 2014.

discussion around them), one might argue that women are overinvesting in education and should accumulate less human capital than men, since education appears to be a less profitable investment because of their disproportionate time spent in home production and because of inadequate market remuneration.

Chiappori, Iyigun, and Weiss (2009) develop a framework to explain how the reversal of the education gap can be thought of as a response to both market incentives (including but not limited to wages) and intrahousehold dynamics. The essence of their framework considers education as a signaling device to the market about ability, which facilitates escaping discrimination. So, although women today still receive lower wages than men and spend more time in the household, they may acquire more schooling because discrimination is lower at higher levels of education. Discrimination against women in the labor market can take several forms. It can be taste based, such that employers have a preference for working with and hiring men. Or it can be statistical, whereby employers believe (correctly or not) that women have a different level of productivity (attitudes, human capital) or incur more frequent absences than men. In the latter case, they prefer to hire men exclusively on productivity grounds.

The notion that education has a signaling value for employers is not new. Why then do we observe these shifts in education and participation behaviors only recently? The second key ingredient in the framework of Chiappori, Iyigun, and Weiss (2009) is that education reaps benefits in the marriage and labor markets, so that more education implies matching with a more educated spouse and being able to extract more marital surplus as a result of greater prospects outside the marriage. This enhanced bargaining power weakens traditional gender roles and divisions of labor in the household, which had women spending more time at home irrespective of their educational attainment. As figures 3.5 and 3.6 illustrate, women's economic role changed dramatically at marriage. Until recently, marriage predicted more than a 20 percentage point drop in a woman's likelihood of participating in the labor force in many countries. In this light, the increasing female education in LAC can be seen as related to weakening conservative values, as documented in chapter 2, and to the "married woman revolution." Indeed, Chiappori, Iyigun, and Weiss (2009) provide a theory underlying the causal mechanism that runs from education to norms. Attanasio and Kaufmann (2012) empirically corroborate the Chiappori, Iyigun, and Weiss (2009) framework in the Mexican context. The authors provide credible and robust evidence of the importance of marriage-market considerations in predicting investments in schooling. In particular, their main results highlight the difference between boys and girls in the determinants of their schooling decisions. Although expected labor market outcomes (that is, the labor market returns to college) are very important for boys, they are less relevant for girls, who instead care more about the returns in the marriage market in their decisions to attend college.

Family formation and its relationship to level of education

At the beginning of the 1960s, marital status determined women's engagement in the labor force almost entirely. The shifts in social norms and identities, as hypothesized by the literature, shaped the evolution of female participation. An indirect proxy for this transformation is provided by the importance of family formation (marriage and fertility) in the decompositions summarized in figure 3.1. Family formation variables make a uniformly positive contribution in explaining the observed trends in female LFP over the four decades. Changes in family characteristics and in their marginal returns to LFP explain between 5 and 22 percent of the change in female LFP between the 1960s and the 2000s. In Argentina, Bolivia, Brazil, and Chile, which experienced the largest female LFP gains in the region, the net effect of family formation variables is as large, or even larger, than the effect of education alone.

More precisely, changes in the marginal effects appear larger than those of endowments, implying that along this margin of economic participation, family formation, traditionally associated with reductions in economic participation, has a smaller negative effect on the decision to participate in the labor market. In all countries but Ecuador, changes in the importance of family characteristics to female LFP are more important than the changes in characteristics themselves.

The reduction in the propensity to withdraw from the labor force as a result of marriage or fertility is consistent with a shift in both norms and job opportunities that are compatible with both marriage and caregiver responsibilities. These shifts often result from the changing sectoral composition of output as countries grow (Mammen and Paxson 2000). In the initial phases of development, women initially move out of the labor force as the economy transitions from agriculture to manufacturing. As countries continue to grow, the nature of jobs available to and acceptable to women tends to change, with the expansion of white-collar or clerical jobs (Goldin 1995). As women invest in more education in response to the greater prevalence of white-collar jobs, the opportunity cost of withdrawal from the labor force upon marriage and family formation increases, whether through the immediate forgone earnings or through forgone future earnings that result from life-cycle interruptions in the accumulation of experience or tenure. This is the heart of the trade-off that women face at the time of family formation: drop out of the labor force to specialize in home production and in the provision of household public goods such as child rearing, with possible benefits to children's development and to their relationship with them, at the expense of forgone present and future wages.

Although the contributions of changes in family characteristics (fertility and marital status) are smaller than those of changes in their marginal effects in explaining the change in female LFP over time, they are not negligible, ranging from a modest 1.6 percentage points in Panama to 7.7 percentage points in Argentina. These figures enrich the evidence summarized by stylized fact 3 from chapter 1. A distinctive feature of the region's fertility decline is that it took place without any major changes in the timing of family formation. More generally, family structure and the onset of family formation have remained fairly stable. This trend is especially relevant in light of women's increased educational investments, which typically delay certain milestones in family formation. In contrast, the "revolution" among married women in the United States and much of Europe was typically accompanied by substantial delays in fertility (Goldin 1995, 2006).

It is often argued that labor force differentials between men and women are not caused by gender alone, but by the fact that women disproportionately face the responsibilities of bearing and raising children. However, the negative association between fertility and female labor supply should not be taken as causal if they are jointly determined, for which considerable evidence exists (Goldin 1990; Moffitt 1984; Rosenzweig and Wolpin 1980; Schultz 1981), or if unobserved factors affect both. For instance, career-minded women may choose to have fewer (or no) children, whereas women with strong preferences for children may also prefer homemaking, so the negative relationship between fertility and LFP could be spurious. With these caveats in mind, figures 3.5 and 3.6 present the relationship between family characteristics and female economic participation by cohort and by level of education, respectively, controlling for other demographic characteristics.

The marginal effect of an additional child on LFP is negative, as expected. It ranges between declines of 3 percentage points in the likelihood of being in the labor force in Chile, where fertility is one of the lowest in the region (with 2.1 children per household),[10] and declines of less than 0.04 percentage points in Brazil, where fertility rates are highest (3.08 children per household, based on IPUMS census data). Further, these effects are (mildly) increasing for younger cohorts.

Whether these correlations reflect causal relationships is open to question, because credible causal evidence on the effect of fertility on LFP is limited. In studies that exploit multiple births (such as twins or changes in fertility induced by preferences for a mixed sibling-sex composition), the negative causal relationship between participation and fertility is much smaller than the raw correlation but remains statistically distinguishable from zero. Following the strategy of Angrist and Evans (1998) of exploiting parents' preferences for the sex composition of their children, Cruces and Galiani (2007) conclude that Angrist and Evans's U.S. results generalize both qualitatively and quantitatively to the populations of Argentina and Mexico. For Argentina, having more than two children reduces maternal labor supply by about 8.1 percentage points, with slightly smaller effects in Mexico (6.3 percentage points), both close to Angrist and Evans's (1998) U.S. estimates for 1990 (8.4 percentage points). Although these are close to twice the correlations reported in figures 3.5 and 3.6, it is worth clarifying that the margins that Angrist and Evans (1998) and Cruces and Galiani (2007) identified are quite different from those reported here. The former authors identify an average causal effect of having an additional child that is specific to women with two or more children, all of whom are the same gender. This margin likely differs substantially from the one in figures 3.5 and 3.6, which is an average correlation across all women and which is not purged of simultaneity and omitted variables biases.

In addition, these figures are based on a model that conditions on an indicator for whether a child in the household is under five years of age, which is not the case in Angrist and Evans (1998) or in Cruces and Galiani (2007). This indicator is likely to soak up much of the effect of fertility on maternal labor supply at the expense of the effect of the number of children in the household because mothers generally interrupt their participation in the labor force for the more time-intensive care of young children. This result is consistent with the hypothesis that new mothers have a preference for and enjoy spending time with their newborns. In the United States, for instance, the demand for formal care increases only after the second year of an infant's life, while informal home-based care is preferred for infants (Leibowitz, Klerman, and Waite 1992; Leibowitz, Waite, and Witsberger 1988).

In addition, reentry into the labor force is delayed by higher household income, which is consistent with a maternal preference for forming early and durable bonds with their children, afforded by higher levels of income. More generally, such delayed reentry is consistent with the possibility that time spent with children is a "normal good."

As hypothesized, having a child under five in the household is apparently related to reductions in LFP in many countries in the sample. The size of the effect is close to 10 percentage points in several countries, which more closely resembles the magnitudes of Angrist and Evans (1998) and Cruces and Galiani (2007; see figure 3.6). In Argentina, where fertility is lowest, the effect exceeds 10 percentage points for four of the cohorts (figure 3.5), reaching almost 15 percentage points for women born between 1949 and 1958. Although it is mild, a slight positive gradient appears, with younger cohorts more responsive to small children. In Ecuador and Panama, young children are associated with increases in labor supply among the oldest cohorts, consistent with a more pressing need for a second source of income among this cohort. All told, although the effects of fertility and family formation can be large, they are often more than offset by the gains from higher education (figure 3.7).

As mentioned, studies of multiple births capture a particular dimension of fertility's effect on economic participation. One might argue that the effect on a mother's labor supply of the third or higher birth-order child would be more muted than that of her first or second child. The behavior of women who already have at least two children may be less responsive to an additional child if they have de facto already specialized in home production. Alternatively, their behavior may be more elastic if the newborn's older siblings are enlisted in childcare and ease the demands on the mother's time or if an additional child places pressure on the household budget, so that a second income is indispensable.

An alternative margin of interest is fertility's effect on mothers with and without children. To tackle this issue, Agüero and Marks (2008) exploit infertility shocks.[11] Infertility appears to be virtually random, in that its incidence is unrelated to a

FIGURE 3.7: Labor force participation returns to education, marriage, and fertility, women ages 25–55

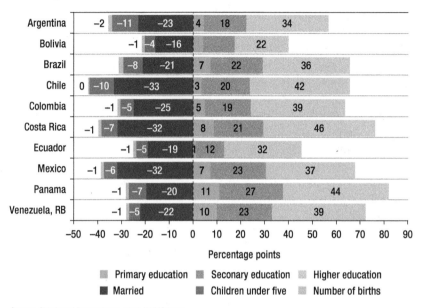

Sources: Chioda and Demombynes 2014; IPUMS 2014.

woman's background characteristics, thereby allowing the authors to credibly identify this causal effect of fertility on female LFP in Bolivia, Colombia, the Dominican Republic, Guatemala, Nicaragua, and Peru (Joffe and Barnes 2000). Infertile women resemble their fertile counterparts along several dimensions. Their LFP rates, their childhood backgrounds, and the age they became sexually active are all statistically indistinguishable from one another. When asked about their desired fertility, no difference exists across fertility statuses.

In the sample used by Agüero and Marks (2008), the raw correlation between female LFP and fertility is such that each additional child is associated with a 3.2 percentage point decline in the likelihood of participation in the labor force, in line with the figure reported in Chioda and Demombynes (2014). However, Agüero and Marks's (2008) estimate that the causal effect of fertility on labor supply is zero, consistent with a situation in which unobserved characteristics of women, such as career ambition, are important.[12] They argue that their identification strategy may be applicable to a broader population than the Angrist and Evans (1998) approach. Indeed, women who prefer a mixed sibling-sex composition appear to be systematically different from the population at large,[13] whereas infertility shocks affect women irrespective of their preferences and circumstances, which helps explain the different conclusions across the two approaches.

The discrepancies in estimates between the Angrist and Evans (1998) and Agüero and Marks (2008) approaches and the divergent populations over which they identify their estimates suggest a discussion about the information content of changes in LFP precipitated by fertility. What are the welfare implications of observing women withdraw from the labor force at the time of childbirth? If single mothers and household heads withdraw at much lower rates than married women with children and are in fact as active in the labor force as men—as they appear to be in the recent years of the Chioda and Demombynes (2014) sample—what information does this carry about the constraints on women?

Conceptually, drawing welfare conclusions based on these outcomes alone is not straightforward. On a purely revealed-preference basis, the fact of married women leaving the labor force after childbirth suggests that such withdrawal is their welfare-maximizing option (in the absence of norms and discrimination), which they can presumably afford because their spouses have not also withdrawn. One reason for a married mother—who may have a comparative advantage in child-rearing relative to her husband—to exit the labor force is that childcare and child-rearing are enjoyable to her, and her spouse's income affords her the possibility to specialize to some degree in home production while he takes on the role of main breadwinner. This gender heterogeneity in preferences and the additional resources (time) invested in children is consistent with evidence from conditional cash transfers, where women's additional resources (cash) translate to more spending on their children. An alternative explanation for a married mother's exit from the labor force is related to intrahousehold bargaining theories. For instance, both parents would prefer to remain in the labor force, but because her husband has a relative advantage in market production (perhaps because of higher wages or better outside options), he also holds greater bargaining power. In a world without frictions or constraints—norms and stigmas related to maternal employment, for example—one would observe maternal withdrawals from the labor force if the husband compensated his wife enough (monetarily or otherwise) to make her at least as well-off as she would be if she returned to the labor force and gained a wage. In both cases the mother's withdrawal from the labor force is welfare maximizing and efficient.[14]

In either scenario, the household is the economic entity that mediates all decisions and plays the critical role in molding outcomes, such as through intramarital transfers of surplus between spouses. As evidence of the relevance of transfers between household members, Amuedo-Dorantes, Bonke, and Grossbard (2010) observe that among couples who pool their incomes and specialize—one earns income while the other engages exclusively in home production—the shared resources should correlate positively with the price of substitutes to home production, such as commercial childcare. In other words, a primary earner should, in theory, compensate his specialized spouse in line with her potential wage if she provided childcare services outside the household. In Denmark, income pooling is more prevalent where outside domestic services are more expensive (Amuedo-Dorantes, Bonke, and Grossbard 2010).

Alternatively, the degree to which household members rely on one another for income and other support may depend on the nature of the relationship between the household heads. In particular, in two-headed households with at least one small child, the maternal labor supply may depend on the characteristics of the second household head and the mother's relationship with him or her. The elasticity of a woman's labor supply to financial need and childcare pressures is responsive to the nature of her relationship to the other household head. Married mothers are better able to draw on the earnings of their partners to reduce their work hours than mothers in other household situations (Abroms and Goldscheider 2002).

Although this evidence does not directly relate to LAC, it suggests that (unobserved) compensating transfers across household members—and spouses in particular—helps shape maternal labor supply, thus complicating direct comparisons between working and nonworking mothers for welfare purposes. As a caution against the desirability of maternal participation in the labor force, Piras and Ripani (2005) report that in their sample of households in Bolivia, Brazil, Ecuador, and Peru, the youngest mothers (ages 14–25 years) participate 10 percentage points more than their equal-age nonmother counterparts. Among those who are unmarried, the difference in LFP rates reaches 27 percent in Bolivia and Peru. These differences may be driven by the economic needs of unmarried young women who must work to support their children (Piras and Ripani 2005).

The complicated association between participation and welfare is further illustrated by certain patterns that emerge from figure 3.6, some of which are familiar. First, across all countries, the negative association between marriage and female LFP is mild at low levels of education, rises (in magnitude) for women with primary or secondary education, and then declines again to its lowest levels for women with tertiary schooling. The U-shaped relationship between the sensitivity of LFP to marriage with respect to education (or socioeconomic status, more broadly) is thus reminiscent of that between development and female LFP, referenced in previous chapters. The similarities go beyond the shape of the relationship and may extend to their underlying mechanisms. Among women with the least education, who on average have low wages and equally poorly educated spouses, a husband's income may not be sufficient to permit their exit from the labor force. If the LFP of low-socioeconomic-status women is somewhat insensitive to marriage, it may plausibly be out of necessity. Those who completed primary and secondary education, in contrast, are less likely to face such binding budget constraints because their spouse's income is on average more elevated, as is their own before marriage. Greater household resources afford them a wider set of options, including the opportunity to reduce their labor supply. The literature has hypothesized a number of possible channels: social norms, preferences (including identities that are more intimately tied to the family), opportunity costs, and broadly defined comparative advantage in home production. Whichever the precise reason, the income effect on women's LFP (from greater spousal resources) is negative and large, and outweighs the substitution effect (from forgone own wages) (Goldin 2006).

In turn, high-socioeconomic-status women, who invested more in their human capital, are by definition more career-minded and more intrinsically attached to the labor force. Furthermore, the opportunity cost of exiting the labor force (measured in forgone wages) is on average considerably higher for women with tertiary education. As a result, marriage is much less likely to draw them out of employment: across all countries, their LFP is the least sensitive to marriage of the four categories of education.

A similar pattern of associations emerges between the sensitivity of LFP to the presence of children under five in the household and education (see figure 3.6, panel b), again plausibly for similar reasons. In interpreting these patterns, considering the presence of a young child in the household as representing a rigid demand on someone's time (given the associated demands of childcare) is useful. For women with low levels of education, the forgone income implied by withdrawal from the labor market when a young child is present is high enough that many remain employed. For these women, formal childcare options are unlikely to be affordable, which means they might seek informal arrangements (such as older siblings or extended family). Highly educated women withdraw at even lower rates, perhaps from a preference for not interrupting their careers and because their more elevated household income implies that formal (nonfamilial) childcare is within their means. In turn, those women in the middle range of education face less-stringent resource constraints than low-socioeconomic-status mothers. If educational investments not only define opportunities in the labor market but also reflect women's aspirations and identities, then primary and secondary education may reveal weaker preferences for attachment to the labor force and thus higher labor force exit rates than their less and more educated counterparts.

If education is viewed as a (rough) proxy for household income, then these patterns become the within-country analog of the U-shaped relationship between per capita income and female LFP emerging from cross-country analysis.

A final remark on figure 3.6 relates to panel a, which depicts the sensitivity of maternal LFP to the number of children in the household across different categories of maternal education, holding constant marital status and the presence of young children in the household. In this instance, the relationship with education is remarkably similar across countries and no longer U-shaped. As education increases, so do the negative association of LFP and presence of children. This observation provides an additional nuance in the labor supply behavior of women in response to fertility. In particular, whereas their LFP decisions are relatively unresponsive to marriage and to having a child under five in the household, highly educated women are instead the most responsive to the *number* of children across all education groups. In some countries, they are as much as 5 percentage points less likely to work for each additional child. One contributing factor in this behavior is that, having not scaled back their labor supply in response to either marriage or an infant in the household, highly educated women have considerable room for reductions in labor supply (that is, they have high baseline LFP relative to less educated women). Furthermore, of all education categories, these women are on average the least income constrained, such that, as mentioned earlier, childcare options outside the home are in all likelihood within their means. Nevertheless, they are most likely to scale back their labor supply with each additional child. These observations, coupled with the fact that their LFP response to the presence of young children—who represent a considerable demand on caregivers' time—is relatively muted, suggest that the labor force withdrawals related to additional births are largely *voluntary* among-high-socioeconomic status women (in line with the labor supply and fertility behaviors of elite professionals documented in developed countries). This pattern contrasts sharply with the labor supply responses of the least-educated women, for instance, whose (in)sensitivity to family structure is likely driven by necessity, complicating interpersonal welfare comparisons on the basis of LFP.

The most striking feature of figures 3.5 and 3.6 is the relative magnitude of the effects associated with marriage and fertility, whether number of children or presence of children under five. All else being equal, marriage implies an average reduction in the probability of LFP of 20 percentage points, or 3 times the effect of children under five and 10 times the effect of the number of children in the household. These marriage effects are *net* of fertility, and the models on which the diagrams are based control for the number of children and the presence of young children in the household. So the large declines associated with marriage cannot be attributed to fertility.

Further, excluding Argentina, Brazil, and the last cohorts in many countries (who may be too unrepresentatively young to support general inferences), most countries' profiles have remained remarkably stable and in many instances have even sloped upward, suggesting that marriage is still important in shaping women's labor supply. These effects are interesting because, although marriage is potentially associated with additional home production, it should not dramatically alter the household burden and crowd out the time allocated to market activities (after controlling for children in the household) so much as to justify large reductions in LFP or crowd it out completely.[15] A possible explanation lies in the social norms discussed in chapter 2. For instance, an important feature of the Chilean labor market over recent years is its relatively low level of female participation, despite its high income per capita and the fact that women in Chile are among the most highly educated in LAC.

Starting from this apparent puzzle and the inability of a standard human capital model to explain the low incidence of women in the labor force, Contreras and Plaza (2010) posit that female labor supply is affected not merely by economic factors but by cultural ones as well. In Chile, "machista" cultural values are relatively strong even among women, and beliefs about the sexes' social roles, including those transmitted intergenerationally by different ethnic groups (Fernández and Fogli 2009; Fernández, Fogli, and Olivetti 2004) have important predictive power in explaining women's LFP decisions. These findings are analogous to those in Fortin (2005), which document a negative association between self-reported conservative beliefs about gender roles and female labor supply. Similarly, the more a woman internalizes traditional cultural values, the less likely she is to join the labor market (Contreras and Plaza 2010).

These effects are strong enough to more than compensate for the positive effects of women's high average levels of education.

Similarly, Araujo and Scalon (2005) present a summary of evidence on cultural characteristics in Brazil. Cultural aspects are so deeply entrenched that they are resistant to change. However, important changes in the organization of family and gender relations are occurring among younger generations. As a result, there is less adherence to traditional attitudes toward gender roles in Brazilian society (Araujo and Scalon 2005).

A substantial proportion of the population maintains more conservative cultural positions toward the societal and familial roles of men and women. Preliminary evidence shows that cultural values of younger generations are in transition and that they affect decisions by both men and women about domestic work and the labor market. These dynamics are corroborated by Chioda and Demombynes (2014), even though for the youngest cohort in Brazil, marriage is still associated with a drop in the likelihood of LFP of 12 percentage points. Nonetheless, the correlation between female education and traditional gender attitudes is negative (Araujo and Scalon 2005; Contreras and Plaza 2010; Fortin 2005). The more educated the female population is, the lower the prevalence of women who self-report as having traditional gender attitudes (in the sense discussed in chapter 1).

Interactions between family formation and education: Single versus married women

The importance of education in married women's LFP decisions not only is evident in the specific LFP returns to education for the married subsample but also contrasts with those of the single subsample (figure 3.8).

Primary education has a much weaker relationship with married women's LFP than with single women's, as evidenced in panel a of figure 3.8, where the difference in returns between married and single women is charted. Several mechanisms could be at play, including more (unobservable) traditional views among married women about the division of labor between spouses. Married women also face lower opportunity costs associated with withdrawals from the labor force, given the presumably positive income of their husbands. Married women may, however, face differential stigma in the labor force relative to single women and face a shorter menu of "socially acceptable" jobs, as was the case in the United States around the early and mid-20th century. For instance, in many countries young unmarried women commonly enter the manufacturing sector of the labor force, where they sometimes account for sizable shares of production workers (Mammen and Paxson 2000).

For secondary education, the differences in returns across single and married women tend to be small and unsystematic. By contrast, higher education unequivocally benefits married women more, with tertiary education on average predicting a

FIGURE 3.8: Differences between marginal effects of education on labor force participation between married and single women by education level, women ages 25–55

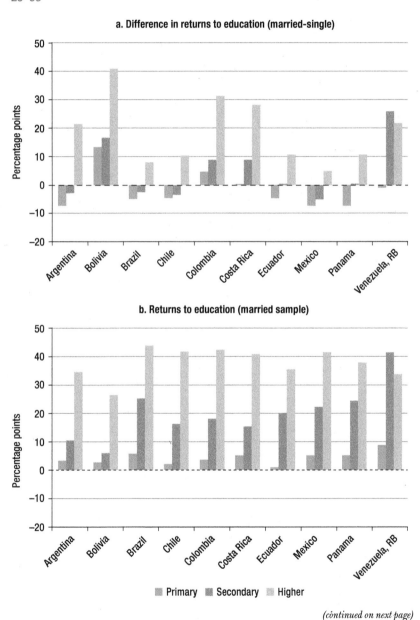

a. Difference in returns to education (married-single)

b. Returns to education (married sample)

Primary Secondary Higher

(continued on next page)

FIGURE 3.8: Differences between marginal effects of education on labor force participation between married and single women by education level, women ages 25–55 *(continued)*

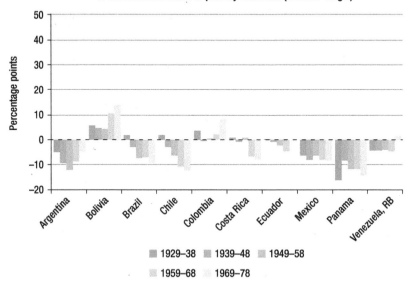

c. Difference in returns to primary education (married–single)

■ 1929–38 ■ 1939–48 ■ 1949–58
■ 1959–68 ■ 1969–78

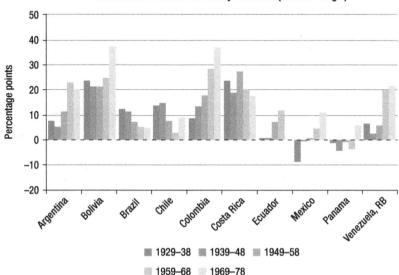

d. Difference in returns to tertiary education (married–single)

■ 1929–38 ■ 1939–48 ■ 1949–58
■ 1959–68 ■ 1969–78

Sources: Chioda 2014; IPUMS 2014.
Note: In Mexico, education levels are not necessarily completed; the omitted category is no education; marginal coefficients are expressed in percentage points.

40 percentage point increase in the likelihood that a married woman will be in the labor force, essentially doubling the marginal effects of singles.

An analysis of the married or single differences in returns to education disaggregated by cohort is also instructive (figure 3.8, panels c and d). Except for Bolivia and Colombia, primary education has higher correlation with participation not only to singles but also to younger cohorts of singles, so there is an increasing gradient in cohort. Among women with some tertiary education, cohort patterns are less systematic.

Concluding that married women with tertiary education work more in percentage terms than the rest of the sample would be wrong. On the contrary, unmarried women's (single, widowed, or with absent spouses) participation rates are considerably higher than their married counterparts, who are less sensitive to education in their labor supply decisions. By contrast, married women exhibit significantly more heterogeneity in their LFP decisions. The results in figure 3.8 merely indicate that attachment to the labor force among married women is on average significantly higher at higher levels of education than at lower levels of education, and that married women are more responsive to higher education in their LFP decisions than single, highly educated women.

As noted earlier, the literature identifies five sets of factors driving the rise in female LFP: rising education levels, changes in marriage patterns and declining fertility, urbanization, increases in the use of time-saving household technology, and changes in the sectoral structure of the economy. Changes in education and in family formation account for two-thirds of the changes in LFP between the 1960s and the 2000s. The relationships between LFP and the remaining factors—urbanization, household technology, and sectoral structure of the economy—are precisely estimated by Chioda and Demombynes (2014) and speak to the trade-offs that women face (see box 3.1 for an analysis of the factors contributing to the declining gap in LFP of single and married women).

BOX 3.1: *The single versus married gap in female labor force participation*

The labor force participation (LFP) gap between single and married women has uniformly shrunk over time for all countries in the sample, as shown in the differential growth rates for married and single women (figure B3.1.1).

Differences in both endowments and coefficients associated with fertility contribute to the gap between single and married women's LFP. The reasons are multiple. Not only has the region experienced an increase in female-headed households with children, but, conditional on fertility, married women also tend to withdraw from the labor market.

(continued on next page)

BOX 3.1: *The single versus married gap in female labor force participation (continued)*

By contrast, single women with children, especially in urban areas, increase their participation, possibly reflecting tighter budget constraints because income cannot be pooled with a second earner.

In addition, single mothers or female-headed households likely systematically differ from married women in some unobservable manner, such as having more progressive views toward gender roles or placing more importance on their careers. These women may feel less social stigma about their labor supply, which may also play a more central role in their identity. Similar arguments about binding budget constraints and diminished social stigma associated with LFP rationalize the much higher participation rates of African American women in the United States since the early 1900s.

FIGURE B3.1.1: Decomposition of single and married gap in female labor force participation, 1960s and 2010s

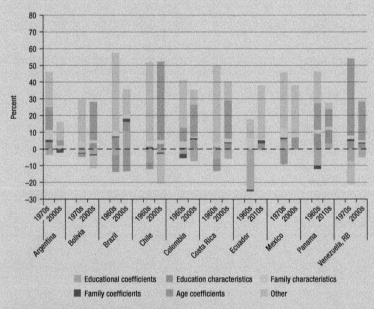

Sources: Chioda and Demombynes 2014; IPUMS 2014.
Note: The "other" category comprises certain household characteristics, such as urban/rural and the presence of household technology such as electricity and piped water.

Sources: Chioda and Demombynes 2014; Goldin 2004.

Urbanization, household technology, and sectoral structure of the economy

Urbanization

Over the 20th century, LAC has evolved from predominantly rural and agricultural economies to largely urban ones. *Urbanization*—the progressive concentration of people in urban areas—has changed the economic opportunities available to women and may have changed social norms, facilitating an increase in the female labor supply. At the same time, urbanization implies a weakening of the extended family, especially for individuals who relocate from rural areas to cities. A social network weakened by a loss of geographic proximity to extended family means a loss of economies of scale in home production, such as household chores and child-rearing. Some analysts have even hypothesized that migration of women from rural areas created a mismatch between demand and supply of skills and contributed negatively to female LFP trends (See Bicerli and Naci 2009).

In the analysis of Chioda and Demombynes (2014), urban settings appear to increase the likelihood of female LFP in the region (excluding Bolivia) by about 8 percentage points, conditional on the other four key drivers. Women in urban settings are between 2 and 12 percentage points more likely to engage in economic activities for pay. As a benchmark, these effects are somewhat larger in absolute value than the (negative) marginal effects associated with the presence of a child under five in the household.

In urban centers, adherence to traditional gender roles may be weaker, and low-income households may face tighter budget constraints (if the cost of living is higher in urban centers, for instance). All else being equal, both of these factors should contribute to higher female LFP in urban areas. In turn, higher-socioeconomic-status households simultaneously face higher opportunity costs from withdrawing from the labor force if wages are higher and economic opportunities abound.

Comparisons of panel a (full sample) and panel b (married sample) of figure 3.9 also indicate a negative and significant association between marriage and urban LFP, because the marginal effects of the urban indicator are typically milder in the married sample than in the full sample. As already hypothesized, weaker social norms regarding women in the workforce and a wider menu of economic opportunities in urban settings are both consistent with this observation. This effect, however, tends to be smaller than the more general marriage effects documented earlier. Although not reported here, the impact of urbanization on the LFP effect of having a child under five in the household is ambiguous. This result could be a reflection of the counterbalancing LFP forces of working more in an urban setting than a rural one, but working less when needing to fulfill childcare responsibilities. The interactive effect of being married and having children is both positive and significant. This observation may reflect additional budget pressures, though the effect of this interaction in urban settings remains unclear.

FIGURE 3.9: Economic participation returns with respect to urban status, house ownership, and time-saving technology, women ages 25–55

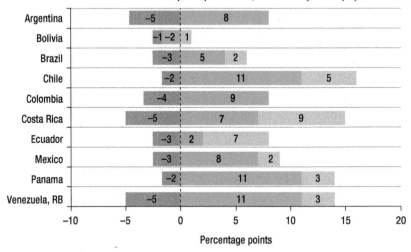

a. Likelihood of participation in the labor force (full sample)

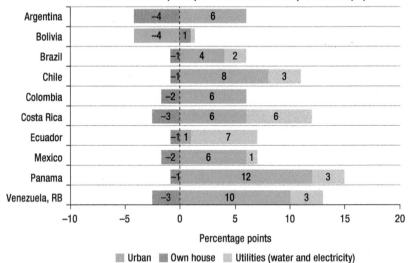

b. Likelihood of participation in the labor force (married sample)

■ Urban ■ Own house ▨ Utilities (water and electricity)

Sources: Chioda 2014; IPUMS 2014.
Note: The variable "access to water and electricity" is not present in IPUMS's standardized censuses for Colombia and Argentina; thus it is omitted.

Household production technology

At the outset of economic development, specialization in the economy manifests itself as economic specialization within the household, where the division of labor in home production is shaped by traditional gender roles. As a result, the burden of home production tends to fall disproportionately on women. The diffusion of time-saving technology (household appliances such as washing machines and microwaves, for example) can increase female LFP as these technologies reduce the demands on homemakers' time and increase the opportunity cost of remaining out of the labor force (figure 3.9).

The household technology revolution played an important role in increasing female LFP rates during the 20th century (Greenwood, Seshadri, and Yörükoğlu 2005). The decline in the relative price of home appliances alone accounted for about 10 percent to 15 percent of the increase in female LFP in the United Kingdom from 1975 to 1999 (Calcavanti and Tavares 2008). In the United States, the decline in home appliance prices accounted for nearly 8.6 percent of the rise in female LFP over the last half-century (Bar and Leukhina 2005). The investigation by Chioda and Demombynes (2014) of the hypothesis that the increasing availability of home appliances was a significant force in the rise in female labor supply is limited by the availability of data in the integrated census. In particular, they can only proxy household production technology with access to electricity and running water, which are necessary inputs to these appliances.[16] This indirect measure is likely to underestimate the real effects of time-saving technologies on female LFP, since it is far from a perfect proxy. Further, one could argue that availability of piped water and electricity in several developing countries also constitutes an indirect measure of household income. To mitigate the confounding effects and attempt to disentangle income effect from home production technology, an indicator of homeownership is included in Chioda and Demombynes's set of controls.

Access to water and electricity is unambiguously associated with a higher likelihood of participation in the labor market. Although modest, the effects are not negligible, ranging between 2 percentage points and 8 percentage points in Costa Rica (in Bolivia they are indistinguishable from zero). To put these figures in perspective, the average reductions in LFP associated with the presence of a child under five and the number of children in the household hover around 5 percentage points and 1 percentage point, respectively. The effects of availability of water and electricity capture LFP decisions for fairly disadvantaged households. Comparisons of married and nonmarried samples reveal only very slightly larger effects for the nonmarried group (approximately 1 percentage point). An important caveat is that the relationship between LFP and access to electricity and running water may be subject to reverse causality if homeownership is only an imperfect measure of income: being active in the labor market implies earning income with which one can purchase access to electricity and water. Nevertheless, these correlations are instructive, and at a minimum the analysis confirms that they are as expected.

To the extent that homeownership is a decent proxy of income, its effect on female LFP can be thought of as a kind of income effect, which would be expected to be negative if leisure is a normal good. This intuition is confirmed with the marginal effects of homeownership across countries ranging between 1 percentage point and 6 percentage points and little difference between the married and single samples.

Sectoral structure of the economy

From the onset, this study has invoked social norms and their potential role in shaping female LFP, in particular among married women. The notion of a "socially acceptable" job that differs according to women's marital status, in LAC as in other developed regions, needs to be internalized asymmetrically by single and married women. For some women, these constraints will be binding. Describing the complete specialization of genders between home and market production at the beginning of the 20th century in the United States, Goldin (1990) states: "The new ideal of womanhood gave rise to what has been called 'the cult of domesticity.' This process left the wife in charge of the domestic realm and her husband in charge of supporting the family." In this environment a married woman's employment signaled that her husband was unable to provide adequately for his family and, consequently, most women exited the workplace upon marriage.

This stigma does not attach to white-collar work, because the women in these jobs typically have more-educated (and white-collar) husbands who are adequate providers. Further, the growing concentration of educated women has diminished the signal that women in the labor force are unequivocally motivated by money and could deflect the perception of inadequate income generated by the husband.

Changes in the sectoral structure of the economy—such as the expansions of tertiary and public sectors relative to manufacturing—are considered one of the main demand-side factors responsible for trends in female LFP in developed countries. These sectors are less bound by the strictures of social norms in manufacturing, so female employment could grow with fewer constraints set by norms. The shift of economies to larger shares of services may thus create more employment opportunities for women.

Unfortunately, the ability to adequately investigate this hypothesis is limited by the available data and by narrow variation in sectoral shares. The details of the IPUMS data permit exploiting only within-country time-series variation in these variables. Nevertheless, with these caveats in mind, a limited set of results is offered here. In Argentina, Bolivia, and Brazil, the sectoral composition of the labor force is unrelated to female LFP, whereas in Chile, Colombia, and Costa Rica, the proportion of workers in the tertiary sector predicts a roughly 15 percentage point increase in female LFP. In turn, expansion in the public sector contributes to female LFP in Ecuador, Mexico, Panama, and the República Bolivariana de Venezuela.

Notes

[1] Exceptions include León (2000) and Duryea, Cox-Edwards, and Ureta (2001), which focus on the 1980s and 1990s.

[2] Because of limitations on available variables in some of the earlier censuses, in most cases the period covered by the decomposition does not begin with the year of the first census used for the summary figures in table 2.1 in chapter 2.

[3] The authors consider five sets of drivers underlying the rise in female LFP: urbanization, rising education levels, changes in marriage patterns and declining fertility, increased use of labor-saving household technology, and changes in the sectoral structure of the economy. To summarize the roles played by these factors, they use an extension of the Oaxaca-Blinder decomposition to nonlinear models based on Fairlie (2005) and Bauer and Sinning (2008). The authors complement the decompositions with a synthetic cohorts panel analysis (Deaton 1985) to examine how changes in LFP by five-year birth cohort relate to measures of the five factors, controlling for a number of other characteristics.

[4] As in standard decompositions, the change in coefficients captures the change in the likelihood that an individual with a given level of education will enter the labor market, holding the level of education constant. The change in endowments captures the change in the underlying characteristics of a given population: in the case of education, the change in the level of women's education over time. The decomposition exercise aims to explain the determinants of the changes in LFP of women. The changes in coefficients answer the question: Do women with a given level of education enter the labor market more or less? In turn, changes in endowments speak to the question of whether changes in female LFP are driven by changes in composition of the population in terms of their level of education, that is, the extent to which women in the 2000s are more educated than women in the 1960s.

[5] Chioda and Demombynes (2014) restrict the sample to women and men ages 25–55 to minimize biases induced by workers transitioning into the labor force or exiting it, either because their schooling is incomplete or because of retirement.

[6] Note that for the purposes of LFP, the educational achievement of women in the latest census waves is not relevant because many women will not have completed their education, so their current status in the labor force can be misleading. For this reason, earlier waves of the World Values Survey are more instructive than the latest one.

[7] The estimated returns for the youngest cohort (born between 1969 and 1978) may be misleading because some women may not have completed their education as of the date of the latest census wave.

[8] All regression specifications include additional controls ranging from indicators for urban/rural status to proxies of income and household characteristics such as marital status and the presence of children in the household.

[9] See Belman and Heywood (1991), Hungerford and Solon (1987), Jaeger and Page (1996), and Park (1999) for the United States. See Ferrer and Riddell (2002) for Canada, Patrinos (1997) for Guatemala, Schady (2003) for the Philippines, and Pons (2006) for Spain.

[10] Chioda and Demombynes (2014) compute fertility statistics based on IPUMS data.

[11] The medical literature defines *infertility* as the failure to conceive after a year of regular intercourse without contraception.

[12] The instrumental variables point estimate (0.003) is close to zero and statistically insignificant, suggesting that the parameter estimated by ordinary least squares is overstated.

[13] Cruces and Galiani (2007) find that women who are induced to have a third child in Mexico and Argentina out of a desire for a balanced sibling-sex mix are less likely to participate in the labor force.

[14] Alternatively, if the relationship between parents is noncooperative, a loss in efficiency (and hence welfare) or equity could arise.

[15] Even in the presence of a discrete change in the hours women devote to household chores upon marriage, the additional time allocated to these activities should not crowd out completely time allocated to labor force participation. Amarante and Rossel (2014) study time use patterns for men and women in four Latin American countries (Colombia, Mexico, Peru, and Uruguay) on the basis of recent time use surveys. They provide stylized facts concerning unpaid household work and its distribution between men and women and the main determinants of this distribution. The most significant jump in household production is associated with the presence of children.

[16] The variable indicating access to water and electricity is not available in Colombia's and Argentina's IPUMS standardized censuses.

References

Abroms, Lorien C., and Frances K. Goldscheider. 2002. "More Work for Mother: How Spouses, Cohabiting Partners and Relatives Affect the Hours Mothers Work." *Journal of Family and Economic Issues* 23 (2): 147–66.

Agüero, Jorge, and Mindy Marks. 2008. "Motherhood and Female Labor Force Participation. Evidence from Fertility Shocks." *American Economic Review Papers and Proceedings* 98 (2): 500–504.

Akerlof, George A., and Rachel E. Kranton. 2010. *Identity Economics: How Our Identities Shape Our Work, Wages, and Well-Being.* Princeton, NJ: Princeton University Press.

Amarante, Verónica, and Cecilia Rossel. 2014. "Unpaid Household Work in Latin America: Unfolding Patterns and Determinants." Paper presented at the 33rd General Conference of the International Association for Research in Income and Wealth, Rotterdam, Netherlands, August 24–30.

Amuedo-Dorantes, Catalina, Jens Bonke, and Shoshana Grossbard. 2010. "Income Pooling and Household Division of Labor: Evidence from Danish Couples." IZA Discussion Paper 5418, Institute for the Study of Labor, Bonn, Germany.

Angrist, Joshua D., and William N. Evans. 1998. "Children and Their Parents' Labor Supply: Evidence from Exogenous Variation in Family Size." *American Economic Review* 88 (3): 450–77.

Araujo, Clara, and Celi Scalon. 2005. *Genero, familia e trabalho no Brasil.* Rio de Janeiro: Editora FGV.

Attanasio, Orazio P., and Katja M. Kaufmann. 2012. "Education Choices and Returns on the Labour and Marriage Markets: Evidence from Data on Subjective Expectations." Working paper, University College London.

Bar, Michael, and Oksana Leukhina. 2005. "Accounting for Changes in Labor Force Participation of Married Women: The Case of the U.S. since 1959." MPRA Paper 17264, Munich Personal RePEC Archive, Munich, Germany.

Bauer, Thomas K., and Mathias Sinning. 2008. "An Extension of the Blinder-Oaxaca Decomposition to Nonlinear Models." *AStA Advances in Statistical Analysis* 92 (2): 197–206.

Belman, Dale, and John S. Heywood. 1991. "Sheepskin Effects in the Returns to Education: An Examination on Women and Minorities." *Review of Economics and Statistics* 73 (4): 720–24.

Bicerli, Mustafa Kemal, and Gundogan Naci. 2009. "Female Labor Force Participation in Urbanization Process: The Case of Turkey." MPRA Paper 18249, Munich Personal RePEC Archive, Munich, Germany.

Cavalcanti, Tiago V. de V., and José Tavares. 2008. "Assessing the 'Engines of Liberation': Home Appliances and Female Labor Force Participation." *Review of Economics and Statistics* 90 (1): 81–88.

Card, David, and Thomas Lemieux. 2001. "Can Falling Supply Explain the Rising Return to College for Younger Men? A Cohort-Based Analysis." *Quarterly Journal of Economics* 116 (2): 705–46.

Cardia, Emanuela. 2009. "Household Technology and Female Labor Force Participation: Evidence from the U.S." Working paper, Université de Montréal, Montreal.

Chiappori, Pierre-André, Murat Iyigun, and Yoram Weiss. 2009. "Investment in Schooling and the Marriage Market." *American Economic Review* 99 (5): 1689–713.

Chioda, Laura. 2014. "How Family Formation Has Shaped Labor Force Participation in LAC." Background paper to this report.

Chioda, Laura, and Gabriel Demombynes. 2014. "The Rise of Female Labor Force Participation Rate in LAC, 1960–2000." Background paper to this report.

Contreras, Dante, and Gonzalo Plaza. 2010. "Cultural Factors in Women's Labor Force Participation in Chile." *Feminist Economics* 16 (2): 27–46.

Crespo, Anna, and Maurício Cortez Reis. 2009. "Sheepskin Effects and the Relationship between Earnings and Education: Analyzing Their Evolution over Time in Brazil." *Revista Brasileira de Economía* 63 (3): 209–31.

Cruces, Guillermo, and Sebastián Galiani. 2007. "Fertility and Female Labor Supply in Latin America: New Causal Evidence." *Labour Economics* 14 (3): 565–73.

Deaton, Angus. 1985. "Panel Data from Time Series of Cross-Sections." *Journal of Econometrics* 30 (1–2): 109–26.

Duryea, Suzanne, Alejandra Cox-Edwards, and Manuelita Ureta. 2001. "Women in the LAC Labor Market: The Remarkable 1990's." William Davidson Institute Working Paper 500, University of Michigan, Ann Arbor.

Fairlie, Robert W. 2005. "An Extension of the Blinder-Oaxaca Decomposition Technique to Logit and Probit Models." *Journal of Economic and Social Measurement* 30 (4): 305–16.

Fernández, Raquel. 2007. "Culture as Learning: The Evolution of Female Labor Force Participation over a Century." NBER Working Paper 13373, National Bureau of Economic Research, Cambridge, MA.

Fernández, Raquel, and Alessandra Fogli. 2009. "Culture: An Empirical Investigation of Beliefs, Work, and Fertility." *American Economic Journal: Macroeconomics* 1 (1): 146–77.

Fernández, Raquel, Alessandra Fogli, and Claudia Olivetti. 2004. "Preference Formation and the Rise of Women's Labor Force Participation: Evidence from WWII." NBER Working Paper 10589, National Bureau of Economic Research, Cambridge, MA.

Ferrer, Ana M., and W. Craig Riddell. 2002. "The Role of Credentials in the Canadian Labour Market." *Canadian Journal of Economics* 35 (4): 879–905.

Fogli, Alessandra, and Laura Veldkamp. 2011. "Nature or Nurture? Learning and the Geography of Female Labor Force Participation." *Econometrica* 79 (4): 1103–38.

Fortin, Nicole M. 2005. "Gender Role Attitudes and the Labour-Market Outcomes of Women across OECD Countries." *Oxford Review of Economic Policy* 21 (3): 416–38.

Goldin, Claudia. 1990. *Understanding the Gender Gap: An Economic History of American Women.* New York: Oxford University Press.

———. 1995. "The U-Shaped Female Labor Force Function in Economic Development and Economic History." In *Investment in Women's Human Capital*, edited by T. Paul Schultz, 61–90. Chicago: University of Chicago Press.

———. 2004. "The Long Road to the Fast Track: Career and Family." *Annals of the American Academy of Political and Social Science* 596 (1): 20–35.

———. 2006. "Quiet Revolution That Transformed Women's Employment, Education, and Family." *American Economic Review Papers and Proceedings* 96 (2): 1–21.

Greenwood, Jeremy, Ananth Seshadri, and Mehmet Yörükoğlu. 2005. "Engines of Liberation." *Review of Economic Studies* 72 (1): 109–33.

Hungerford, Thomas, and Gary Solon. 1987. "Sheepskin Effects in the Returns to Education." *Review of Economics and Statistics* 69 (1): 175–77.

IPUMS (Integrated Public Use Microdata Series, International). 2015. Version 6.4 [Machine-readable database]. Minneapolis: University of Minnesota, Minnesota Population Center.

Jaeger, David A., and Marianne E. Page. 1996. "Degrees Matter: New Evidence on Sheepskin Effects in the Returns to Education." *Review of Economics and Statistics* 78 (4): 733–40.

Joffe, Michael, and Isobel Barnes. 2000. "Do Parental Factors Affect Male and Female Fertility?" *Epidemiology* 11 (6): 700–705.

Leibowitz, Arleen, Jacob Alex Klerman, and Linda J. Waite. 1992. "Employment of New Mothers and Child Care Choice: Differences by Child Age." *Journal of Human Resources* 27 (1): 112–33.

Leibowitz, Arleen, Linda J. Waite, and Christina Witsberger. 1988. "Child Care for Preschoolers: Differences by Child Age." *Demography* 25 (2): 205–20.

León, Francisco. 2000. "Mujer y trabajo en las reformas estructurales latinoamericanas durante las décadas de 1980 y 1990." Economic Commission for Latin America and the Caribbean, Santiago.

Mammen, Kristin, and Christina Paxson. 2000. "Women's Work and Economic Development." *Journal of Economic Perspectives* 14 (4): 141–64.

Moffitt, Robert. 1984. "Profiles of Fertility, Labour Supply, and Wages of Married Women: A Complete Life-Cycle Model." *Review of Economic Studies* 51 (2): 263–78.

Park, Jin-Heum. 1999. "Estimation of Sheepskin Effects Using the Old and the New Measures of Educational Attainment in the Current Population Survey." *Economics Letters* 62 (2): 237–40.

Patrinos, Harry Anthony. 1997. "Differences in Education and Earnings across Ethnic Groups in Guatemala." *Quarterly Review of Economics and Finance* 37 (4): 809–21.

Piras, Claudia, and Laura Ripani. 2005. "The Effects of Motherhood on Wages and Labor Force Participation: Evidence from Bolivia, Brazil, Ecuador, and Peru." Sustainable Development Department Technical Paper, Inter-American Development Bank, Washington, DC.

Pons, Emar. 2006. "Diploma Effects by Gender in the Spanish Labour Market." *Labour* 20 (1): 139–57.

Rosenzweig, Mark R., and Kenneth I. Wolpin. 1980. "Life-Cycle Labor Supply and Fertility: Causal Inferences from Household Models." *Journal of Political Economy* 88 (2): 328–48.

Schady, Norbert R. 2003. "Convexity and Sheepskin Effects in the Human Capital Earnings Function: Recent Evidence for Filipino Men." *Oxford Bulletin of Economics and Statistics* 65 (2): 171–96.

Schultz, T. Paul. 1981. *Economics of Population*. Reading, MA: Addison-Wesley.

Weiss, Andrew. 1995. "Human Capital vs. Signalling Explanations of Wages." *Journal of Economic Perspectives* 9 (4): 133–54.

4

Family Structure and Patterns of Duration and Transition across Occupational States

Introduction

The decision to participate in the labor force is an important margin and one that remains very sensitive to education and family circumstances. It is particularly elastic to changes in marital status. By contrast, participation patterns of single women, with or without children, have been catching up to those of men at a fairly steady pace—from the onset of the "quiet revolution" in the 1970s and 1980s.

So far we have focused on labor force participation (LFP) without distinguishing between the various occupational states. To deepen the understanding of female economic participation, this chapter considers the extent to which women and men differ in their patterns of transition across occupational states (such as formal employment, informal employment, unemployment, and out of the labor force) and in the amount of time they spend in each occupational state.

The distribution of workers across sectors can have multiple causes. Differences in occupational choices can be traced back either to issues of human capital or to differences in preferences over job characteristics (Boeri, Del Boca, and Pissarides 2005; Dolado, Felgueroso, and Jimeno 2002). Together, these lead to differences in the comparative advantages across jobs that a well-functioning labor market will allocate differentially across sectors. Alternatively, employers may discriminate explicitly against women, effectively rationing them into less desirable jobs. In fact, these two hypotheses are not mutually exclusive. Different levels of human capital that appear to drive occupational choice may actually be driven by low expectations of possible job opportunities. Women's preferences for certain types of jobs may be driven by social norms concerning, but not limited to, traditional division of labor within the household (Akerlof and Kranton 2000).

These considerations lead to the debate in the literature surrounding the *informal sector*, defined as workers not covered by formal labor benefits. The informal sector accounts for roughly half of Latin America's labor markets. One view, broadly analogous to the dual labor market literature in the United States, sees informality as disguised unemployment. In this view, the informal sector receives workers who have comparative advantage in formal sector jobs but have lost one or are unable to find one, perhaps because of discrimination. An alternative view sees workers as indifferent toward formality—transitioning between it and informality to take advantage of profitable opportunities (see Lucas 1978).

Marital status and fertility decisions appear to play crucial roles in explaining the gender differences in transition and duration patterns. Men experience different transitions and durations from married women but similar transitions and durations to single women. Family formation is negatively correlated with formal sector participation but is positively correlated with informal self-employment. These empirical regularities further corroborate the household perspective approach undertaken here, highlighting the importance of intrahousehold allocation of resources and implicitly assigning relevance to the underlying decision-making processes.

The rest of this chapter presents evidence of gender heterogeneity across occupational states. It then explores these gender differences and attempts to discern whether the observed patterns of mobility reflect discrimination against women or underlying patterns of comparative advantage.

How men and women differ in their transitional behaviors

The perceived overrepresentation of women in informal jobs (compared with formal jobs) is a leitmotif in the gender literature in developing countries (Cunningham 2000a, 2000b). On the one hand, female participation in informal jobs may result from barriers to formal jobs, such as discrimination. On the other, the internalization of traditional gender roles, comparative advantage, and economic efficiency may shape the household decision-making process, leading women to specialize in home production. In particular, child rearing may constrain economic participation in the formal sector, largely through the need for flexibility to tend to household responsibilities. In this view, women have a comparative advantage in informal labor.

Bosch and Maloney (2011) characterize transition and duration patterns for Argentina, Brazil, and Mexico (box 4.1).[1] In particular, the authors examine how patterns of labor market mobility differ between women and men and why this might be. They look at whether barriers to the formal sector force women into the informal sector or whether, in the household decision-making process, women become responsible for child rearing, which constrains their participation in formal jobs largely through the resulting need for flexibility.

BOX 4.1: *Patterns of labor market mobility: Definitions and sample*

Bosch and Maloney (2010) develop a search model to inform a set of statistics useful for examining labor market dynamics. In particular, it nests two competing views of the informal sector within a simple search model that can also incorporate household constraints that workers may face.

Definitions: The authors follow the International Labour Organization in dividing employed workers into three employment sectors: informal salaried (I), informal self-employed (SE), and formal sector (F).

The remainder of the sample is divided into two nonemployment groups identical to those in the advanced country literature: those outside the labor force (OLF) and the unemployed (UNM). As is standard, these groups are distinguished by whether the individuals are actively looking for a job.

Sample: The sample is divided into three age groups: less than 24 years of age, 24 to 40 years of age, and more than 40 years of age. The surveys are sampled monthly for Brazil, quarterly for Mexico, and biannually for Argentina; yearly transitions are computed as the common transition interval.

This analysis requires panel data, and the number of countries covered is therefore limited. Argentina, Brazil, and Mexico account for 70 percent of the Latin American workforce and include a range of potentially segmenting labor market legislation and institutions that would lead to queuing, such as minimum wages and union power. Generalization to the rest of Latin America may not be straightforward, but Argentina, Brazil, and Mexico are not obviously outliers among developing countries and their experience is likely to be relevant (see Botero and others 2004; Heckman and Pagés 2004).

Several patterns emerge, suggesting that women are substantially different from men in their transition behavior:

- Women spend substantially more time out of the labor force.
- Women transition less often into formal employment than into self-employment.
- Women experience a particularly dynamic channel of transition between informal self-employment and being out of the labor force.

These findings are consistent both with a theory of discrimination against women in formal employment and with the hypothesis that women's comparative advantage (in this case, preference for distinct types of jobs) changes with family formation. The next section attempts to disentangle the relative importance of the two hypotheses.

Bosch and Maloney (2011) divide the female sample into several subcategories of single or married and with or without children.[2] If family considerations—not discrimination against women—drive these patterns, one might expect that single women would have mobility patterns similar to those of men.

As with economic participation decisions, Bosch and Maloney (2010) find that both the sectoral allocation of women and their patterns of transition vary greatly with marital status and fertility decisions. Single women are overrepresented in formal employment by perhaps 15 percentage points. These figures considerably weaken the argument that women are uniformly discriminated against in the labor market. Married women (with and without children), however, tend to be underrepresented in the formal sector (*preference discrimination* in economist Gary Becker's terminology). The search intensity summary statistics of single women now very closely mimic those of men. Most of the difference in the duration of time spent outside the labor force can be explained by marital status. In fact, Argentine single women now spend less time outside the labor force than men. In Mexico single women spend 3.13 years outside the labor force, compared with 5.10 for their gender overall, far closer to the mean time of men, at 2.57 years.

Further, transitions from self-employment to inactivity seem correlated with family formation, suggesting either a changing comparative advantage or possibly discrimination. For instance, if an employer observes that, on average, women with children are more likely to be absent and thus less productive, the employer might prefer to hire men or other women, given a choice (*statistical discrimination* in Becker's terminology). Alternatively, because of social norms and even economic circumstances, women may consider it optimal to increase home production by fully specializing or by opting for a more flexible work arrangement afforded by the informal sector in the absence of other formal sector part-time work arrangements.

How flows between the informal and formal sectors reflect rationing versus choice

A simple comparison of transition probabilities would not distinguish between rationing and choice. Hence, Bosch and Maloney (2011) build a comparative advantage statistic (C-statistic), which intuitively rescales the raw transition probabilities by controlling for search intensity (separation probabilities) and openings of employment opportunities in the "receiving" sectors.[3]

The alternative views of the role of the informal sector suggest the shape of flows between states of employment. If, for instance, women are rationed out of formal employment for reasons of discrimination such that the informal jobs they take are inferior, flows toward formal jobs should occur but few in the reverse direction.[4] If, in contrast, flows are driven by households' calculations that determine the comparative advantage a worker has in each sector, such asymmetries of flows should not exist. Thus, the symmetry of the C-statistic offers a potential test between the two views of informality (figure 4.1).

FIGURE 4.1: A test for bilateral symmetry based on comparative advantage statistics

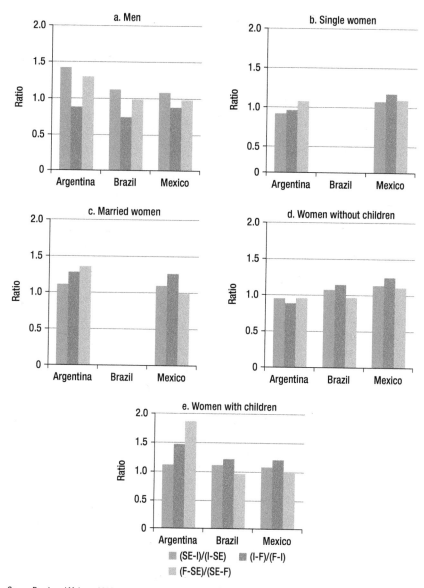

Source: Bosch and Maloney 2010.
Note: Each bar corresponds to the ratio of comparative advantage statistics for the bilateral movements between two sectors. For Brazil the married-single distinction is not available. SE = self-employed; I = informal salaried; F = formal sector employed.

For competitive markets where workers have allocated themselves freely across sectors, a high C-statistic for the self-employment sector for a worker in the formal sector implies that the worker has a comparative advantage in the self-employment sector. Symmetry should be expected across sectors: whatever preferences, abilities, or household constraints led a worker who chooses self-employment to have a comparative advantage in formal sector employment should also lead to an equivalent measure of comparative advantage from formal sector employment to self-employment.

This symmetry would not necessarily occur in the presence of barriers to mobility or gender discrimination where one sector dominates the other. The distortion alters the C-statistic by changing the relative attractiveness of formal and informal positions. If markets are segmented, relative C-statistics capturing largely unidirectional flows from informality into formality should be observed. The symmetry of the C-statistic is thus informative in determining which of two views of why women are found more in the informal sector as they marry and have children is likely to explain the sectoral distribution of men and women.

Figure 4.1 presents a graphical test of symmetry, emerging from the comparison of comparative advantage statistics for both bilateral flows for two given sectors (the ratio of C-statistics from the formal to the informal salaried sector, divided by the C-statistic for the reverse movement). Symmetry in the bilateral movements implies a ratio in the neighborhood of one.

For *men,* the ratio of C-statistics for all the cross-sectoral transitions is close to one, suggesting reasonably unobstructed flows, with the exception of Argentina, where breaking into self-employment seems difficult. In all three countries, the ratio of comparative advantages for transitions between the informal and formal sectors is less than one, suggesting perhaps some queuing to enter formal employment from informal employment.

Disaggregating women by family status does not reveal dramatic asymmetries in most cases. The transition of greatest interest—between the ubiquitous self-employment and formal sector employment for single women and women without children—is symmetrical in all cases and greater than one, suggesting that women do not face even the queuing that males do in Argentina. When women marry or have children, things change somewhat, but only in Argentina. The ratio for married women rises from 1.07 to 1.35 and then, with the arrival of children, jumps to 1.86. This observation suggests that in Argentina women with family responsibilities find themselves increasingly behind in the queue. By contrast, no such evidence appears in either Mexico or Brazil, where symmetry appears to be the rule.

The ratios present some interesting results. For single women in Argentina and Mexico, access seems easier than for men, perhaps reflecting a preference for some unobservable skills, such as discipline, if young women are on average more disciplined than young men (Sklair 1993; Tiano 1994).

What is surprising is that for married women in Argentina and Mexico, and women with children in all three countries, the ratios strongly favor transitions from informal self-employment to formal employment, suggesting, if anything, a barrier to the flows into informal self-employment. The consistency of the result across countries and the steady rise in Argentina are puzzling. The surprisingly low ratios for women with no children may reflect some mix of coupled but unmarried women in this category. The ratios reflect a high degree of symmetry, even in Argentina, suggesting few barriers to mobility between the two sectors of informality, regardless of family structure.

This exercise sheds additional light on the finding that patterns of mobility change according to family structure. The relative symmetry across family structures in Mexico and Brazil suggests that this change is not because of a sudden lack of access to formal jobs, for instance.

In countries of the Organisation for Economic Co-operation and Development, Boeri, Del Boca, and Pissarides (2005) document a strong relationship between household formation and part-time work (see chapter 6). The analogy to the developing-country case is strong on all points. Using cross-sectional data from Mexico, Cunningham (2000a) found single women to be overrepresented in the formal sector but married women to be underrepresented, suggesting that household formation may play an important role. The labor code restrictions on part-time work (that are common across the region) have also been postulated as a reason for the low LFP of women in Chile. In the same way that such restrictions lead to higher rates of self-employment and family labor in southern Europe, they may likewise lead to informal employment in developing countries. In a companion paper discussed in detail in chapter 6, Bosch and Maloney (2011) find support for this hypothesis in Argentina. Using a difference-in-difference approach to exploit the legislation liberalizing part-time work, they find that women with children were 5 percentage points more likely to shift into formal part-time work than married women without children after the legislation was enacted.

Evidence across the business cycle

To further test the robustness of their results, Bosch and Maloney (2011) exploit time-series variations across the business cycle as an identification strategy, since a standard segmentation view would suggest that during upturns increased access to formal jobs and fewer flows back into informality occur. They find this standard view not to be supported by evidence for men in Mexico. Rather, flows are overall symmetrical and procyclical, consistent with rematching across sectors, as has been found in industrialized countries with cyclical rematching within formal employment. Replicating this exercise for women, the pattern holds and does not weaken with childbearing.[5]

More generally, women's patterns across the business cycle are broadly consistent with those of men and with the view of Bosch and Maloney (2010) on adjustments in

Latin American labor markets. Inactivity is highest among married women and women with children, is relatively acyclical, and shows a secular decrease between 1987 and 2005, consistent with an increase in female LFP rates documented earlier in this report (see stylized fact 1 in chapter 1).

Unemployment patterns in the aggregate are broadly similar for men and women, though single women and women without children show higher levels than men, perhaps reflecting their apparent comparative advantage for formal work and hence a reluctance to take on informal work.

Women exit all sectors of employment and become inactive at much higher rates than men; for self-employment, the female exit rate is higher than the male rate by a factor of 10. Evidence also exists of greater cyclicality among women, consistent with added worker effects whereby women hold onto their jobs in downturns to supplement family income.

Women also share the countercyclical movements in separations into unemployment and the sectoral patterns of volatility. For men, formal employment is the state with the least volatility in separations, whereas informal salaried employment is the state with the highest volatility (Bosch and Maloney 2011). Women exhibit more muted cyclical patterns across all sectors. No evidence exists, at least in Mexico, that women are disproportionately dismissed in downturns.

Consistent with recent research, the patterns of accession to employment—in this case, formal employment—are what drive overall aggregate movements, not separations (Shimer 2006, 2009). For men, hiring into formal employment from outside the labor force is far more volatile than either of the other two sectors, or than separations. The same is true for accessions from unemployment. So what drives the movements in relative shares across the business cycle is not the increase in separations, which is relatively invariant, but the fact that formal employers cease to hire while informal employment continues.

The pattern for women is similar, but with a twist. A clear secular increase occurs in transitions from outside the labor force to both informal sectors. This drives both the decline in the incidence of being outside the labor force and the falling formality rates: the rising participation is largely into the informal sectors. Abstracting from this trend, formal hiring clearly adjusted most during the 1995 downturn. If anything, accessions from unemployment are slightly more muted among women, although they do not appear to share fully in the post-2000 recovery.

In sum, behavior across the business cycle reveals two points. First, in Mexico and Brazil, women's extreme relationship to self-employment—and its shift with family status—is a function of changing comparative advantage, not discrimination. In Argentina, evidence indicates queuing and suggests increased family responsibilities may delay selection from the queue. Second, the evidence from Mexico does not suggest that women behave particularly differently from men across the business cycle, either in separations from formal employment or in accessions to formal employment from outside the labor force and unemployment. Once the different average rates of transition are acknowledged, the proportional movements do not seem particularly different between the two genders.

What explains young women's overrepresentation in formal employment?

The finding of an absence of rationing, along with the overrepresentation of single women in formal employment, suggests that single women are perceived as being better suited for formal employment. In fact, in the tourism, teleservices, and in-bond (or *maquila*) industries, women are employed in higher proportions than men, and the literature suggests that this situation responds to employer demand.

In Mexico's *maquila* industry, women were perceived as "docile and dexterous," traits necessary for a highly competitive, repetitive assembly process (Sklair 1993; Tiano 1994). In the teleservices industry in Jamaica, young women are assumed to be more productive at secretarial work because of their greater patience, dexterity, and flexibility in learning new skills (Pearson 1997). In the tourism industry, women are assumed to be more productive because of their presumed docility, reliability, punctuality, flexibility, diligence, patience, domestic skills, cooperative disposition, and willingness to take orders (Chant 1991).

The shift from formal work into self-employment and inactivity occurs when women form families. Differences in LFP and sector of employment can be heavily influenced by norms (Goldin 1995; Mammen and Paxson 2000). If these norms exist, they appear to apply to wives but not to unmarried women or at least to be less binding for unmarried women. In many countries, young unmarried women commonly work in factories, where they sometimes account for sizable shares of production workers.

Why should social norms dictate that white-collar jobs are acceptable for married women, whereas blue-collar jobs are not? One explanation is that women dislike factory work and avoid it if possible; norms may simply reflect women's preferences. Descriptions of long work hours and poor health standards in Mexican maquiladoras could render marriage and exit from the labor force relatively attractive (Cravey 1998). Nonetheless, factory work does confer some financial independence on women that may not otherwise be available, and why factory work should be inherently more distasteful to women than to men is not clear.

Another explanation is that societies stigmatize the husbands of women in blue-collar jobs (Goldin 1995). In the view of the prevailing culture, "only a husband who is lazy, indolent, and entirely negligent of his family would allow his wife to do such labor" (Goldin 1995, 71). Why would such a stigma exist? Goldin (1995, 71) hypothesizes that this stigma reinforces a "powerful social norm that obliges men to provide for their families." A wife who takes a blue-collar job signals that her husband is shirking his obligations. The stigma does not apply to white-collar work, because women in these jobs typically have more educated (and white-collar) husbands who are adequate providers.

Notes

[1] The exercise can easily be extended to other countries, but the need for panel data limited the regional coverage. Data sources were Argentina: Permanent Household Survey, 1993–2001; Brazil: Monthly Employment Survey, 1985–2002; and Mexico: Urban Employment Survey, 1987–2002. All surveys have yearly periodicity. The analysis of gender differences in labor market dynamics is akin to the revealed-preference approach in microeconomics and to revealed comparative advantage in international trade. This approach is generally favored over a parametric one when sufficient data are available, because it relies on observed behavior and fewer behavioral assumptions.

[2] Ideally, one would simply have a division of single, married, and married with children, but the Brazil data do not include a marital status variable.

[3] C-statistic can be seen as the worker's probability of transiting from sector k into sector l over its probability of leaving sector k, relative to the analogous ratio for all the sectors. Thus, the C-statistic approximation takes the same form as Balassa's (1965) measure of revealed comparative advantage in trade, where the measure is a country's exports of a good over total exports relative to the global analogue.

[4] If markets are segmented, we should see relative Cs capturing largely unidirectional flows from informality into formality: workers are born, enter informality, graduate to formality, and retire.

[5] Insufficient data make testing this impossible in Argentina, where one might expect a different outcome.

References

Akerlof, George A., and Rachel E. Kranton. 2000. "Economics and Identity." *Quarterly Journal of Economics* 105 (3): 715–53.

Balassa, Bela. 1965. "Trade Liberalisation and 'Revealed' Comparative Advantage." *Manchester School* 33 (2): 99–123.

Boeri, Tito, Daniela Del Boca, and Christopher Pissarides. 2005. *Women at Work: An Economic Perspective.* Oxford, UK: Oxford University Press.

Bosch, Mariano, and William F. Maloney. 2010. "Comparative Analysis of Labor Market Dynamics Using Markov Processes: An Application to Informality." *Labour Economics* 17 (4): 621–31.

———. 2011. "Women on the Move: Female Labor Market Dynamics in the Developing World." Background paper for this report, World Bank, Washington, DC.

Botero, Juan C., Simeon Djankov, Rafael La Porta, Florencio López-de-Silanes, and Andrei Shleifer. 2004. "The Regulation of Labor." *Quarterly Journal of Economics* 119 (4): 1339–82.

Chant, Sylvia. 1991. *Women and Survival in Mexican Cities: Perspectives on Gender, Labour Markets, and Low-Income Households.* Manchester, UK: Manchester University Press.

Cravey, Altha J. 1998. *Women and Work in Mexico's Maquiladoras.* Lanham, MD: Rowman & Littlefield.

Cunningham, Wendy. 2000a. "Mexican Female Small Firm Ownership: Motivations, Returns, and Gender." World Bank, Washington, DC. http://web.worldbank.org/archive/website00955A /WEB/PDF/FEMALE_S.PDF.

———. 2000b. "Unemployment Insurance in Brazil: Unemployment Duration, Wages, and Sectoral Choice." World Bank, Washington, DC. http://info.worldbank.org/etools/docs/library/76164 /dc2001/proceedings/pdfpaper/cunninghamp.pdf.

Dolado, Juan J., Florentino Felgueroso, and Juan Francisco Jimeno. 2002. "Recent Trends in Occupational Segregation by Gender: A Look across the Atlantic." CEPR Discussion Paper 3421, Centre for Economic Policy Research, London.

Goldin, Claudia. 1995. "The U-Shaped Female Labor Force Function in Economic Development and Economic History." In *Investment in Women's Human Capital*, edited by T. Paul Schultz, 61–90. Chicago: University of Chicago Press.

Heckman, James J., and Carmen Pagés. 2004. "Introduction." In *Law and Employment: Lessons from Latin American and the Caribbean*, edited by James J. Heckman and Carmen Pagés, 1–108. Cambridge, MA: National Bureau of Economic Research.

Lucas, Robert E. Jr. 1978. "On the Size Distribution of Business Firms." *Bell Journal of Economics* 9 (2): 508–23.

Mammen, Kristin, and Christina Paxson. 2000. "Women's Work and Economic Development." *Journal of Economic Perspectives* 14 (4): 141–64.

Pearson, R. 1997. Global Change and Insecurity: Are Women the Problem or the Solution? In *Searching for Security: Women's Responses to Economic Transformations*, edited by I. Baud and I. Smyth, 10–23. London: Routledge.

Shimer, Robert. 2006. "On-the-Job Search and Strategic Bargaining." *European Economic Review* 50 (4): 811–30.

———. 2009. "Convergence in Macroeconomics: The Labor Wedge." *American Economic Journal: Macroeconomics* 1 (1): 280–97.

Sklair, Leslie. 1993. *Assembling for Development: The Maquila Industry in Mexico and the United States*. San Diego: Center for U.S.-Mexican Studies, University of California.

Tiano, Susan. 1994. *Patriarchy on the Line: Labor, Gender, and Ideology in the Mexican Maquila Industry*. Philadelphia, PA: Temple University Press.

5
Gender Differences in Earnings

Introduction

A striking feature of the physiognomy of the trends in female labor force participation (LFP) in Latin America and the Caribbean (LAC) since the early 1960s is the separate trajectories of single and married women. Further analyses of the underlying determinants of participation (Chioda and Demombynes 2014) and occupational states (Bosch and Maloney 2010) confirm that the decision regarding labor market participation is intertwined with decisions regarding marital status and fertility.

This chapter aims to shed light on the dimension of economic activity embodied by market wages, which ultimately determine the market returns to human capital investments and represent the opportunity cost of specialization in home production.[1] Market wages are one of the major ingredients in decisions regarding occupational sector and, ultimately, participation. The standard neoclassical view of the family and labor supply would explain LFP in terms of the costs and benefits of participation in the labor market. Although this framework constitutes a good approximation to male LFP, several authors have argued that female labor force decisions hinge on more complex trade-offs, as discussed in the introduction of this book. After documenting a large drop in the own-wage elasticity of labor supply of married women in the United States between 1980 and 2000 as well as a decline in its responsiveness to husband's wages, Blau and Kahn (2006) conjecture these declines may result from factors such as changing identities and career-mindedness, as described by Goldin (1990).

Wage comparisons across different sets of occupations can be misleading. Workers value and take into account numerous other important characteristics (pecuniary or otherwise) when making their labor supply and sectoral decisions. These characteristics include, but are not limited to, riskiness, stability over the business cycle, opportunities for promotion, career advancement, learning, and on-the-job training. All of these elements are reflected in differences in the wage-earnings profile and, perhaps most important for women, the flexibility associated with each job.

Fortin (2005), for instance, finds that nonwage characteristics of jobs are better predictors of women's employment in a sample of the Organisation for Economic Co-operation and Development (OECD) countries. Specifically, women value whether a job is "useful for the society" and, in the case of part-time occupations, a job's "working hours." In contrast, "good pay" is not correlated with the labor market participation decision. In a later study, Fortin (2008) investigates the role of greed and altruism in explaining the gender wage gap. She relies on longitudinal data that allow her to capture premarket psychological attributes and therefore minimize after-the-fact rationalizations by respondents. Women tend to score higher on most factors that are predictive of financially less attractive labor market outcomes. For example, women hold more altruistic values than men and rank opportunities to "help others or be useful in society" higher in their career selection.

These observations not only provide insight and help contextualize the evidence described in this chapter, but also set the stage for a discussion of recent research, proposing a new set of explanations for gender differences in labor market outcomes: differences in men's and women's psychological attributes and preferences that may make some occupations more attractive to women and others more attractive to men.

Finally, unfavorable attitudes toward women have been shown to soften as countries grow and more women enter the labor force (Fernández and Fogli 2009; Fernández, Fogli, and Olivetti 2004; Goldin 1995; stylized fact 4 in chapter 1). Bosch and Maloney (2010) and Chioda and Demombynes (2014) present additional evidence consistent with the hypothesis. In fact, single women's participation rates and behavior in the labor market are very similar to those of men, suggesting that even if a discrimination argument can be made, it does not apply to *all* women. This report does not downplay or dismiss the role of discrimination in the labor market nor its policy relevance, but we highlight alternate theories because they are relevant for policy and welfare and essential to understanding gender differences in participation, even in the desideratum of no discrimination.

In light of these caveats, interpreting gender earnings gaps as evidence of discrimination against women, whether outright or statistical, is difficult, because the unexplained component of earnings will include differences caused by the unobserved characteristics of both workers and jobs.

Recent findings on gender wage gaps in Latin America and the Caribbean

For nearly two decades the increase in female LFP was accompanied by a slow but steady rise in wages[2] relative to men and in market returns to education, such that women in most countries contribute about one-third of households' incomes (Duryea, Edwards, and Ureta 2004).

In an analysis of 15 countries in the region with data covering the end of the 1980s, Psacharopoulos and Tzannatos (1992) show that human capital accounts for one-third of gender wage differentials, leaving a large portion of wage gaps unexplained. By the middle of the current decade, however, most Latin American countries had closed the gender gap in educational attainment (Duryea and others 2007; Hausmann, Tyson, and Zahidi 2009), motivating in part an updated analysis of the current gender wage gap.

Most studies agree that to manage their housework and child care responsibilities, women may permanently or temporarily withdraw from the labor market or choose occupations with flexible or fewer working hours (Tenjo, Ribero, and Bernat 2006). To a certain extent, the results from the previous chapters call for a more nuanced view, because fertility is not a perfect predictor of participation.

Hoyos and Ñopo (2010) undertake a comprehensive analysis of the wage gaps[3] in 18 countries in LAC (Argentina, Bolivia, Brazil, Chile, Colombia, Costa Rica, Dominican Republic, Ecuador, Guatemala, Honduras, Mexico, Nicaragua, Panama, Peru, Paraguay, El Salvador, Uruguay, and the República Bolivariana de Venezuela) that, together, account for almost 90 percent of the region's population.[4] The authors repeat the exercise in 1992 and 2007 to study changes over time.[5]

Table 5.1 shows relative labor earnings of males and females during the two periods in the study. In each year, earnings are normalized so the average for females is set to equal 100. The average male earnings (minus 100) can then be directly interpreted

TABLE 5.1: Relative wages for different segments of the population, circa 1992 and circa 2007

	Period 1 (circa 1992)		Period 2 (circa 2007)	
	Male	Female	Male	Female
All	116.32	100.00	108.80	100.00
Age				
15–24	78.37	72.55	71.07	69.11
25–34	120.99	110.50	106.01	101.00
35–44	139.17	115.86	121.00	109.24
45–54	134.37	105.91	132.53	114.14
55–64	113.43	86.68	119.01	104.66
Education				
None	61.98	52.61	55.83	52.31
Primary incomplete	90.71	65.14	73.96	61.17
Primary complete	104.76	80.56	84.07	67.25
Secondary incomplete	106.40	83.56	87.85	72.95
Secondary complete	147.98	124.23	116.23	90.65

(continued on next page)

	Period 1 (circa 1992)		Period 2 (circa 2007)	
	Male	Female	Male	Female
Tertiary incomplete	193.79	157.42	156.70	132.21
Tertiary complete	271.56	214.88	242.63	203.57
Presence of children in the household				
No	119.37	102.25	110.92	101.52
Yes	100.29	82.56	86.97	79.18
Presence of other wage earner in the household				
No	124.37	107.84	109.75	103.91
Yes	111.09	98.09	108.30	98.94
Urban				
No	78.37	66.12	71.69	69.24
Yes	130.44	107.21	116.98	103.83
Type of employment				
Employer	197.83	181.85	195.88	187.87
Employee	113.57	103.66	107.42	102.43
Self-employed	104.54	83.04	92.22	81.45
Time worked				
Part time	148.27	121.04	130.43	114.87
Full time	120.80	102.38	111.34	101.17
Overtime	96.98	61.13	93.47	69.66

Source: Hoyos and Ñopo 2010.
Note: Base: average female wage = 100. The "time worked" category denotes whether the worker is employed full time or part time, with part time defined as working fewer than 35 hours per week.

as the gender wage gap. Between 1992 and 2007 the average male earnings dropped from 16.3 percent to 8.8 percent of average female wages. Note that the table provides average relative earnings for different segments of the labor markets without controlling for any observable characteristics that are presumably linked to productivity (and hence earnings). In that sense, the table shows only referential information about how relative wages are distributed across the labor markets for males and females.

Analogous figures for the United States help place these gaps in context. Since the 1990s, women in the United States have earned roughly 75 cents for every dollar earned by men. In the metric employed by Hoyos and Ñopo (2010), this represents a gender gap of 33 percent. The latest census statistics (released September 16, 2010) imply that the gap had declined very slightly to 30 percent, based on the median earnings of full-time, year-round workers in 2009. For the European Union and the United Kingdom, the corresponding figures are 22 percent and 26 percent, respectively.

The life-cycle pattern of earnings and earnings gaps is of interest. Working youth show the lowest earnings and lowest earnings gaps, perhaps reflecting in part no differences in experience at the beginning of their working lives. As individuals age, however, earnings improve up to a maximum and decline slightly thereafter. As expected, a clear pattern of increasing earnings in educational attainment also exists (figure 5.1).

The presence of children (age six years or younger) in the household is related to lower labor earnings for both men and women, with women's earnings staying roughly constant and men's earnings declining. However, whereas for men the presence of another wage earner in the household implies higher earnings, a second wage for women implies lower earnings.

Hourly earnings are consistently higher in urban areas for both genders, nearly twice those of their rural counterparts. More important, the large urban gender gap of 23.23 percent in 1992 dropped dramatically to 13.15 percent in 2005. Part-time wages are dramatically higher than the average, with the gap still favoring men, which may signal that part-time arrangements are more common for workers at the top of the earnings distribution. High part-time wages may also signal that informal workers may

FIGURE 5.1: Confidence intervals for the unexplained gender wage gap for different subgroups of the Latin American and Caribbean population, by education, presence of children under six in the household, and employment type

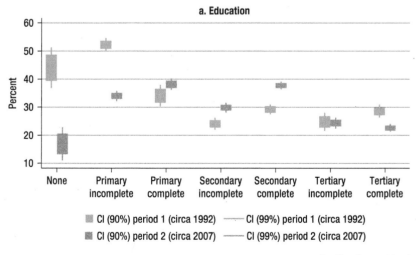

(continued on next page)

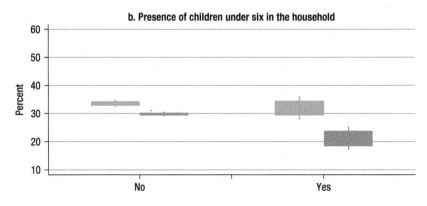

b. Presence of children under six in the household

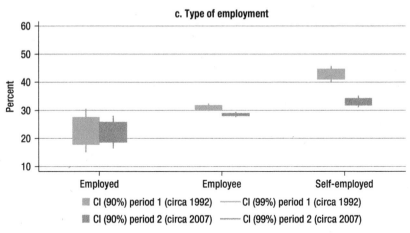

c. Type of employment

■ CI (90%) period 1 (circa 1992) —— CI (99%) period 1 (circa 1992)
▓ CI (90%) period 2 (circa 2007) ⋯⋯ CI (99%) period 2 (circa 2007)

Source: Hoyos and Ñopo 2010.
Note: Confidence intervals (CI) for the unexplained wage gaps are shown, controlling for full set of characteristics.

be working more than 35 hours per week or are less likely to report that they are working fewer than 35 hours per week.

The overall wage gap dropped from 16.32 percent of average female wages to 8.8 percent over this 15-year span. The reduction of the unexplained earnings gaps during the 15-year span is statistically significant and robust to different specifications. The reductions in unexplained earnings gaps can arise from a uniform trend of narrowing gaps for all segments of the labor markets or from changes over time in the distribution of individuals' observable characteristics. Hoyos and Ñopo (2010) provide evidence that in the hypothetical situation of no changes over time in the distribution of characteristics across men and women, the drop in unexplained earnings gaps would have been even greater than was actually observed.[6]

Going beyond the average difference, Hoyos and Ñopo (2010) cut the sample along several dimensions and analyze how earnings differentials have evolved for specific subgroups. In their matching methodology, gender gaps can then be decomposed into four parts: (a) differences in observable characteristics of matched males and females (denoted ΔX); differences in the characteristics of (b) males that cannot be matched to females (ΔM) and of (c) females that cannot be matched to males (ΔF); and (d) a residual ($\Delta 0$), which cannot be attributed to differences in observable characteristics and could result from discrimination (table 5.2).

The results show that the gender gaps decreased for all age groups, but especially for those between ages 25 and 44, possibly because social norms are less ingrained in younger workers. In education, the earnings gaps increased for those in the middle of the distribution of educational attainment and dropped for those at the extremes, most dramatically among those with no education, for whom the confidence interval for unexplained wage gaps dropped from 40–49 percent to 13–21 percent of female wages.[7] Finally, the unexplained gaps declined significantly among people with children under six at home, in rural areas, and among self-employed and part-time workers.

TABLE 5.2: Gender wage gap decompositions for circa 1992 and circa 2007

Percent

			a. Period 1 (circa 1992)				
	Age	+ Education	+ Presence of children in the household	+ Presence of other wage earner in the household	+ Urban	+ Type of employment	+ Time worked
Δ	16.32	16.32	16.32	16.32	16.32	16.32	16.32
$\Delta 0$	13.44	25.17	25.42	23.96	25.00	23.99	33.68
ΔM	0.00	0.39	0.50	0.80	0.02	2.23	1.29
ΔF	0.00	−0.01	0.05	−0.02	0.13	0.26	−1.43
ΔX	2.88	−9.23	−9.65	−8.41	−8.83	−10.16	−17.22
Percent CS males	100.00	99.46	98.20	93.47	89.34	79.62	65.55
Percent CS females	100.00	99.88	99.52	98.88	97.40	92.79	80.66

(continued on next page)

TABLE 5.2: Gender wage gap decompositions for circa 1992 and circa 2007 *(continued)*

b. Period 2 (circa 2007)

	Age	+ Education	+ Presence of children in the household	+ Presence of other wage earner in the household	+ Urban	+ Type of employment	+ Time worked
Δ	8.80	8.80	8.80	8.80	8.80	8.80	8.80
Δ0	9.73	22.21	22.21	21.88	22.56	20.75	29.56
ΔM	0.00	0.03	0.04	−0.25	−0.89	−0.33	−2.07
ΔF	0.00	0.01	0.02	0.07	0.16	0.37	0.43
ΔX	−0.92	−13.44	−13.47	−12.90	−13.03	−11.98	−19.12
Percent CS males	100.00	99.86	99.26	97.42	95.28	89.61	79.42
Percent CS females	100.00	99.97	99.78	99.41	98.74	96.36	89.04

Source: Hoyos and Ñopo 2010.
Note: "Time worked" label denotes whether the worker is employed full time or part time, in particular part-time workers working fewer than 35 hours per week. ΔX denotes differences in observable characteristics of matched males and females; ΔM denotes differences in the characteristics of males that cannot be matched to females; ΔF denotes differences in the characteristics of females that cannot be matched to males; and Δ0 is a residual that cannot be attributed to differences in observable characteristics.

As in previous work, Atal, Ñopo, and Winder (2009) show that the unexplained gender wage gap widens after taking into account gender differences in observable characteristics. In particular, when controlling for education, the portion of the gap that is not accounted for by differences in characteristics increases by 12 percentage points in both periods.

How might we interpret this result? A gap that widens after controlling for education implies that women and men in the labor force differ systematically in their educational attainments. It is well established—see previous chapters and existing literature—that more highly educated women are more likely to join the labor force. This hypothesis is corroborated by the summary statistics of Hoyos and Ñopo (2010), which confirm that LFP rates are higher among the more highly educated.

Controlling for the level of education is equivalent to answering the following counterfactual question: What would happen to the wage gap if women and men had comparable education? A widening of the wage gap implies that women on average receive lower wages than men of similar education, bringing the education-adjusted wage gap to 25 percent in 1992 and 20 percent in 2005.

The literature on gender wage gaps, however, has demonstrated the importance of the *type* of education (technical fields and major field of study) in addition to the quantity of education. For instance, an individual with 16 years of education who studied finance in tertiary education is not expected to earn the same wage as a person with 16 years of schooling focused on literature classics. The fact that this information is not observed here implies that the identified gaps may overstate the true gaps that account for field of study.

The unexplained gender wage gap is lower among those with tertiary education, possibly because of the wider menu of working options offered to individuals with higher degrees of education. In addition, higher educational attainment plays a key signaling role in relation to the labor market, resolving potential employers' uncertainty about candidates' preferences over attachment to the labor force. As noted, the value of this signal may be higher for women (Chiappori, Iyigun, and Weiss 2009), implying that returns to education may go beyond the actual wage rate. A complementary explanation might be that more-educated women fill positions in firms that have less room for discretionary wage-setting.

When accounting for differences in work arrangements (part time compared with full time), the gender earnings gaps increase by approximately 3 percentage points in 1992 and 4 percentage points in 2005. Controlling for additional household characteristics such as the presence of children and additional wage earners leaves the gap virtually unchanged.

Atal, Ñopo, and Winder (2009) are able to explore a richer set of controls by limiting their analysis to 2005, and their results complement the previous findings. In particular, controlling for job-related characteristics (type of employment, formality, occupations, and small firms) only slightly reduces the unexplained component of wage gaps. These findings challenge the popular belief that occupational segregation positively contributes to measured gender wage gaps, reinforcing previous evidence on this matter (Barrientos 2002).[8] If we restrict the analysis to informal workers and those in small firms, we observe much larger gaps in earnings between men and women, which further contradict the view that occupational segregation matters when measuring gender earnings gaps.

The gap along the earnings distribution

Turning to the distribution of the unexplained components of the earnings gap, figure 5.2 compares the unexplained gaps along the percentiles of the earnings distribution for the two periods. This figure suggests that most of the decline in the average unexplained gender wage gaps in LAC countries results from declines at both extremes of the earnings distribution. The unexplained gender earnings gaps at the middle of the distribution (between percentiles 35 and 60) are mostly unchanged.

The gaps at the bottom of the distribution dropped about 10 percentage points (for instance, at the fifth percentiles of the distributions of earnings, the unexplained gender gaps dropped from 48 percent to 38 percent of average female earnings). In turn, the gaps at the top of the distribution dropped between 3 and 9 percentage points (for instance, at the 90th percentiles of the distributions of earnings, the unexplained

FIGURE 5.2: Unexplained gender wage gap by wage distribution percentiles in all Latin American and Caribbean countries

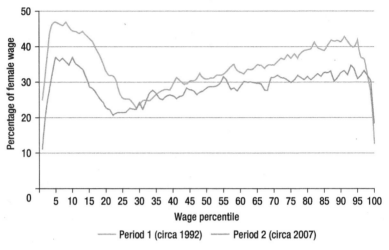

Source: Hoyos and Ñopo 2010.
Note: Matching by the full set.

gender gaps dropped from 42 percent to 33 percent of average female earnings in the 90th percentile).

The V-shaped curve of unexplained gender earnings gaps that was relatively clear in 1992 has smoothed somewhat in 2007 and is now more homogenous along the distribution. Nonetheless, a pattern of higher unexplained earnings gaps at the bottom of the distributions of earnings persists. Therefore, the regional averages suggest that gender wage gaps are associated with poverty and low income.

Heterogeneity within LAC

While figure 5.2 reports the mean wage gaps (across countries in the sample) along the distribution of income, the regional averages mask substantial heterogeneity both across and within countries. In most countries, the mean gap fell between 1992 and 2007, although Argentina, Mexico, Nicaragua, and the República Bolivariana de Venezuela are exceptions. In Nicaragua, the deterioration has been especially severe, with the unexplained gap rising from roughly 10 percent of female wages in 1992 to 25 percent in 2007. In Guatemala, the gap has been virtually eradicated since the early 1990s. Whereas El Salvador and Guatemala have average unexplained gender gaps below 10 percent, in Brazil the gap is on the order of 40 percent in 2007. With this exception, the gender wage gaps in all countries reported in figure 5.3 are currently

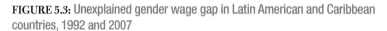

FIGURE 5.3: Unexplained gender wage gap in Latin American and Caribbean countries, 1992 and 2007

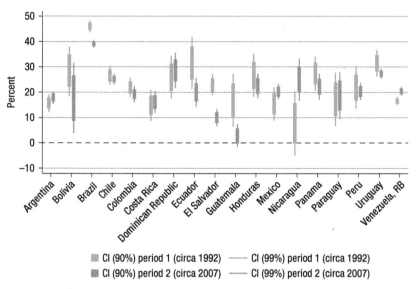

■ CI (90%) period 1 (circa 1992)   —— CI (99%) period 1 (circa 1992)
■ CI (90%) period 2 (circa 2007)   —— CI (99%) period 2 (circa 2007)

Source: Hoyos and Ñopo 2010.
Note: The figure shows confidence intervals (CIs) of 90 and 99 percent for the unexplained gender wage gaps in 1992 versus 2007, controlling for the full set of characteristics.

exceeded by that of the United States, where women earn 78 cents for each dollar made by a man (though this figure represents the raw gap, unadjusted for worker characteristics).

The heterogeneous experiences of countries are further highlighted by country-specific versions of figure 5.2, wherein each country's unexplained wage gap is plotted at every percentile of the wage distribution. The subset of countries portrayed in figure 5.4 provides a snapshot of typical shapes and dynamics of wage gaps as a function of the earnings distribution.

The regional averages of figure 5.2 most resemble the patterns in Brazil, which also exhibits a (slightly) V-shaped gap in both 1992 and 2007 and experienced its greatest improvements at the low end of the wage distribution. In many other countries, the change in mean wage gap over time was similarly driven by equalizations at the lowest end of the wage distribution (Ecuador, El Salvador, Honduras, and Paraguay). As an illustration, the wage gap in Ecuador was hump shaped at the low end of the distribution, with men at the 15th percentile earning close to 70 percent more than their female counterparts. By 2007, however, that difference had fallen substantially, leaving a 20 percent gap.

FIGURE 5.4: Unexplained gender wage gap by wage distribution, selected Latin American and Caribbean countries

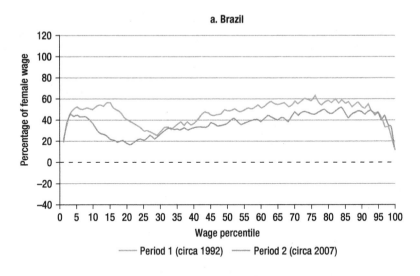

a. Brazil

Period 1 (circa 1992) —— Period 2 (circa 2007)

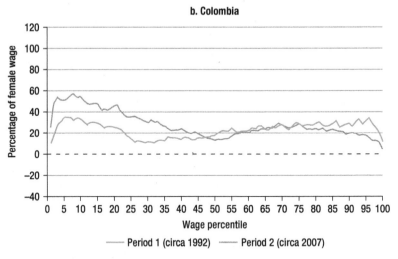

b. Colombia

Period 1 (circa 1992) —— Period 2 (circa 2007)

(continued on next page)

FIGURE 5.4: Unexplained gender wage gap by wage distribution, selected Latin American and Caribbean countries *(continued)*

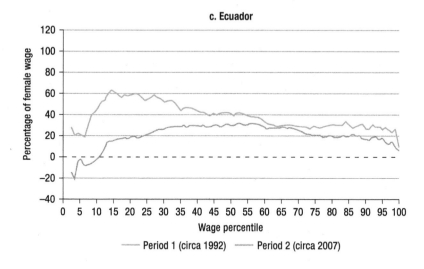

c. Ecuador

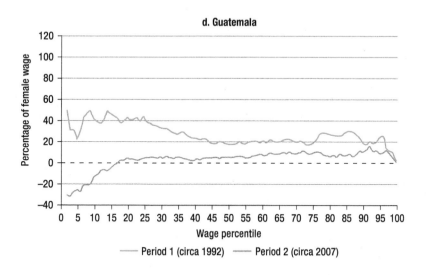

d. Guatemala

(continued on next page)

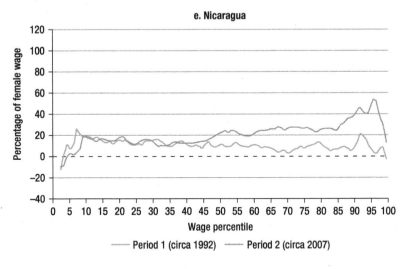

e. Nicaragua

Period 1 (circa 1992) ——— Period 2 (circa 2007)

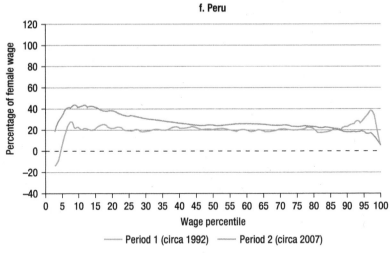

f. Peru

Period 1 (circa 1992) ——— Period 2 (circa 2007)

Source: Hoyos and Ñopo 2010.

In other countries, the converse relationship holds: deteriorations in the wage gap at the low end of the distribution are largely responsible for stagnation in the mean gap in Argentina, Colombia, and Peru, for instance. In turn, Nicaragua's widening gap is driven entirely by progressively stronger erosion in the upper half of the wage distribution: below the median wage, the gender gap in 2007 was unchanged relative to 1992 but opens up by roughly 10 percentage points at the 50th percentile and is 20 percentage points more elevated than in 1992 at the 95th percentile.

As a final remark on country-specific gender gaps, the relationship between the wage and education gaps is interesting. In particular, as noted earlier (chapter 1), an enrollment gap among 6- to 11-year-olds exists that favors boys in only four LAC countries: Bolivia, Guatemala, Mexico, and Peru. In three of these countries (Peru in 1992, and Mexico and Guatemala in 2007), the wage gap surprisingly favored women at the bottom of the wage distribution, such that women received a premium over men. In Guatemala, the female wage premium is as large as 40 percent at the 1st percentile and persists until at least the 15th percentile of the wage distribution, while it disappears much faster in Mexico and Peru.

Arguably, the education and gender gaps may be related: since low-skilled women receive a higher wage than their low-skilled male counterparts, this premium constitutes a disincentive for them to pursue further education, because they are more readily drawn out of school and into the labor force. This in turn may explain girls' enrollment deficits relative to boys' in these countries.

The role of experience

In the literature on gender pay gaps, information on actual labor force experience is scarce but makes a significant difference to the measured size of the gap. Several studies that include true measures of work experience conclude that experience can explain roughly a third of the difference in earnings (Blau and Kahn 2000).

Gender differences in labor market experience are generally attributed to biological differences between men and women, which are further reinforced by traditional divisions of labor within the household. For example, it clearly falls on female workers to take time off from work for childbirth and child care in the first few months of newborns' lives. But an alternative explanation highlights the role of gender discrimination in the workplace and cultural biases in the allocation of family duties. For example, in the presence of returns to experience in the labor market and in home production, gender discrimination can result in substantial differences in the labor market experiences for men and women, even in the absence of any inherent gender differences in productivity.[9] Empirically, distinguishing between truly exogenous differences between men and women and the endogenous responses to gender-specific labor market conditions is difficult.

With this caveat in mind, Hoyos and Ñopo (2010) peer into the relationship between wage differentials and attachment to the labor force. Data on job tenure for the studied period limit the analysis to six of the 18 countries in their sample (Brazil, Ecuador, Nicaragua, Panama, Paraguay, and Uruguay). Job tenure may not fully capture the role of experience accumulated over longer periods of time, but it can be seen as a proxy for labor force attachment.

The total gender earnings gap for this subsample is similar to that for the whole sample in the first period but slightly higher in the second period (table 5.3). In this case the drop in total earnings gap for the 15-year span is 5.5 percentage points instead of 7.5. Similarly, the 15-year drop in unexplained earnings gaps after controlling for different sets of observable characteristics is smaller for the six-country subsample than for the whole 18-country sample. The leitmotif of this table, however, is the last column, which uses job tenure as a matching variable on top of the previous characteristics. The table shows that the addition of job tenure reduces the unexplained gender gap in earnings by 7.35 percentage points for period 1 and by 4.88 percentage points for period 2. Gender differences in job tenure seem to explain a substantial part of gender earnings gaps (table 5.3).

Why is there a wage gap or why should there not be a wage gap?

As mentioned in the introduction to this chapter, wage gap analysis does not consider two key elements:

- First, wage gap analysis does not account for the underlying selection process that led women to invest in human capital and participate in the labor market, and the circumstances of their participation (sector, field, degree of career

TABLE 5.3: Distribution of the female and male labor force by job tenure, 1992 and 2007

percent

Tenure	Period 1 (circa 1992)		Period 2 (circa 2007)	
	Males	Females	Males	Females
Less than 1 year	19.53	21.81	19.39	22.96
1 year	12.20	13.87	11.59	13.18
1–5 years	28.81	31.27	27.67	29.54
5–10 years	16.51	15.58	16.31	15.00
10–20 years	14.85	12.70	15.38	12.66
More than 20 years	8.10	4.77	9.65	6.66

Source: Hoyos and Ñopo 2010.

interruption, and so on). In essence, individual participation in the labor market entails a series of complicated choices that reflect one's preferences and existing or perceived constraints.

- Second, jobs are bundles of characteristics, and wage comparisons are somewhat limiting. This problem would be only partially overcome by accounting for all those characteristics (time arrangements, leadership, sector of employment, and quality of peers, among others), simply because a key piece of missing information is the private valuation that each individual assigns to the various job characteristics.

The bundled nature of occupations and the selection process complicate the analysis and interpretation of wage gap studies, because their effects on results depend on the preferences, norms, and constraints of the specific context.

The literature on gender differences in developed countries has recently moved to complement traditional decomposition-based analyses with studies that attempt to shed light on gender differences in the primitives that underlie economic decisions, such as preferences. Over the last decade new classes of explanations for gender differences in labor market outcomes have gained popularity. Particularly relevant for labor market outcomes is the finding that men and women differ significantly in psychological traits and preference parameters, rendering some occupations inherently more attractive to women than to men and vice versa. In particular, attitudes toward risk, competition, and negotiation, as well as the strength of other-regarding behavior, appear to differ systematically between men and women (Bertrand 2011). As a result, the field is provocatively leaning toward a rephrasing of the core question surrounding gender wage gaps, away from the traditional "Why is there a wage gap?" to "Why should there not be a wage gap?"

As an illustration of the importance of differences in risk preferences to labor market outcomes, Bonin and others (2007) show that more risk-averse individuals tend to select occupations with less variable earnings. These safer occupations typically pay less, because of compensating wage differentials in uncertain environments, whereby workers are rewarded with higher average earnings for assuming more risk. For instance, if women tend to sort into low-risk (as to wage and health) positions, such as in the education sector, whereas men more readily accept risky environments, such as on offshore oil platforms, men will command a wage premium for the additional risks they bear. In other words, risk preferences may play an important role in the determination of wages (and wage gaps), above and beyond the traditional factors typically included in compensation studies.

A rich literature exists in experimental economics and psychology on gender differences in risk preferences, as shown by the thorough review of Croson and Gneezy (2009). They hypothesize that systematic gender differences in emotional or affective reaction to risk may affect the utility that one experiences while making choices under uncertainty, providing an explanation for gender differences in risk preferences.

Women exhibit more stress, fear, or dread when faced with the uncertain prospect of a negative outcome. According to Fehr-Duda, Gennaro, and Schubert (2006), women's apparent higher risk aversion can be sourced to a greater tendency than men to underestimate large probabilities of gains. This would be consistent with Loewenstein and others' (2001) hypothesis of "risk as feelings," in which women's stronger emotional reaction to a risky decision manifests itself as pessimism. A similar pessimism may likewise induce women to overestimate the likelihood of negative outcomes, as in Flynn, Slovic, and Mertz (1994) and Finucane and others (2000).

Related to the discussion of gender differences in risk attitudes is the gender discrepancy in overconfidence. Although both sexes are prone to overconfidence, men are particularly overconfident about tasks they perceive as more masculine in nature (Beyer and Bowden 1997), which may render them more inclined to enter riskier situations.

Gaps in the sexes' tendencies to negotiate are also documented. Conceiving of negotiation as a competition over the distribution of resources between parties, several authors have placed increasing importance on situational or contextual factors in explaining gender differences in negotiation (Stuhlmacher and Walters 1999; Walters, Stuhlmacher, and Meyer 1998). For instance, Bowles, Babcock, and Lai (2007) document that negotiating intensity depends upon whether subjects are told that they are negotiating for themselves or for others, with women's performance improving substantially when negotiating for someone other than themselves. In turn, the performance of men is unaffected by whether they negotiate for themselves or for others. In their sample of close to 200 working adults, Babcock and others (2006) report that men initiated wage negotiations two to four times more frequently than women. Among MBA students, more than half the male students negotiated their job offer, compared with only 10 percent among female students. The differences in the aggressiveness with which the sexes pursue compensation, whether inherent or socialized, have important implications for interpretations of the measured gender gaps in wages.

Different labor market trajectories may also result from the biological differences that distinguish the sexes. For instance if men are comparatively better suited to physically demanding occupations, we would expect a certain degree of occupational segregation along gender lines, with corresponding differences in earnings. Links have also been established between biological differences and gender differences in life-cycle experience profiles. Childbirth, for instance, necessarily entails disruptions and discontinuities in women's labor force experiences, which, in turn, affect their outcomes. Some studies have demonstrated the value of medical progress by documenting that technologies that mitigate the effects of such biological differences have helped close the gender gaps in education and LFP (Albanesi and Olivetti 2009; Bailey 2006; Goldin and Katz 2002).

In Europe, women take approximately 7.6 more sick days per year than men of the same age with the same occupation and level of education. In the United States and Canada, the corresponding figures are 3.1 and 5.2 days, respectively. Although family-related commitments explain part of this gender gap in absenteeism, even among unmarried workers with no children, women still take significantly more sick days than men. Taking these observations as a starting point—and exploiting the personnel data set from a large Italian bank, which contains the exact date and duration of every employee absence from work—Ichino and Moretti (2009) document that the likelihood of an illness-related absence increases significantly for females relative to males 28 days after the previous absence. The authors show that absences with 28-day cycles explain roughly one-third of the gender gap in days of absence and more than two-thirds of the overall gender gap in the number of absences; they conclude that these differences have small but nontrivial consequences for women's careers and earnings.

Whether physical or preference related, these differences between genders can translate into sizable career and earnings differentials, even among individuals with elite education or at the top of the potential wage distribution. Bertrand, Goldin, and Katz (2010) assess the wage gap and career choices of elite MBA students in the United States. Top MBA graduates are likely to be very similar along several unobservable dimensions, including high motivation and ability, and have strong career orientations. Although male and female MBAs have comparable labor incomes at the outset of their careers, a gap soon opens. Five years after completion of their MBA, men's annual earnings are 30 percent higher than women's, a difference that nearly doubles in another five to 10 years. The proportion of female MBAs who are out of the labor force also rises substantially in the decade following MBA completion.

Bertrand, Goldin, and Katz (2010) identify three main factors underlying the large and rising gender gap in earnings: differences in training prior to MBA graduation, differences in career interruptions, and differences in weekly hours worked. The authors document that the presence of children in the household is the main reason for these women's more frequent career interruptions and more modest job experience, as well as their shorter work hours. Although differences in the productive characteristics of male and female MBAs are small at baseline, the wage penalties from shorter hours and career discontinuities are large.

Worth noting is that women who select into elite business schools in all likelihood have relatively progressive views of home production and the division of household labor, as likely do their spouses. Furthermore, given these women's expected (favorable) position in the income distribution, they probably could afford high-quality child care by relying on the dual incomes of the spouses that would result from not withdrawing from the labor force. Nevertheless, they opt to leave the labor force, choosing to incur the pecuniary penalties documented by Bertrand, Goldin, and Katz (2010).

To economists, this outcome may appear paradoxical and puzzling. These women could have it all. Of course, common sense suggests that women attach value to raising their children and the rewards from doing so are not comparable to a salary. In the United States, trends in female LFP show that it began to level off in the mid-1990s, peaking around 72 percent in the late 1990s, before retreating below 70 percent in 2004. This phenomenon has received considerable press recently. On the option to withdraw from the labor force, Wallis (2004) writes:

> For most mothers—and fathers, for that matter—there is little choice but to persevere on both fronts to pay the bills. Indeed, 72 percent of mothers with children under 18 are in the work force. ... But in the professional and managerial classes, where higher incomes permit more choices, a reluctant revolt is under way. Today's women execs are less willing to play the juggler's game, especially in its current high-speed mode, and more willing to sacrifice paychecks and prestige for time with their family. Most of these women are choosing not so much to drop out as to stop out, often with every intention of returning. Their mantra: You can have it all, just not all at the same time.

Here, the ability of mothers to choose to stay home and afford to care for their children themselves is framed as a luxury.

Similar evidence comes from Sweden, which is traditionally invoked by economists and social scientists as the gold standard in child care provision, parental leave policies, and family-friendly employment policies. Sweden is also lauded for its progressive views on gender parity. Despite these achievements, only 1.5 percent of senior managers are women, compared with 11 percent in the United States. Three-quarters of Swedish women work in the public sector, while three-quarters of men work in the private sector. Among the most-cited reasons for these choices are the availability of part-time opportunities, a relatively flat wage scale with respect to tenure, and the ease of transitions in and out of the sector. Even full-time positions tend to have fairly light loads in terms of hours. Media commentators (including *The Atlantic* and *The Economist*) have concluded, "As the allure of public-sector and part-time work reveals, women make professional choices based on more than just their qualifications!" (Allan 2010).

These two examples are particularly compelling. Even when they do not face binding budget constraints, women with career aspirations reduce their labor supply and consequently incur wage penalties from lost experience. This finding is consistent with Hoyos and Ñopo's (2010) results: women on average seem to be paid less because of sorting and less accumulated labor force experience.

If women at the very top of the income distribution are willing to forgo experience (one of the key determinants of the gender wage gap) or choose professions that pay less to benefit from more flexible arrangements, then the same logic should apply to women who face lower opportunity costs (lower wages) and who, as Wallis (2004) points out, simply cannot afford that option.

Beyond the inescapable biological differences between the sexes lies the question of whether more subtle gender differences—such as differences in preferences and personality traits—also have biological origins ("nature") or whether they are the products of environmental influences ("nurture"). Evidence suggests at least some role for environmental influences, which implies a margin of behavior amenable to policy intervention to improve women's labor market outcomes.

Notes

[1] Wage gap analyses are by definition carried out on segments of the population that are active in the labor market. However, if a gendered selection process into the labor market operates such that working and nonworking women are significantly different from working and nonworking men, then wage gap analyses may not capture the full extent of the gaps. For instance, if low-productivity men are more likely to work than low-productivity women, the wage gap may be understated. Examples of the importance of gendered sample selection in Colombia and the United States are Badel and Peña (2010) and Machado (2012), respectively. In other words, gaps may be underestimated if the sample of women is positively selected compared to that of men. However, the matching decomposition methods adopted by Hoyos and Ñopo (2010) de facto aim at minimizing the concerns of gendered selection issues. The common support assumption of the matching estimator de facto trims the sample in such a way that the two groups are "on average" close to each another in terms of their observable characteristics and minimizes the discrepancies in terms of unobservables.

[2] The analysis of gender wage gaps is easier in countries whose labor markets are dominated by formal salaried employment. To the extent that most workers are either self-employed or employees in family enterprises, or are employers, the analysis of gender wage gaps is less comparable to the literature from developed countries, where most of the labor force is employed in formal salaried positions. In particular, some of the earnings reported by self-employed workers and employers may not correspond just to labor earnings but may include capital income.

[3] Throughout the report the terms *gender wage gap* and *gender earnings gap* are used interchangeably. In the analysis, the measure used corresponds to hourly earnings, which include wages for salaried employees and income from self-employed workers and employers.

[4] The samples are representative of each country's total population, except in the cases of Argentina and Uruguay, where they are only representative of the urban population.

[5] The decomposition is undertaken only after hourly earnings in local currencies are converted to 2002 dollars using purchasing power parity exchange rates and nominal GDP deflators—to express them in a common, constant currency. The same observable characteristics are used in every country to match women and men, such that the components of the wage gap are comparable across countries. The econometric procedure used by Hoyos and Ñopo (2010) follows the methodology of Ñopo (2009), which is an extension of the Blinder-Oaxaca decomposition, using a nonparametric matching approach. In its application to gender gaps, women and men are matched when they have the same combination of observable characteristics.

[6] Significant heterogeneity also exists across countries in the magnitudes of both the unconditional gender earnings gaps and the unexplained component of the earnings gaps. Brazil, the Dominican Republic, Honduras, Nicaragua, Peru, and Uruguay register the greatest unexplained wage gaps, while Colombia, Ecuador, and Paraguay register the lowest.

[7] A number of studies have documented a "convexification" of the returns to education in LAC, whereby the wage returns to secondary education have declined whereas those to tertiary education have increased. Recent findings point to a combination of supply- and demand-side factors: the substantial rise in the supply of workers having completed secondary education depressed their wages relative to other workers, while the demand for workers with tertiary education expanded, thereby inflating their wages (see Binelli 2014; Manacorda, Sánchez-Páramo, and Schady 2010).

Others argue that demand-side factors play the more prominent role (see Gasparini and Lustig 2011, for instance). The pattern documented by Hoyos and Ñopo—and discussed previously—of widening gender gaps in the middle of the education distribution and narrowing at the extremes is consistent with the hypothesis that the convexification of the returns to education was more dramatic for women than for men. That is, both the decline in the returns to secondary education and the rise in the returns to tertiary education were sharper for women than for men.

[8] Gender segregation in economic sectors is not by itself the source of wage differentials. The authors conjecture that the results could potentially be driven by males' overrepresentation in agriculture, which in turn is the sector with the lowest average wages.

[9] That is, if greater experience in either the labor market or home production makes someone more productive in that particular endeavor (perhaps through a process of learning by doing), discrimination that forms an initial barrier to women's entry into the labor market may reinforce occupational segregation, as both men and women become more productive in their respective sectors despite not having an initial comparative advantage in either. As a result, men's and women's labor market experiences may differ considerably.

References

Albanesi, Stefania, and Claudia Olivetti. 2009. "Production, Market Production and the Gender Wage Gap: Incentives and Expectations." *Review of Economic Dynamics* 12 (1): 80–107.

Allan, Nicole. 2010. "Have Women Really Taken over the Workforce?" *Atlantic,* January 12, 2010.

Atal, Juan Pablo, Hugo Ñopo, and Natalia Winder. 2009. "New Century, Old Disparities: Gender and Ethnic Wage Gaps in Latin America." RES Working Paper 4640, Inter-American Development Bank, Washington, DC.

Babcock, Linda, Michele Gelfand, Deborah Small, and Heidi Stayn. 2006. "Gender Differences in the Propensity to Initiate Negotiations." In *Social Psychology and Economics*, edited by David De Cremer, Marcel Zeelenberg, and J. Keith Murnighan, 239–62. Mahwah, NJ: Erlbaum.

Badel, Alejandro, and Ximena Peña. 2010. "Decomposing the Gender Wage Gap with Sample Selection Adjustment: Evidence from Colombia." *Revista de Análisis Económico* 25 (2): 169–91.

Bailey, Martha J. 2006. "More Power to the Pill: The Impact of Contraceptive Freedom on Women's Labor Supply." *Quarterly Journal of Economics* 121 (1): 289–320.

Barrientos, Armando. 2002. "Women, Informal Employment, and Social Protection in Latin America," IDPM General Discussion Paper 66, Institute for Development Policy and Management, University of Manchester, Manchester, U.K.

Bertrand, Marianne. 2011. "New Perspectives on Gender." In *Handbook of Labor Economics*, Volume 4B, edited by Orley Ashenfelter and David Card, 1543–90. Amsterdam: North-Holland/Elsevier.

Bertrand, Marianne, Claudia Goldin, and Lawrence F. Katz. 2010. "Dynamics of the Gender Gap for Young Professionals in the Financial and Corporate Sectors." *American Economic Journal: Applied Economics* 2 (3): 228–55.

Beyer, Sylvia, and Edward M. Bowden. 1997. "Gender Differences in Self-Perceptions: Convergent Evidence from Three Measures of Accuracy and Bias." *Personality and Social Psychology Bulletin* 23 (2): 157–72.

Binelli, Chiara. 2014. "How the Wage-Education Profile Got More Complex: Evidence from Mexico." Discussion Paper 1404, University of Southampton, Southampton, U.K.

Blau, Francine D., and Lawrence M. Kahn. 2000. "Gender Differences in Pay." *Journal of Economic Perspectives* 14 (4): 75–99.

———. 2006. "The U.S. Gender Pay Gap in the 1990s: Slowing Convergence." IZA Discussion Paper 2176, Institute for the Study of Labor, Bonn, Germany.

Bonin, Holger, Thomas Dohmen, Armin Falk, David Huffman, and Uwe Sunde. 2007. "Cross-Sectional Earnings Risk and Occupational Sorting: The Role of Risk Attitudes." *Labour Economics* 14: 926–37.

Bosch, Mariano, and William F. Maloney. 2010. "Comparative Analysis of Labor Market Dynamics Using Markov Processes: An Application to Informality." *Labour Economics* 17 (4): 621–31.

Bowles, Hannah Riley, Linda Babcock, and Lei Lai. 2007. "Social Incentives for Gender Differences in the Propensity to Initiate Negotiations: Sometimes It Does Hurt to Ask." *Organizational Behavior and Human Decision Processes* 103 (1): 84–103.

Chiappori, Pierre-André, Murat Iyigun, and Yoram Weiss. 2009. "Investment in Schooling and the Marriage Market." *American Economic Review* 99 (5): 1689–713.

Chioda, Laura, and Gabriel Demombynes. 2014. "The Rise of Female Labor Force Participation Rate in LAC, 1960–2000." Background paper to this report, World Bank, Washington, DC.

Croson, Rachel, and Uri Gneezy. 2009. "Gender Differences in Preferences." *Journal of Economic Literature* 47 (2): 448–74.

Duryea, Suzanne, Alejandra Cox Edwards, and Manuelita Ureta. 2004. "Women in the Latin American Labor Market: The Remarkable 1990s." In *Women at Work: Challenges for Latin America*, edited by Claudia Piras, 27–60. Washington, DC: Inter-American Development Bank.

Duryea, Suzanne, Sebastian Galiani, Hugo Ñopo, and Claudia Piras. 2007. "The Educational Gender Gap in Latin America and the Caribbean." Working Paper 4510, Inter-American Development Bank, Washington, DC.

Fehr-Duda, Helga, Manuele de Gennaro, and Renate Schubert. 2006. "Gender, Financial Risk, and Probability Weights." *Theory and Decision* 60 (2–3): 283–313.

Fernández, Raquel, and Alessandra Fogli. 2009. "Culture: An Empirical Investigation of Beliefs, Work, and Fertility." *American Economic Journal: Macroeconomics* 1 (1): 146–77.

Fernández, Raquel, Alessandra Fogli, and Claudia Olivetti. 2004. "Preference Formation and the Rise of Women's Labor Force Participation: Evidence from WWII." NBER Working Paper 10589, National Bureau of Economic Research, Cambridge, MA.

Finucane, Melissa L., Paul Slovic, C. K. Mertz, James Flynn, and Theresa A. Satterfield. 2000. Gender, Race, and Perceived Risk: The 'White Male' Effect. *Healthy Risk and Society* 2 (2): 159–72.

Flynn, James, Paul Slovic, and C. K. Mertz. 1994. "Gender, Race, and Perception of Environmental Health Risks." *Risk Analysis* 14 (6): 1101–8.

Fortin, Nicole M. 2005. "Gender Role Attitudes and the Labour-Market Outcomes of Women across OECD Countries." *Oxford Review of Economic Policy* 21 (3): 416–38.

———. 2008. "The Gender Wage Gap among Young Adults in the United States: The Importance of Money versus People." *Journal of Human Resources* 43 (4): 886–920.

Gasparini, Leonardo, and Nora Lustig. 2011. "The Rise and Fall of Income Inequality in Latin America." Working Paper 1110, Department of Economics, Tulane University, New Orleans, LA.

Goldin, Claudia. 1990. *Understanding the Gender Gap: An Economic History of American Women.* New York: Oxford University Press.

———. 1995. "The U-Shaped Female Labor Force Function in Economic Development and Economic History." In *Investment in Women's Human Capital*, edited by T. Paul Schultz, 61–90. Chicago: University of Chicago Press.

Goldin, Claudia, and Lawrence F. Katz. 2002. "The Power of the Pill: Oral Contraceptives and Women's Career and Marriage Decisions." *Journal of Political Economy* 110 (4): 730–70.

Hausmann, Ricardo, Laura D. Tyson, and Saadia Zahidi. 2009. *The Global Gender Gap Report 2009.* Geneva, Switzerland: World Economic Forum.

Hoyos, Alejandro, and Hugo Ñopo. 2010. "Evolution of Gender Gaps in Latin America at the Turn of the Century: An Addendum to 'New Century, Old Disparities: Gender and Ethnic Wage Gaps in Latin America." Background paper prepared for the Regional Study on Gender in LAC, World Bank, Washington, DC.

Ichino, Andrea, and Enrico Moretti. 2009. "Biological Gender Differences, Absenteeism, and the Earnings Gap." *American Economic Journal: Applied Economics* 1 (1): 183–218.

Loewenstein, George F., Christopher K. Hsee, Elke U. Weber, and Ned Welch. 2001. "Risk as Feelings." *Psychological Bulletin* 127 (2): 267–86.

Machado, Cecilia. 2012. "Selection, Heterogeneity, and the Gender Wage Gap." IZA Discussion Paper 7005, Institute for the Study of Labor, Bonn, Germany. http://ftp.iza.org/dp7005.pdf.

Manacorda, Marco, Carolina Sánchez-Páramo, and Norbert Schady. 2010. "Changes in Returns to Education in Latin America: The Role of Demand and Supply of Skills." *Industrial and Labor Relations Review* 63 (2): 307–26.

Ñopo, Hugo. 2009. "The Gender Wage Gap in Peru 1986–2000: Evidence from a Matching Comparisons Approach." Research Department Working Paper 675, Inter-American Development Bank, Washington, DC.

Psacharopoulos, George, and Zafiris Tzannatos. 1992. "Latin American Women's Earnings and Participation in the Labor Force." Policy Research Working Paper 856, World Bank, Washington, DC.

Stuhlmacher, Alice F., and Amy E. Walters. 1999. "Gender Differences in Negotiation Outcome: A Meta Analysis." *Personnel Psychology* 52 (3): 653–77.

Tenjo, Jaime, Rocío Ribero, and Luisa Bernat. 2006. "Evolución de las diferencias salariales de género en seis países de América Latina." In *Mujeres y Trabajo en América Latina*, edited by Claudia Piras, 149–98. Washington, DC: Inter-American Development Bank.

Wallis, Claudia. 2004. "The Case for Staying Home." *Time Magazine*, March 22.

Walters, Amy E., Alice F. Stuhlmacher, and Lia L. Meyer. 1998. "Gender and Negotiator Competitiveness: A Meta-Analysis." *Organizational Behavior and Human Decision Processes* 76 (1): 1–29.

Part III

6

A Closer Look at Dynamics within the Household

Introduction

In the analysis of previous chapters, family formation emerges as important in shaping female economic participation, along several dimensions. Transitions in and out of the labor market, across sectors, and between formality and informality are all affected by marriage and fertility decisions, providing a compelling reason to improve researchers' understanding of household decision making.

In recent decades, households in Latin America and the Caribbean (LAC) have faced structural and policy changes that are likely to have affected their labor force decisions and the allocation of their resources. As documented in the previous chapters, female labor force participation (LFP) has risen steadily, providing women with a direct source of income. Investments in education have also grown steadily, with important consequences not only for women's earnings potential but also for their identities and aspirations. Education also affects women's prospects in the marriage market and ultimately their bargaining positions within the household: greater earning potential implies that women's options outside the couple are better and broader, thus commanding greater leverage in the current household. In addition, over the past two decades, several countries in the region have adopted poverty reduction policies that directly or indirectly benefit women's access to income and economic assets, such as conditional cash transfer (CCT) programs, expansions of microcredit programs targeting women, and changes to the institutional environment that promote gender equality.

Studying household decision making is complicated because experimentally altering the bargaining power of one spouse and then following how households later redistribute resources (consumption, leisure, and so on) is difficult. For instance, women who have more progressive views and who value their careers more are more likely to invest in their human capital and ultimately have higher earnings. They are then more likely to marry a spouse with higher education and more liberal views. In essence, the empirical difficulty with studying household decisions is that many outcomes, including female LFP and income, are often the result of decisions earlier in life that reflect both spouses' preferences and expectations, rather than random variation in present-day resources or bargaining power. These differences confound comparisons across individuals.

This chapter explores the determinants and consequences of female economic participation and sheds light on the mechanisms through which they operate, focusing on interactions within the household. It exploits social policies and interventions that exogenously relax women's constraints (time and budget) either by endowing them directly with additional resources or by manipulating the prices and opportunities they face.

The lenses for studying these interventions are economic theories of the family, some of which explicitly allow stakeholders to have diverging interests and preferences. Why is understanding how households operate and providing an accurate theoretical description of interactions within households worthwhile? Understanding household dynamics and decision making is not only essential to shed light on the evolution of LFP and to make statements about welfare—but it is also essential for policy purposes. Intrahousehold decisions mediate the effects of policy, so insights about how decisions are made and resources are allocated can illuminate the path for effective policy.

As discussed, different assumptions on the household decision-making process and on the household members' potentially conflicting interests predict very different household behaviors and allocations, particularly in the face of policies. If the interests of household heads do not align, the distribution of bargaining power across spouses may affect household choices. In that event, public policy might generate both desired and perverse outcomes, depending on whom the policy targets and how. The policies considered here are of interest precisely because they alter the bargaining position of women, sometimes experimentally, thus shedding light on the consequences of female economic empowerment.

CCTs are one such policy. They generally disburse income to families with children on the condition that eligible children attend school and regularly visit health clinics. They explicitly place the additional resources in the nominal control of women on the assumption that mothers make better decisions for their children than fathers and that the transfers endow mothers with greater authority in allocating household resources. Does this assumption bear out? Does nominal control over resources enhance a woman's bargaining position relative to her spouse in making consumption and labor supply decisions? Does reducing men's say in household choices have any costs, intended or otherwise?

Child care subsidies can also improve women's position in the household indirectly by making a market option to self-provide child care more affordable and increasing the opportunity cost of time spent in home production. A couple that takes advantage of the subsidy frees the time otherwise spent on child care, relaxing the household's time constraints, particularly women's, because responsibilities for child rearing typically fall on women. What are the responses to cheaper market provision of child care? By reducing demands on women's time, do subsidies indirectly give them more control in allocating their time and facilitate their integration into the labor force?

Legislation that permits part-time employment in environments in which it was previously prohibited operates similarly by increasing opportunities for formal employment while preserving some flexibility to meet demands at home. Although such legislation in principle applies to both sexes, in practice it affects female household members, who typically carry the load of domestic production. How do these work arrangements affect women's labor supply? Do they draw women who otherwise specialize in home production into the labor force by allowing them to combine market work with family responsibilities, at least partially realizing their earnings potential? Do they instead segregate the labor market into full-time and part-time work along gender lines? Or are part-time positions filled by informal sector workers, who have already committed to participation in the labor market but place a high value on flexibility?

Finally, with positive labor market returns to education, exogenous increases in educational attainment caused by changes in compulsory schooling laws render women more productive and their time in the labor market more valuable, again boosting the opportunity cost of remaining out of the labor force. Do these policy-induced changes in education afford women more opportunities in the labor market? Do they make women more likely to join the labor force or increase their labor supply? Do nonmarket gains to education occur in the form of "better" suitors in the marriage market—or of improved bargaining power within their relationships, including greater control over their fertility?

This chapter analyzes these (and other) themes in LAC, exploiting policies that, while not designed to address such inquiries, permit researchers to study them. The chapter first reviews theories of intrahousehold allocation, emphasizing their implications for household outcomes and labor supply. It then reviews the empirical evidence, highlighting the role of intrahousehold dynamics in shaping policy impacts. It then turns to policy interventions that exogenously alter household endowments and the trade-offs between women's specialization in home production and participation in the labor force, considering the impact of exogenous changes in the following:

- Economic resources nominally controlled by women (CCTs)
- The opportunity costs of specializing in home production (subsidized child care)
- Labor market rigidities (part-time work legislation)

Intrahousehold allocations: Theory and practice

As referenced in the introduction to this book, classical economic models of consumer demand and labor supply begin (uncontroversially) with a single individual choosing actions and consumption bundles that maximize his or her welfare within what is permitted by his or her budget. In reality, however, people tend to exist, work, and consume within the context of families and households, where resources and household production may be shared and decisions made collectively. How can researchers reconcile the individualistic theory of the consumer with this collective reality? A first pass is to treat the family as if it were a single decision maker, with a single pooled budget constraint and a single utility function that includes the consumption and leisure time of every family member. This is the *unitary*, or *consensus*, approach (Becker 1974, 1991; Samuelson 1956).

Unitary models and income pooling: How they fare in practice

The basic unitary model of a two-person household assumes that each partner has an individual utility function that depends on his or her private consumption of goods, but that, by consensus, they agree to maximize a common welfare function incorporating their individual utilities, subject to a joint budget constraint that pools the income received by the two spouses. The result is an aggregate household expenditure pattern that resembles an individual demand function and that can be analyzed in the classical way, as though the family were a single agent maximizing a single utility function, yielding a set of demand functions that depend only on prices and total family resources.

In this theory of the household, an increase in women's market wages affects outcomes only in that it relaxes the family budget constraint, increasing the total amount of household consumption (among normal goods). In turn, a part of this increase may be passed on to women and children through a higher allocation for them. Thus the unitary model's assumption that all household resources are mechanically aggregated into a single budget constraint, referred to as *income pooling*, implies that only total income will affect demand and that changes in women's earnings affect intrahousehold allocations only through changes in the overall family budget constraint.

How does the unitary model fare as a description of household behavior? The income-pooling hypothesis provides much of the basis for testing the validity of the unitary model, because it asserts that the identity of the income earner is immaterial to ultimate allocations and demand functions: the impact on household demand for goods and services of an additional unit of income earned by wives should precisely match that of an additional unit of income contributed by husbands. Equivalently, household demand functions should be invariant to redistributing income nominally controlled by husbands to their wives because such redistribution leaves total family income unchanged.

Empirical tests of pooling invariably conclude that income controlled by husbands and wives has significantly different effects on family behavior, whether measured by expenditures on categories of goods and services, such as food, or by outcomes, such as child health.[1] In Brazil, resources in the hands of mothers improve children's health significantly more than those in the hands of fathers, and that difference can be sizable: the effects of mothers' unearned income on child survival probabilities is almost 20 times that of fathers' income (Thomas 1990). Interestingly, the effects differ according to the sex of the child: fathers' income affects mostly boys' health whereas that of mothers improves the health of girls. This heterogeneity is interesting not only because it refutes the unitary model's income-pooling postulate but also because it points to parents' unequal concerns for their children along gender lines. Similar findings of gender differences in expenditure patterns using comparable methods are found in French data (Bourguignon and others 1993) and Canadian data (Browning and others 1994).

Though these results are intriguing, one might be concerned that differences in unearned income might reflect not just random differences across households but also unobserved family background, entrepreneurship, or preferences. Several studies have subsequently considered the income-pooling hypothesis with data from a variety of countries, making clever use of policies and natural shocks that effectively make observationally equivalent households face different environments.

Lundberg, Pollak, and Wales (1997), for instance, examine the effects of a curious policy in the United Kingdom that transferred a substantial child allowance from husbands to wives in the late 1970s. The transfer provides an almost ideal setting to test the unitary model's income-pooling requirement. That is, it left each household's total budget constraint unaltered, but by making transfers "from the wallet to the purse," it expanded wives' nominal control. The authors find robust evidence that greater expenditures on women's and children's clothing coincided with this income redistribution, contradicting the unitary model's premise that the distribution of income within the household is irrelevant. As noted in the introduction to this book, these gender-specific preferences appear to be persistent and to span generations. They operate not only from parent to child but also from grandparent to grandchild, as shown by Duflo (2000, 2003) and Edmonds (2005), who investigate the effects of an extension of the South African Old Age Pension on children's health, nutrition, and educational attainment. Although making these payments to grandmothers has measurable benefits, it may also be associated with (opportunity) costs. Although Duflo (2000, 2003) does not identify any benefits along anthropometric measures of granddaughter's health, Edmonds (2005) estimates some human capital benefits of disbursement to grandfathers. He considers the impact of the reform on schooling and education investments by comparing the school enrollment of adolescents in families where an elderly member is eligible for the pension with that in families that have an ineligible elderly member. He finds that, compared with children in families with ineligible elders, children are more likely to be in school when they live with an eligible man than with an eligible woman. Thus, the identity of the income holder matters, and an apparent trade-off emerges, with men making educational investments in their grandchildren and women making nutritional investments in their granddaughters. Both results reject a unitary framework for multigenerational families and provide a nuanced picture of how children benefit from male versus female control of household resources. This evidence calls for theoretical alternatives to the unitary (or consensus) model. The most common alternatives are spousal-bargaining models that explicitly model the diverging interests of spouses.[2]

Alternatives to the unitary model: Cooperative bargaining

Under an alternative (bargaining) hypothesis, males and females may have conflicting preferences and unequal bargaining powers, such that the same lump-sum redistribution of income can improve the woman's ability to tilt outcomes according to her preferences.

In Mexico's Oportunidades (Opportunities) anti-poverty program, the source of income matters, with changes in female-controlled CCT income substantially and positively affecting expenditures on food and on children's goods—and changes in income driven by rainfall shocks having a smaller influence on household public goods outlays (Bobonis and Castro 2010). In Ecuador's Bono de Desarrollo Humano (Human Development Voucher), an unconditional cash transfer program targeting rural mothers, women favor spending on nutrition (Schady and Rosero 2008).[3]

Several studies of the expenditure patterns of CCT recipients in LAC have identified a surprising regularity among CCT beneficiaries, namely, that the food share of total spending remains invariant to total income. This would be of little interest were it not for Engel's law, which holds that a negative relationship should exist between total expenditures and the budget share of food. The law holds almost universally in the developed world.

According to Engel's law, the expectation is for food budget shares to fall following exogenous expansions in household income, consistent with a unitary model in which food is a necessity. Why then are recipient households of CCTs the exception? Among these households, the income effect (that is, the expected drop in food budget share) appears to be offset by some other aspect of the program, such that the net effect of the CCTs on the share of food is nil or, in some cases, positive.

After an analysis of Mexico's Oportunidades program, in which they give several data and methodological obstacles particular attention, Attanasio and Lechêne (2010a, 2010b) confirm the observation that food commands equal or greater shares of spending among program beneficiaries.

They then consider the following long set of mechanisms that could account for the observed changes: an increase in the price of food in response to CCT receipt, food being a luxury, homothetic preferences, changes in preferences leading to the purchase of better food, differential "labeling" of money (for example, mental accounts), and changes in decision making among beneficiary households. Their analysis rejects all but the last hypothesis, pointing to a failure of the unitary model among Oportunidades's beneficiaries.

They show that CCTs have a dual effect on choices. The first, induced by the addition to total household income, is the expected drop in the budget share of food (in accordance with Engel's law), having shown that food is a necessity. The second is to raise the budget share of food by an amount matching the decrease induced by the preceding income effect.[4] The only aspect of CCT (and similar) programs that can resolve the puzzle is that the transfer is placed in the hands of women, who appear to have greater concern for nutrition. CCTs, often designed to place nominal control over resources in the hands of mothers, appear to alter the balance of control such that women's preferences are better represented in consumption. This assumption underlies some of the gendered targeting in CCTs.

Cooperative bargaining models of marriage from game theory typically consider a family consisting of two members, a husband and a wife. Each has a utility function that depends on his or her consumption of private goods (Manser and Brown 1980; McElroy and Horney 1981). If agreement is not reached on the consumption allocation, each receives a payoff represented by his or her "threat point"—the utilities associated with his or her best outside option of divorce.[5] This dependence is the critical empirical implication of bargaining models: family demands depend not only on prices and total family income but also on determinants of the threat point. In an alternative bargaining model, the "separate spheres" model, the threat point is internal to the marriage, not external as in divorce-threat bargaining models, with divorce being the ultimate threat available to marital partners in disagreement (Lundberg and Pollak 1993). Unlike unitary models, cooperative bargaining does not necessarily imply income pooling.

Bargained outcomes depend on the threat point, and the income controlled by husband and wife will affect family behavior (and the relative well-being of men and women within marriage), assuming that this control influences the threat point. Critically, this dependence implies that public policy (for example, taxes and transfers) need not be neutral in its effects on distribution within the family. In addition, changes in welfare payments available to divorced mothers or in the laws defining marital property and regulating its division on divorce can affect the distribution of allocations between men and women in two-parent families through their effect on the threat point.

In sum, the model that best approximates household behavior can have important implications for policy because alternative models imply different allocations to household members. These allocations include not only consumption but also labor supply and investments in the human capital of the next generation. In the following subsection, another margin of control among female beneficiaries of CCTs is examined—their decisions regarding time allocations and LFP.

How additional control over resources could increase female labor force participation

As discussed in the previous section, empirical tests of income pooling using data from a variety of countries are invariably rejected. Resources nominally controlled by the husband and wife have substantial bearing on family behavior, whether measured directly by the composition of expenditures or indirectly by such outcomes as children's health. This accumulation of evidence represents a powerful refutation of the view that households behave as a single individual would and instead favors a perspective that individual family members can have conflicting interests and exert independent power on household decisions. His or her bargaining power determines how much the individual influences outcomes, and the evidence suggests that an important determinant of this influence is the share of household resources under the individual's nominal control.

Discrepancies in bargaining power linked to control over resources appear to emerge from the gendered division of labor within the family and, in particular, to the allocation of responsibility for the care of children to mothers. This difference can arise from a model of marital gains to specialization and exchange among spouses that is directly analogous to models of international trade that define comparative advantage and the gains from trade. If a two-person family produces and consumes two types of outputs—market and nonmarket (such as home production)—and one family member is relatively more productive in one sector than the other (because of endowments, previous investments, or how they are remunerated by the market), at least one member will completely specialize and devote all of his or her time to either market or nonmarket production. In these traditional models of specialization, even minute differences between otherwise identical spouses can generate completely gender-segregated divisions of labor.

To the extent that women continue to perform more household work than their spouses and to earn lower market wages as a result, nonunitary models of the family predict that women will receive a smaller share of household resources than they would in the absence of gender specialization. But what if their resources were inflated for reasons unrelated to their behavior? According to these nonunitary models, CCTs can reverse some of these consequences of gender specialization by targeting women directly, exogenously endowing them with a greater share of resources.

With their increased bargaining power, how do CCT recipients respond in terms of labor supply? Do increases in unearned income lead women to seek further improvements in bargaining power by joining the labor force and earning yet more income? Do they exercise their increased power by way of reductions in their involvement in home production?

This section considers how an exogenous transfer of resources, nominally assigned to women, may alter the division of labor within the household. In principle, the increased resources controlled by mothers can affect female labor supply through three channels:

- *Income.* Theoretically, one might expect a reduction in labor supply in response to an exogenous increase in nonlabor income through its income effect on leisure. To the extent that leisure is a normal good, greater income should result in greater consumption of leisure, in the form of either reduced hours or no further participation in the labor force. So a pure income effect would predict an unambiguous reduction of labor supply, larger for wives than for husbands as a result of their increased bargaining power.

- *Increased shadow price of home production.* This exogenous change in income controlled by women is associated with conditionalities such as children's school attendance and visits to health clinics (as with Mexico's Oportunidades program), which impose certain demands on household members' time and limit eligible children's role in home production. Thus, remaining household members must reallocate the extra responsibilities among themselves. If mothers assume these responsibilities, one might mechanically expect a reduction in their labor supply.

- *Bargaining power.* The additional resources (and bargaining power) provided by CCTs could "buy" women more discretion in the allocation of their time. Women who previously specialized in home production might try their hand in the labor market or in entrepreneurship. In this view, the CCTs offer an option to further increase their household bargaining position by seeking yet more earnings in the labor market.

Several studies have considered the effect of CCTs on female LFP. By and large, they find no effect on LFP among CCT recipient households (Maluccio and Flores 2005). Maluccio and Flores (2005) exploit a randomized, community-based intervention in Nicaragua (Red de Protección Social (Social Protection Network)) and find no negative impact on female LFP. Skoufias and Di Maro (2008), exploiting the experimental design of PROGRESA—a conditional cash transfer program in rural Mexico—consistently estimate that the program has no significant impact on adult labor supply.

But households participating in Mexico's Oportunidades program increase investments in productive enterprises and expand their income-generating opportunities. The program raised the probability of female microenterprise activity by roughly 3 percentage points, a significant increase from the mean baseline of 5.1 percent (Gertler, Martinez, and Rubio-Codina 2006).

Conditional cash transfers and heterogeneity in women's labor supply responses

In 2005, Peru introduced the CCT program Juntos (Together) in rural areas. Like other CCTs in the region, Juntos disburses a fixed monthly amount to mothers—roughly US$33, about 13 percent of monthly household income—if their children comply with basic education and health requirements (Perova and Vakis 2009, 2011). Families are in the program for a maximum of four years.[6] Program conditions include regular health visits for pregnant women and children under five years of age, at least 85 percent school attendance for children between ages six and 14 years who have not completed elementary education, and completion of identification documents for women and children covered by the program. Eligible households are identified in three stages: geographic targeting, household targeting, and community validation of potential beneficiaries. Roughly 450,000 families in 638 districts were eligible for the program (Perova and Vakis 2009).

A short-term evaluation of Juntos's impact on a number of outcomes reveals no effect on employment rates or hours worked (Perova and Vakis 2009). But women who have been in the program for more than a year (13–25 months) have a 9-percentage-point higher probability of being employed; men show no similar effect.

What stands out is that the average employment rate of women in this rural Peru sample (about 70 percent) is much higher than that of women in the evaluation samples of the Mexican and Nicaraguan programs (Sinha and Montes 2010). In the poor communities targeted by CCT programs, women's LFP rates are typically very low. In Mexico, Parker and Skoufias (2000) report that female LFP rates before the introduction of the program were 15 percent to 18 percent (women ages 18 and older). Similarly, in Nicaragua, Maluccio and Flores (2005) report baseline female LFP rates of 25 percent (among women ages 15 and older) in treatment and control communities in Nicaragua. Male LFP rates, in contrast, were close to 90 percent.

In line with the previous research, Sinha and Montes (2010) find Juntos does not affect men's employment rate but raised female rates by a significant 4.5 percentage points.[7]

This central tendency, however, masks considerable heterogeneity in the age and education of household heads. The largest impacts, roughly an 8.5 percentage point increase, are for those 14–19 and 20–30 years of age. Individuals in these two age groups play different roles in the household. The 20- to 30-year-olds are likely young mothers, potentially benefiting from additional time made available by the improved health of their children or the diminished requirements of child-rearing activities because of their children's young ages, which, coupled with the additional source of income, is associated with increased economic participation, mainly in terms of informal occupations and self-employment.

In turn, the 14- to 19-year-olds are likely older siblings of eligible children. So even if the older siblings are not eligible for the CCT program, they may be affected by the conditionality to the extent that their younger (eligible) siblings' attendance at school frees up their own time by not having to care for their siblings during the day. That additional time may be filled by joining the labor force. Siblings may also indirectly benefit because of the additional resources the CCT program brings into their household. However, if resources are not equally allocated within the household, the benefits to ineligible siblings might be limited; or worse, parents may decide to concentrate most of their educational investments on eligible children, possibly leading to adverse outcomes for those who are not eligible (Blundell, Chiappori, and Meghir 2005; Oster 2007). These results are consistent with a reallocation of academic opportunities and labor market responsibilities across family members.

In Bogotá, Colombia, siblings (particularly sisters) of treated students work more and attend school less than students in families that received no assistance, implying that the decisions of parents reinforce, rather than compensate for, unequal human capital investment opportunities among sibling children (Barrera-Osorio and others 2011).[8] Barrera-Osorio and others (2011) investigate the magnitude of peer effects within the household and across households, in the context of the Subsidios Condicionados a la Asistencia Escolar (Conditional Subsidies for School Attendance) pilot established by Bogotá, Colombia, to improve student retention, lower dropout rates, and reduce child labor. Although the authors document positive spillover effects across neighboring households, they find some evidence that the subsidies can cause responsibilities to be reallocated within the household.

Unintended consequences: Domestic violence

The overwhelming evidence from countries' experiences with CCTs is that women's control over additional resources improves outcomes for children and, in some cases, for the women themselves. But the increased bargaining power of women may not yield only dividends. The subsequent reductions in the influence of men may come at the cost of emotional or physical well-being if husbands react to their loss with threats or acts of violence.

Theoretically, reliance on the assumption of Pareto-efficient outcomes within the household requires good information sharing within families (or at least that it not be asymmetric) and that members be able to make binding, costlessly enforceable agreements and commitments regarding household allocation of goods and responsibilities. But because legal institutions do not provide external enforcement of contracts for consumption, labor supply, and distribution of resources and welfare within marriage, the binding-agreement assumption may not be desirable or appropriate.

As a result, economists have invoked arguments from noncooperative game theory that focus on self-enforcing agreements and that can achieve Pareto-efficient outcomes under certain conditions. Indeed, one of the benefits of modeling interactions within a marriage as a noncooperative game is the opportunity to treat efficiency endogenously, such that it results internally from the bargaining environment and potentially depends on the institutions and social context of the particular application—and on the characteristics of the marital partners. The prevalence of such destructive phenomena as domestic violence and child abuse, as well as the demand for marriage counseling and family therapy, provide compelling evidence that family behavior is sometimes inefficient, a possibility that must be considered in a theory of the family that accounts for such events.

Some researchers have pointed to gender segmentation in many countries—even in the presence of gender-specific comparative advantage in the management of businesses or agricultural plots—as evidence of an essentially noncooperative, and possibly inefficient, family environment. Udry (1996) provides one piece of evidence, finding that in Burkina Faso the marginal product of land controlled by women is less than that of land controlled by men. This fact violates notions of efficiency, which require these marginal productivities to equalize. The author concludes that the household allocation of inputs to male- and female-controlled agricultural plots is inefficient. A further source of inefficiency is that household members cannot always provide insurance for each other. In Côte d'Ivoire, women and men grow different crops and are thus affected differentially by the same rainfall. Some years are good for men, while others are good for women. If the household is efficient, household members fully insure each other against short-term variation in individual income. Therefore, nonpersistent, idiosyncratic (across spouses within the household) income shocks should not result in differences in the allocation of resources within the household. Yet in years when the production of women's crops is greater, the household spends a larger share of its budget on food and private goods for women. In years when the production of men's crops is greater, the household spends a larger share on alcohol, tobacco, and private goods for men (Duflo and Udry 2004).

Gelles (1976) pioneered work on women's income and violence against women, finding that women with fewer resources are less likely to leave an abusive relationship.[9] The study, as well as many that have followed, ignores the potential endogeneity of women's income in this context. In particular, omitted variables associated with both women's wages and the likelihood of being in an abusive relationship (such as education) might explain the negative relationship with violence. Alternatively, the relationship may simply reflect reverse causality, with declines in abuse increasing a woman's productivity and earnings (Aizer 2010).

The background paper by Bobonis and Castro (2010) considers the long-term effects of CCT receipt on the incidence of family violence. The shift in control over household resources, induced by gendered CCTs, may come at an unintended cost if, for instance, it also increases the incentives of male partners to use threats of violence to (re)gain control over household decision making.[10] Researchers have identified two patterns of domestic violence in Mexico's Oportunidades program. In the short run, women in beneficiary households experienced a 33 percent drop in the incidence of physical abuse, but a 60 percent increase in the incidence of emotional abuse (with no associated physical abuse) relative to nonbeneficiary women (Angelucci 2008; Bobonis, González-Brenes, and Castro 2013). In the longer run, however, five to nine years after the start of the program, women in beneficiary households appear equally likely to experience physical, sexual, or emotional abuse as women in nonbeneficiary households (Bobonis and Castro 2010).

One candidate explanation for these patterns is the possibility that marital selection—selective survival and dissolution of marital relationships as a result of the program—plays an important role. In the short-term experimental evaluation of the PROGRESA program, the predecessor to Oportunidades, couples eligible for the program experienced a modest increase in marital dissolution rates, with most of the effect concentrated among young and relatively educated women's households (Bobonis and Castro 2010).[11]

The patterns of marital dissolution and subsequent formation in response to CCT-induced improvements in control over household resources are consistent with the cooperative bargaining models of household behavior that treat divorce as the external threat point, as well as the noncooperative separate spheres variants in which the threat is instead a breakdown in cooperation without necessarily dissolving the relationship. In either case, the relative increase in the wife's control over resources improves her options and welfare in the event of dissolution, thereby lowering the threshold for dissolution and increasing its frequency (Bobonis and Castro 2010).

This finding has implications for policy, because it provides a mixed view of CCTs' effects on women's condition in the household and highlights some unintended consequences of shifting the locus of power in marital relationships, especially where the option to exit a union is either unfeasible or prohibitively costly (perhaps because of social norms or because the legal framework for marital dissolution is missing).

Recently, Aizer (2010) emphasized the relevance of what the household-bargaining theory refers to as "potential outside options." Bargaining power is determined not only by the actual distribution of resources among household members, but also by their potential earnings outside the union, that is, in the outside option. A shrinking wage gap in a woman's local labor market, driven by an increased demand of goods in sectors of the economy traditionally populated by women, is associated with declines in domestic violence in the United States. These findings highlight the importance of relative labor market conditions of women in general measured by the wage rate, rather than women's actual earnings. Within this framework, improvements in women's labor market conditions have the potential to alter household bargaining power and decrease violence even in households where women do not work (Pollak 2005).

These observations and evidence urge caution and mindfulness of the cultural context in which programs are implemented. In the short run, the Oportunidades program had the effect of increasing women's exposure to violent threats by 60 percent, which is likely to compromise their emotional health and other aspects of their well-being. But in the long run, endowing women with greater control over household resources may have empowered them to dissolve abusive relationships and establish healthier new ones. These effects may not generalize to other countries, and their magnitude may depend on social attitudes toward domestic violence and on the institutional environment—such as the existence of a legal framework that allows marital dissolution and on the enforcement of domestic violence laws. For instance, a shift in the locus of control to women may have much more severe repercussions in societies where a stronger tradition of male control and dominance exists—and where domestic violence is tolerated more.

Time is money: Competing demands on women's time and economic participation

Bargaining positions in the household are affected by more than control over monetary resources. In collective-bargaining models (both cooperative and noncooperative), spousal decisions and the allocation of resources depend on the threat points and outside options. For instance, spousal education; divorce laws; ability to control fertility; and arrangements and technologies that alter productivity in home production, child rearing, and the labor market all can affect spousal dynamics and the subsequent allocation of resources in the household. Influencing the outside options are legislation governing marital dissolution and women's property rights and even labor market laws, among other things in the institutional environment. Interventions that affect the value of and demands on women's time include subsidized child care, compulsory schooling laws (box 6.1 provides an illustration of the importance of compulsory schooling in shaping gender outcomes), and part-time employment legislation.

The focus here is on women's labor market outcomes, to enhance understanding of decisions to participate in the labor market and form a family.

BOX 6.1: *Compulsory schooling in Colombia*

In 1991, Colombia promulgated a new constitution, which made education compulsory for children from 5 to 15 years of age and recommended one year of prekindergarten training, without mandating completion of secondary schooling. Starting in 1992, all children enrolled in school the previous year had to complete at least 10 years of schooling. This institutional change arbitrarily raised the probability that children born in 1977 would complete at least 10 years of schooling relative to those born in 1976. The law thus generated an exogenous change in younger cohorts' education.

The new law had little impact on the average educational attainment of men but increased women's completed education by roughly 0.85 years. This coarse policy change thus appears to have benefited women disproportionately. In addition, evidence from quantile regressions indicates that those most affected by the law were those at the lower centiles of the conditional education distribution; that is, the law raised the "education floor."

(continued on next page)

BOX 6.1: *Compulsory schooling in Colombia (continued)*

This exogenous increase in schooling allows Chioda (2011) to evaluate the causal effect of education on a variety of outcomes among women in Colombia. She finds nonzero returns to education in both the labor and marriage markets:

- Female labor force participation rises by 3.4 percentage points from a base of 49.8 percent in response to an additional year of schooling.

- Although an additional year has no measurable effect on women's hourly wages, it causes a 3.1-hour increase in the number of hours worked per week, or an increase of 14 percent from a base of 22 hours a week, implying a 14 percent increase in weekly earnings.

- Little causal evidence exists that an additional year affects the likelihood of being married, the probability of having children, or the number of children in the household, independent of marital status.

- Conditional on being married, an additional year of schooling yields large returns to women. In particular, married women have improved fertility outcomes (the number of children in the household falls on average by 0.12), and their husbands have better characteristics, suggesting that education improves prospects in the marriage market. Their husbands have 0.7 more years of education and, although their corresponding hourly wages are no higher, they work on average six more hours per week.

Thus an additional year of schooling yields multiple dividends for women in household earnings, because they are more likely to be employed, and both their weekly hours and those of their husbands increase (without reductions in wages).

When repeating the analysis with census data, Chioda (2011) faced a trade-off between the number of observations (and thus the precision of estimates) and the detail of individual information. Overall, the preceding results are confirmed and seldom strengthened. For the full aggregate sample:

- The change in compulsory schooling increases the average years of schooling of the younger cohort of girls by 0.38 years. This is associated with a 7-percentage-point increase in their likelihood of being employed in 2005 (where the baseline participation rate was 30 percent). The effect is both statistically and economically significant.

- The impact of the reform on fertility is also important. The causal effect of an additional year of schooling is a 0.25 reduction in the average number of children per woman in 2005. The size of this effect is all the more surprising given the local nature of the identifying variation, which compares women born just one year apart.

Source: Chioda 2011.

Women's labor supply and child care: A summary of the channels

As shown in earlier chapters, the presence of children in the household has a stable and statistically significant correlation with the likelihood of women's participation in the labor market. Parenthood reduces aggregate household involvement in the labor market by increasing the value of time spent at home relative to time in the market.

Whether by choice (desire to care for and rear their children) or comparative advantage (resulting from biological or market conditions), an efficient division of labor in the presence of children tends to be affected by reduced market wages resulting from potential lost experience and forgone tenure owing to withdrawals from the labor force to care for children and the competing demands on working mothers. In a collective-bargaining model, this leads to some segmentation of market and home production activity between spouses almost entirely caused by gender characteristics. In practice, however, the optimal amount of specialization in a marriage depends on the relative productivities of husband and wife in market and home endeavors, their preferences, and their ability to substitute market inputs for home time. As their real wages rise and their opportunities in the market improve, married women may prefer to allocate more time to market work and less to home production, thus reducing marital specialization.

As documented earlier, the substantial advances in female LFP in recent decades have been concentrated among married and better-educated women. Further, the labor supply behaviors of men and women without children are increasingly similar (especially among singles). But substantial husband-wife specialization persists among couples and couples with children, especially in households with women with primary or secondary education. Husbands and wives tend to specialize into gendered roles— into market and home production, respectively. Marriage is associated with a drop in the probability of being in the labor force of roughly 20 percentage points for women among the majority of countries, while the presence of children under five reduces this probability to a much smaller (yet still economically significant) degree, between 5 and 10 percentage points (Chioda and Demombynes 2014). With an average baseline LFP rate of 50 percent among married women, the presence of children under age five represents a 10 percent reduction in female LFP. Moreover, some of these negative correlations are larger for women with primary and secondary education but are considerably lower for women with tertiary education.

An interesting feature of the relationship between family formation and women's likelihood of being in the labor force is its remarkable stability across age cohorts and over time, suggesting the stability of the underlying reasons, including preferences and social norms. The negative correlation between fertility and the likelihood of being in the labor force exhibits moderate variation across levels of education. In accordance with the importance of fertility and family formation in the labor market, the penalties associated with fertility are far from restricted to low-socioeconomic-status women or to women with limited career prospects.

Even among highly educated women (MBAs from highly selective U.S. schools), who are unlikely to be resource constrained, the presence of children is associated with less job experience, greater career discontinuity, and fewer work hours. As a result, although disparities in the productive capacities of male and female MBAs are small or nothing, the pecuniary penalties related to family formation from fewer work hours and career discontinuities are sizable (Bertrand, Goldin, and Katz 2010). Where women's choices are likely not constrained, the reduction in current and future wages can be interpreted as monetized valuation (shadow price) for rearing their children.

Impact of child care on LAC women's attachment to the labor force

The persistent negative correlation between fertility and women's LFP, along with the (mixed) evidence from a number of Organisation for Economic Co-operation and Development (OECD) countries that large-scale expansions in the market supply of child care can encourage female LFP, has contributed to the view that the main obstacles to women's economic participation are the difficulties balancing it with the demands of child care and home production. This view seems to be confirmed by results from the Bolivian Enterprise Survey as well as focus groups of women beneficiaries of a program in Mexico (box 6.2).

BOX 6.2: *Mexico's child care program to support working mothers (programa estancias infantiles para Apoyar a Madres Trabajadoras)*

The main objective of the program is to provide support for working mothers and single parents with preschool children to gain access to or continue in the labor market (or school) by expanding the supply of day-care centers and providing subsidized care for children. An impact evaluation is still in progress, but the following preliminary results have emerged from a qualitative study based on focus groups:

- Cultural barriers feature prominently in program take-up with many feeling that "it is the responsibility of women to raise their children." These sentiments vary widely by location and are strongest in the south.

- Among participants, the benefits most cited are affordability and greater flexibility to look for work, especially in the formal sector, which has more rigid work schedules.

- Among the employed, the benefits most cited are higher productivity on the job, given fewer concerns about children; a feeling of empowerment and more flexibility in allocating household income; and more quality time with children.

Source: Angeles and others 2012.

The belief in the efficacy of child care provision as a tool to foster female LFP has also found support in a handful of simulation studies whose findings have to be carefully interpreted because they are often based on efficient provision. For instance, in Chile, political interest in the Bachelet administration's dramatic expansion in the supply of day-care centers stimulated ex ante evaluations of the measure, which often report large impacts on female LFP.

Bordón (2006), for example, uses a Chilean household survey to characterize the determinants of female labor supply. She predicts that doubling the supply of day-care centers (the Bachelet plan expanded them by 240 percent between 2005 and 2007) would increase women's LFP by 5.7 percentage points. This represents a sizable effect, considering the low baseline participation rate among Chilean women (43.3 percent in 2006).

Using a survey designed to measure the potential use of day-care facilities, Bravo, Contreras, and Puentes (2012) find that a subsidy of about US$100 with a copayment of US$35 would increase female LFP by 15 to 20 percentage points—again, a large effect.

Ex post evaluations of the same program differ in their conclusions, however. Medrano's (2009) evaluation of the impact of the dramatic expansion in the supply of day-care centers after 2005 reveals no evidence of an effect on female LFP. She hypothesizes that the expansion instead induced women already in the labor force to substitute formal day-care arrangements for informal day-care arrangements, though the data do not permit a formal assessment of this conjecture.

The apparent incongruence of these empirical results underlines the importance of carefully identifying and estimating the effects of these policies.

In a household-bargaining perspective, fertility-induced changes in the total hours of market work of husbands and wives reflect the degree of substitutability between own and market-provided child care—and the household's perceptions of the relative costs of these two alternatives. Thus, both household's preferences (including their perceptions regarding outsourcing child care) and market conditions (including the availability, affordability, and quality of care, and the conditions faced by women in the labor market) play roles in the decision to rely on formal day-care arrangements. Is limited access to child care the obstacle to women's economic participation and to a more equitable division of responsibilities among spouses? Would an increase in the availability and affordability of child care facilitate and encourage women's entry into the labor force? Do preferences and social norms play a role in the observed division of labor within the household?

In principle, the public provision or subsidization of child care has the potential to provide more equitable access to quality child care and may indeed confer benefits in the form of higher labor supply among households' secondary earners. But the effectiveness of such policies in fostering maternal labor supply depends on the answers to two questions. First, does public financing affect the quality or quantity of care provided, or does it merely lead to substitution from one form of care to another?

Second, should a net increase in child care use result, is it accompanied by increases in LFP of parents? The credible empirical evidence of access to day-care facilities and female LFP is inconclusive or often contradictory. Although the evidence from developed nations is richer than that from developing countries, both sets tell intriguingly similar stories.

Studies of the elasticity of female labor supply to child care costs in the United States deliver estimates that vary greatly, ranging between −0.36 and 0.06 (Blau and Currie 2006). This variability exists not only across studies that use different data sources but also within studies depending on the econometric specification and subsample in question. The uncertainty surrounding the size of the elasticity is disquieting from a policy perspective because meaningful design of interventions intended to improve women's opportunities in the labor market depends on this parameter.

A closer look at the factors governing child care and female LFP decisions reveals the importance of social norms—and the feasibility of substituting between formal (market-provided) and informal (provided by a family member or friend) child care arrangements. Also important is distinguishing between labor supply responses along the extensive margin (whether or not to participate) and the intensive margin (how many hours to work, conditional on participating).

Overall, the impact of universal provision of child care on use appears to be sizable. But these effects are attenuated considerably or eliminated almost entirely once substitution between informal child care arrangements and the new, cheaper, formal option is taken into account. Thus the large demand for formal child care appears to come from women who have already made the decision to participate in the labor market and who merely readjust their existing child care arrangements in favor of the cheaper form of formal care.[12]

The labor supply responses to expansions in child care facilities or subsidies are nuanced. The maternal response is often found to be along the intensive margin (hours worked) rather than along the extensive margin (participation). This outcome obtains because previously working women appear not only to favor subsidized child care options to informal arrangements but also to work more hours in response.

In Argentina, although maternal participation in the labor market is not especially elastic to the availability of child care, hours worked appear quite responsive: conditional on working, mothers are 19.1 percentage points more likely to work more than 20 hours a week (that is, more time than their children spend in school), and they work on average 7.8 more hours per week as a consequence of their youngest offspring attending preschool.[13]

These results are in line with what is documented in focus groups, especially among mothers who already participate in the labor force: conditional on having made the decision to enter the labor market, improved access to formal child care affords them increased flexibility and potentially allows them to seek employment in the formal sector. Consistent with this explanation is the negative relationship in Guatemala

City between hours worked and cost of formal day care (Hallman and others 2005; Quisumbing, Hallman, and Ruel 2007).[14] Although expanding availability of child care appears to fulfill an unmet demand for formal child care services among previously working mothers, it does not seem to induce those not in employment to enter the labor force. The evidence from experimental or quasi-experimental interventions thus challenges the widely held belief that lack of access to formal child care is the primary barrier to maternal employment across a number of LAC countries, but supports the argument that improved access relaxes a constraint on those mothers already in the labor force by enabling them to work more hours.

A closer look at the determinants of day-care choice by type reveals that household structure and a child's age are important determinants of the type of child care arrangements. In the United States, the demand for formal care increases after the second year of life, whereas informal home-based care is preferred for infants (Leibowitz, Klerman, and Waite 1992; Leibowitz, Waite, and Witsberger 1988). Interestingly, although it is accelerated by higher wages, reentry into the labor force is delayed by higher household income, which is consistent with a maternal preference for forming early and durable bonds with their children, afforded by higher levels of income. These observations are consistent with findings by Cascio (2009). She documents a large positive effect of an implicit kindergarten subsidy for single women whose youngest child is at least five years old, but no effect among single mothers with younger children or married women. Taken together, these patterns suggest that the decision to enter the labor force may not be constrained by price or availability of child care among single women with young children and married women—at least not in the United States in the three decades ending in the early 1990s (Cascio 2009). Analogously, Hallman and others (2005) study the correlates of mothers' LFP and child care use in the slums of Guatemala City, using a survey of randomly selected mothers with preschool children. They document that higher household wealth reduces a mother's likelihood of being in the labor force but does not significantly affect her hours of work. Staying at home and caring for young children, therefore, thus shares properties of normal goods in that its "consumption" rises with income (Hallman and others 2005).

Female labor force participation and subsidized child care in Rio de Janeiro

Brazilian women have entered the labor force at an increasing rate over the past few decades, but especially since 1990. The LFP rate for women ages 15 and older rose from 38 percent in 1980 to 59 percent in 2007 (figure 6.1), driven mainly by married women (Soares 2002) and women with children, including small children (Bruschini and Lombardi 2003). The trend has not been offset by a decline in the proportion of working fathers. Women in Brazil participated in the labor market at almost the same rate as those in the OECD (65 percent) and at much higher rates than those of most

FIGURE 6.1: Brazilian women have rapidly entered the labor force since 1990

Female labor force participation in Brazil and in Latin America and the Caribbean (not including Brazil), since 1960

a. Female labor force participation rates, 1980–2013

——— Brazil   ——— LAC (without Brazil)

Source: World Bank data.

b. Female labor force participation rates by marital status, 1960–2010

——— LAC single (without Brazil)   ——— Brazil single
——— LAC married (without Brazil)   ——— Brazil married

Source: Chioda 2014 data from Integrated Public Use Microdata Series (IPUMS).

other Latin American countries at similar incomes (only 44 percent in Chile and Mexico). The quality of Brazilian women's participation in the labor force remains an issue, however. Gender wage gaps remain high in Brazil by regional standards (Atal, Ñopo, and Winder 2009; Salas and Leite 2007). Informal employment is much more common among women than men: 53.1 percent versus 46.2 percent (CEDLAS and World Bank 2014). And unemployment is higher among women, particularly young women.

Although no evaluation of the impact of actual access to child care on labor supply has been done, earlier studies have looked at the negative effects of the presence of children on maternal LFP and how this interacts with having alternative caregivers in the household (Connelly, DeGraff, and Levison 1996; Sedlacek and Santos 1991). Generally across the region, the presence of children has a negative impact on mother's LFP, mediated by the presence of other adult females in the family. In addition, estimates of the correlation of LFP, child care services, and earnings in low-income areas in Rio de Janeiro suggest that expanding the supply of low-cost child care could increase mothers' LFP and earnings (Deutsch 1998). These studies do not, however, provide robust measures of the impact of unmet child care needs on women's decision to work and on earnings. By estimating the impact of child care indirectly through the composition of the household, they most likely are overestimating the impact of unmet child care needs on females.[15]

A key limitation of the evidence in Latin America—especially in light of the current push to expand child care coverage—is the lack of studies that jointly estimate the economic impacts and the impacts on children's development outcomes.[16] Carvalho and others (2010) exploited a randomized experiment to analyze the relationship between Rio de Janeiro's subsidized child care program and female LFP. The public day-care is an integrated early childhood development program for children up to age three years living in low-income neighborhoods. To improve knowledge about good parenting, it has 244 well-equipped and properly managed day-care centers in most of these neighborhoods, including full-time day care, health services, food, and instructional toys and materials for children.

In 2007, as in previous years, demand for these slots far outstripped supply: more than 25,000 families applied for 10,000 new slots. To ensure equality of opportunity, a lottery assigned the slots among all eligible applicants (about 24,000 of the 25,000). New beneficiary children started receiving services in March 2008.

A first-round household survey was carried out between April and June 2008. If one ignores the imbalance in the preprogram LFP of women[17] and considers only postprogram information, a 17 percentage point impact on female LFP is found. That is, although 48 percent of women in the treatment group worked at least once after the program started in March 2008 and before the end of the survey in August 2008, only 31 percent of women in the control group did. Note, however, that this estimated 17 percentage point impact on female LFP is very similar to the 16 percentage point preprogram difference obtained with recall data.[18] A double-difference approach indicates that the program had no statistically significant impact on female LFP.

For the subpopulation of women who did not work before the program in 2007,[19] the estimated impact on female LFP was 8 percentage points. Although 17 percent of women in the treatment group who did not work in 2007 were found working in 2008, the figure was only 9 percent for women in the control group.

In sum, the results did not show an increase in overall female LFP, but they appear to indicate that access to free day care induces women who did not previously work to enter the labor force. However, because of the apparent baseline imbalance in preprogram female LFP, one cannot robustly conclude that access to day care keeps women in the labor force.

Preliminary results on the intensive margin reveal a positive but insignificant effect of access to child care on mothers' number of hours worked. A closer look at the diary data from fieldwork confirms this finding, such that the new child care arrangement appears associated with a roughly four-hour reduction in time that mothers previously spent with their children. Whether the newly available time is now spent commuting to work, substituting between jobs with better characteristics, or simply dedicated to search for a new job is unclear. Once again, a significant substitution effect occurs between informal or private child care and the new publicly subsidized option.

What do social norms have to do with female labor force participation and child care services?

Values and attitudes that reflect a combination of preferences and social norms play a key role in explaining economic activity and employment decisions in the presence of children. A large empirical literature has argued that such attitudes and beliefs, broadly defined as *culture*, are an important determinant of LFP (see Fogli and

Fernández 2009; Fernández, Fogli, and Olivetti 2002; Fortin 2005). Of course the (un)availability of detailed and reliable data has complicated the task of applied economists attempting to understand the nature of the joint decision to work and use formal child care. Van Dijk and Siegers (1996) formalize the link between child care use, LFP, and social norms. They find evidence that social norms and positive attitudes toward women's active roles in the marketplace influence actual LFP and that this in turn generates demand for child care services. They fail to find evidence of reverse causality: the supply of day-care centers does not appear to increase women's LFP.

Similar results are found in Nicodemo and Waldmann (2009), who analyze the relationship between child care and female LFP in southern European countries. They argue that social norms in southern Europe play a large role in the persistently low LFP rates of women, who continue to take the traditionally gendered role of child care. The apparently large elasticity of female labor supply to child care use is driven by the availability of informal child care arrangements (mainly relatives), rather than by the presence of subsidized child care options, especially for younger children. These results echo those of Deutsch (1998) in Brazil and of Hallman and others (2005) for Guatemala. Child care arrangements, particularly informal ones involving grandparents, are correlated with having more time to participate in the labor market. But in other countries, such as Greece, Italy, and Spain, children spend few hours in paid child care. If a response to child care provision does exist, it seems to appear at high incomes and wages, suggesting a possible weakened influence of social norms at higher incomes and de facto crowding out of informal arrangements.

In Latin America, the evidence on the relationship between child care provision and female LFP is growing rapidly and benefiting from expanding the impact evaluations of large-scale early childhood development programs. The growing literature has documented benefits of early childhood development on children's outcomes.[20] However, evidence of their indirect effects on female LFP paints a more subtle picture. Evidence from LAC (Argentina, Brazil, Chile, Colombia, and Guatemala), while more limited, is consistent with the patterns described: the correlations between LFP and child care provision shrink once causal relationships are isolated. In particular, after taking into consideration the likelihood that expansions in some of the child care services are endogenously placed to respond to existing demand for these types of services, significant impacts along the extensive margin are no longer observed. Instead, considerable substitution from informal to formal or subsidized child care arrangements is found, sometimes coupled with an increase in hours worked.

In OECD economies, education and the absence of children appear to have strong positive effects on LFP, whether controlling for stated preferences for traditional gender roles or not (Fortin 2005). These preferences have significant and negative effects and contribute a great deal of explanatory power to a regression model. The patterns and stylized facts emerging from the World Values Survey suggest that the aggregate effects of social norms on female LFP may be sizable even in the LAC region. Although LAC has experienced significant improvement in terms of the so-called discriminatory views, both men and women in the region show a strong attachment to more traditional views of women in the household and child rearing.

Finally (and interestingly), the stated belief by women that working women are not perfect substitutes for their nonworking counterparts in providing child care and rearing children has a negative and significant effect on LFP. This suggests that economic costs of child care, such as price and availability, will play a bigger role for women who have already sorted into the labor force based on their values and preferences for economic participation. In fact, job characteristics and wages play at best a minor role in explaining their participation (Fortin 2005).

Although social norms tend to move slowly, they are by no means static or predetermined, and their dynamics are a potential interesting margin along which to design effective policies. On the effects that a woman's decision to work has on her children and their beliefs, the extent to which LFP trades off her children's future utility is unknown (Fogli and Veldkamp 2011). However, strong evidence from the United States indicates that women pass on their beliefs about the importance of nurture to their children. Each generation updates those beliefs, using a set of observations on other children's outcomes.

But observations are only informative about the cost of LFP if women from the previous generation work. Initially, very few women participate in the labor market; information about the role of nurture diffuses slowly, and beliefs are nearly constant. As information accumulates and the uncertainty surrounding the effects of LFP dissipates, more women participate, learning accelerates, and LFP rises more quickly. As beliefs converge to the truth, learning slows down and participation levels off. In this view of the intergenerational transmission of beliefs, a mother's position in the household and her ability to make her own decisions about economic participation is important in the dynamics of social norms. To the extent that policies such as CCTs and child care subsidies facilitate women's economic participation and endow them with more control over their economic lives, such policies may also generate momentum in changing social norms, though their effects would appear in the long run.

Labor market rigidities: Part-time work arrangements and economic participation

Sweden is traditionally invoked by many economists as the standard in terms of child care provision, parental leave policies, and its family-friendly employment policies. It is also lauded for its progressive views on gender parity. Despite this, only 1.5 percent of senior managers are women, compared with 11 percent in America. Three-quarters of Swedish women work in the public sector; three-quarters of men in the private sector. Why is the public sector so popular for women? Among the most cited reasons are the availability of part-time opportunities, a relatively flat wage scale with respect to tenure, the ease of transition in and out of the sector, and fairly light loads in terms of hours, even in full-time positions.

The presumed female comparative advantage in home production can be attributed to a gender gap in market wages and to a productivity advantage in household activities, including the care of children. These may come from biological factors, preferences, or early training in domestic tasks. In the bargaining model, women's preferences for flexible work arrangements can be ascribed to the attempt to achieve an optimal division of time between market and home production and to social norms and attitudes toward traditional or progressive gender roles. Cultural factors, such as *machista* or conservative values, reduce female LFP in Chile (Contreras and Plaza 2010). Fernández, Fogli, and Olivetti (2004) stress the importance of intergenerational transmission of norms and attitudes: wives of men whose mothers worked are more likely to work, either because the husband is less averse to his wife working, or because he is more willing to share or is more productive at housework. For any given set of social norms, the initial gains to specialization will be reinforced over time as husband and wife acquire skills specific to the market or domestic sectors in which they specialize. This will be true particularly if labor market institutions are so rigid as to force full specialization—say, by inhibiting occasional or part-time market work by the spouse specializing in the domestic sphere. So the specialization in the household is also influenced by options in the labor market and by the extent to which choices along the intensive margin of labor supply are feasible—that is, by whether flexibility exists in choosing how many hours to engage in market work. This section sheds new light on part-time institutional arrangements and their impact on female LFP. The evidence on flexible work opportunities comes largely from OECD economies, with relatively little work on LAC, where few countries offer regulated part-time options. As such, this case study of Argentina provides insight on the importance of flexible labor market institutions.

This section asks the following questions: Is the informal sector enabling women to balance demands on their time between market and home production and thus avoid full specialization in one sector or the other? Does demand exist for part-time work arrangements? Are part-time employment and informality substitutes that offer solutions to balancing competing demands on women's time?

Women experience substantially longer spells out of the labor force, transition less often into formal employment, and experience particularly dynamic transitions between informal self-employment and being out of the labor force (Bosch and Maloney 2011). These features of gender transitions appear largely related to family formation and household structure (and the very presence of the informal sector). Single women, in fact, are far more similar to men in their transitions and are generally overrepresented in the formal sector relative to married women. It has been hypothesized that the restrictions on part-time work embedded in the labor codes of many countries in the region contribute to their low female LFP rates and to the overrepresentation of women in the informal sector. This hypothesis would be consistent with static findings that women are underrepresented in jobs protected by labor legislation (formal jobs) and overrepresented in those that are not (informal jobs) (see Boeri, Del Boca, and Pissarides 2005; Dolado, García-Serrano, and Jimeno 2002).

Who is working part time in OECD countries?

In several European countries, the percentage of women who work part time because of family responsibilities (which include child care and care for elderly family members) is quite high, exceeding 40 percent in Austria, Germany, Switzerland, and the United Kingdom (2001 European Labor Force Survey). Thus, the option of part-time employment may play a role in the LFP of women who face such circumstances. This observation is likely to hold outside Europe—and particularly in LAC, where the responsibilities for family and household production fall disproportionately on women.

The reasons underlying different gender-specific occupational representations can broadly be broken down into human capital endowments and preferences for the characteristics of one type of job over another (Boeri, Del Boca, and Pissarides 2005). Together, these lead to differences in the comparative advantages across jobs that a well-functioning labor market will allocate differentially across sectors.

Boeri, Del Boca, and Pissarides (2005) find a strong relationship between household formation and part-time work. In the United Kingdom, for example, single women without children are 5.5 percent more likely than single men without children to hold a part-time job, but the disparity rises to 23.5 percent for those married without children and to 50.1 percent for those married with small children. Documenting the patterns across OECD economies, Boeri, Del Boca, and Pissarides (2005, 53) conclude that

[I]n northern and central Europe, part-time work among women is explained largely by family ties (especially when there are very young children), and it is unlikely to be perceived as the consequence of a market constraint on the number of hours worked. On the contrary, in southern European countries (including France) the explanatory power of family ties in female part-time employment is lower, and single women are more likely to be involuntarily part-time than are single men. The results for the southern countries are much easier to reconcile with discrimination against women in regular, full-time jobs than with gender differences in preferences or comparative advantages.

As an alternative work arrangement, part-time work lifts a constraint between the extremes of unemployment and full-time employment, allowing for greater flexibility in the labor market. Beyond this mechanical benefit, part-time work may be seen as a means to facilitate the integration of women in the labor market, by allowing them to combine market work with family responsibilities and by enabling the accumulation of human capital while meeting such family demands. Conversely, the social value of part-time work may come into question if the labor market segregates into full-time and part-time work along gender lines, perhaps because of barriers such as social norms or discrimination. That is, in some countries part-time jobs may marginalize women in the labor market. This may occur when part-time jobs are characterized by poor wages and benefits, low job tenure, and the absence of training, thereby reducing women's prospects of promotion and putting them at a higher risk of dropping out of the labor force.

Interestingly, some evidence exists of a wage penalty among voluntary part-time workers, as if part of the compensation in the voluntary case (northern Europe) is the added flexibility. Accordingly, workers are willing to be "remunerated" with flexibility and forgo some of the pecuniary compensation. After controlling for a number of earnings determinants and job characteristics, Pissarides and others (2005) find evidence of an hourly earnings penalty for part-time jobs in northern Europe, where part-time work is considered voluntary. However, in southern Europe, where part-time work is perceived as involuntary, the wage gaps are reversed, and the authors report a wage premium in Austria, Germany, and southern European countries.

Marginalization might be measured by a difficulty to move to full-time jobs or weak attachment to the labor market. O'Reilly and Bothfeld (2002) find that only a small proportion of women in Germany and the United Kingdom can use part-time work as a bridge back to full-time employment. Instead, a substantial percentage drops out of employment, especially mothers of more than one child. For the United States, Miller (1997) finds that part-time experience increases the probability of part-time employment and decreases the probability of full-time employment, even if part-time work was taken up temporarily because of the presence of children. In contrast, Blank (1989) and Farber (1999) conclude that part-time work and temporary work are often part of the transition out of unemployment, leading to regular full-time employment in the future.

Although several measurable disadvantages and penalties are associated with part-time work (as detailed previously), whether the overrepresentation of women in part-time employment results from societal constraints and welfare-reducing frictions in the labor market (such as discrimination or perceptions of lower productivity) or from optimizing behavior by households is unclear. For instance, the observed distribution of genders across employment modalities may obtain if households optimally split their time between market and home production and husbands and wives are differentially productive in the two sectors, with women (on average) holding a comparative advantage in home production and child rearing.

Booth and van Ours (2008, 2009, 2010) study the relationship between hours of work and self-reported job and life satisfaction and happiness in three countries. In Australia (Booth and van Ours 2009), they find that women working part time are more satisfied with working hours than women working full time. Partnered women's life satisfaction increases if their partners work full time. Male partners' life satisfaction is unaffected by their partners' market hours but increases if they themselves are working full time.[21] For the United Kingdom, Booth and van Ours (2008) report that women prefer part-time jobs irrespective of whether their hours are many or few.

In the Netherlands, where the share of women workers ages 25–54 years who are working part time is 54 percent, Booth and van Ours (2010) analyze the relationship between part-time work and life satisfaction and between job satisfaction and preferred working hours, using panel data on life and job satisfaction for a sample of partnered women and men. The authors exploit time-use data to consider the distribution within the household of market work and housework. Their main results indicate that partnered women in part-time work have high job satisfaction, have low desire to change their working hours, and live in partnerships with highly gendered household production. Booth and van Ours (2010, 1) conclude that the results suggest that part-time jobs are "what most Dutch women want."

In OECD economies, women work less than full time by choice and with some satisfaction, rather than as a result of social forces or constraints in the job market (Booth and van Ours 2008, 2009, 2010). This finding contrasts with the only comparable evidence from Latin America, where the share of women working part time increased 30 percent between the mid-1990s and the early 2000s. Unlike the preceding results from OECD economies, López Bóo, Madrigal, and Pagés (2009) do not find a preference for part-time work among women. In Honduras, both women and men tend to prefer full-time work, though the preference for working longer hours is more intense for men (López Bóo, Madrigal, and Pagés 2009). In addition and somewhat surprisingly, partnered women with children are more likely to prefer full-time work than partnered women without children. The authors hypothesize that women may be labor supply constrained, working part time not by choice but rather because the demand for labor is lacking. And working full time is likely to be preferred because it generates more per capita household income. The contrasting results between developed countries and Honduras point to a need for a better understanding of demand-side constraints on labor and of worker flows across modalities of work.

Although the discussion here has centered on the full-time or part-time margin of choice, many of the arguments regarding the trade-offs apply similarly to the distinction between formal and informal work. While work in the formal sector often entails (explicit) benefits, such as social insurance and some degree of job security (depending on the regulatory regime and the rigidities built into the labor market), it can be inflexible and impose restrictions on time and child rearing.

How does part-time work legislation affect female labor force participation in Argentina?

Argentina's legalization of part-time work in 1995 provides an opportunity to distinguish between different hypotheses concerning why women with children are overrepresented in the informal sector, relative to their counterparts without children.[22] The first is that women with children may be rationed out (discriminated against) of formal employment. The second is that the need to balance family and work responsibilities may require increased flexibility with respect to hours of work.

Before 1995, formal employers were prohibited from offering part-time contracts, leaving informal work and, in particular, self-employment as the only option for women with children seeking flexible employment. A more flexible contract added another alternative. If formal employers systematically discriminated against women on the basis of gender, an increase in formal employment should not be expected simply because they could be hired for fewer hours.[23]

In line with the previous chapters, married women differ from single women beyond merely marital status. Single women with no children both participate more and tend to use more full-time contracts than their married counterparts, although they have no significant differences in degree of formality. But on having children, unmarried women converge more toward married women on both measures.

For both single and married women, formal employment is correlated with higher rates of full-time employment. This correlation is particularly dramatic in the case of single women without children, for whom 86 percent of formal positions are full time, compared with 67 percent in informal employment. Finally, part-time work was becoming increasingly prevalent over 1993–2001 for all categories of women, though more conspicuously for women with children.

Focusing on married women (the bulk of the sample), several observations are noteworthy. First, a slight increase in participation is observed over this period— 7 percent for those without children and 4 percent for those with children. Second, formality remained constant across the two periods for those without children. For married women with children, however, it increased initially by around 5 percent and then substantially by around 9 percent in formal part-time jobs.

Single women show similar patterns—though less striking. Participation rose for those with and without children. Informality fell for both classes as well. And, again, the increase in formal employment was accompanied by a rise in part-time work for both.

To investigate the impact of Argentina's part-time reform, Bosch and Maloney (2011) divide the sample by women's marital status and the presence of children. In addition, they distinguish between women with one or two children and women with more than two children, to explore possible nonlinearities in the effects of family responsibilities on the labor supply decisions.

Participation

Bosch and Maloney (2011) report no significant effect of the change in part-time legislation on overall participation in part-time work. These results hold for the whole sample as well as for subsamples segregated by fertility and marital status. Either workplace flexibility was not a factor in participation decisions or the informal sector provided the necessary flexibility for those willing to work.

Single women with and without children seem to be less elastic to the change in legislation, along the intensive and extensive margins: conditional on being active in the labor market, this group does not exhibit a preference for a more formal flexible work arrangement. This pattern could reflect a more binding budget constraint relative to married women, who have the option to pool resources with spouses, hence adjusting the intensity of their participation.

Substitution

However, important changes in the allocation between informal and formal employment emerge across the period. In particular, for married women with family responsibilities, the authors find a significant increase in formal employment (8.6 percentage points) at the expense of self-employment (−7.2 percentage points), compared with married women without children. Given the dominance of the married women with children category, this represents a decline in female informality of roughly 4 to 5 percentage points.

To shed light on whether the rise in take-up of part-time formal work was driven by the appeal of formality as a job characteristic, the authors consider substitutions across part-time work arrangements only: informal self-employment, informal salaried, and formal part time. A significant 5.3 percentage point increase in the probability of women with children being in part-time formal employment is recorded after the reform, relative to those without children. The result appears to be driven mostly by married women with one or two children, once again at the expense of a reduction in self-employed part-time contracts.[24]

Conclusions

In sum, the authors find strong evidence that the law increased formal sector employment at the expense of informal self-employment and that this change was driven by the uptake in part-time work in the formal sector.

These results are consistent with formality being preferred, but before the change in legislation, only informal work offered the flexibility necessary to accommodate family responsibilities. The rise in formality appears to be driven primarily by married women with one or two children, with a more muted and insignificant effect recorded for those with more children. The substitution patterns apparently driven by the uptake in formal part-time work suggest, first, that informality was a flexible option to (the more rigid) formal employment before the change in legislation, and, second, that well-designed legislation, which recognizes the realities of the demands on households' time, can significantly affect the level of informality.

This set of results is consistent with evidence from Fortin (2005), who considered the determinants of part-time occupation. The absence of children and being single are associated with large reductions in the probability of working part time, as noted in previous sections, such that the correlates of single women's labor supply resemble those of men. Interestingly, females' stated preferences for a more traditional division of labor between sexes are also negatively related to the probability of being employed part time. Finally, the presence of children coupled with the belief (stated preference) that mothers provide better care for children is strongly and positively correlated with part-time work, suggesting that part-time work may afford women some flexibility in balancing maternal and professional roles.

An indirect measure of the role of part-time arrangements in balancing the competing demand on women's time is the fact that, unlike full time participation, women's part-time participation is significantly related to job characteristics. Unsurprisingly, "good wages" are predictive of part-time work (implying that the income can be dedicated to outsourcing home production). More surprising is the fact that "good hours" are even more predictive: flexible work hours increase the probability of working part time by 5 percentage points, after controlling for demographics, gender attitudes, and education. The division of labor within the household and the relative bargaining positions of spouses are influenced not only by relative comparative advantages, strength of assets brought into the marriage (Hallman and others 2005), and social norms—but also by institutions and, more generally, by the options available outside the household.

In Argentina, institutional reform highlights unmet demand for flexible work arrangements, which is otherwise met by the informal sector. In particular, the addition of a formal option with flexible hours seems to attract new female workers who may otherwise be deterred by the informal status. Thus the lack of an option to choose the intensity of labor supply apparently may force some women into specializing in home production because of their comparative advantage.

This natural experiment highlights that reforms successfully encouraging female LFP recognize the differences between men and women in their preferences and in their comparative advantages in home or market production. This enables policy makers to design effective gender policies by recognizing and exploiting these differences to allow free and unconstrained choices.

Notes

[1] Testing the pooling hypothesis requires a measure of the husband's and wife's relative (nominal) control over resources. Relative labor earnings might seem a natural candidate for this measure, because labor income is frequently the largest component of family income and earnings data are readily available. But the trouble with this approach is that earnings are the product of wage and hours worked, the latter being a choice variable in the household's time allocation decisions. As a result, households with different ratios of the wife's earnings to husband's earnings are likely to face different wages and prices and have different preferences. In that event, relative labor income would reflect differences across households in prices or preferences rather than the desired degree of control over resources.

[2] A necessary condition for the unitary model to break down is differences in preferences across spouses. As illustrative evidence that men and women differ in their preferences (and therefore in their self-interest), see Croson and Gneezy (2009) and Bertrand (2011). Both authors offer a review of experiments and existing evidence on gender differences in tastes. Briefly, they report systematic

and sizable differences in tolerance for risk and in social preferences (altruism, inequality aversion, reciprocity, and trust).

[3] In a recent working paper, Camacho and Rodríguez (2012) study the effect of Familias en Acción, the Colombian CCT, on the self-reported decision-making responsibility of men and women in the household with regard to children's schooling, consumption, and health visits. The authors find that the CCT did not lead beneficiary women to report increased decision-making responsibility in any of the dimensions in question. The authors interpret the findings as suggestive of a reduction in bargaining power of women.

[4] Attanasio and Lechêne (2010a) was part of the background material prepared for this report.

[5] The threat points depend on a set of exogenous factors that influence individual well-being in the event of divorce. Through a process of (Nash) bargaining, these factors—which may include individual wages, unearned incomes, and the resources of prospective mates in the remarriage market—in turn determine each spouse's demands. The utility received by husband or wife in the bargaining equilibrium depends on the threat point: the higher one's utility at the threat point, the higher one's utility in the Nash bargaining solution.

[6] Most of the difference in employment rates between women in Juntos and those in control groups is concentrated among women with low education; the difference for the highest quartile is not statistically significant. Single mothers are more likely than women in couples to be employed in both Juntos and control samples, not surprising since single mothers are the breadwinners for their households.

[7] This result is likely related to the previously mentioned high baseline female participation rate in Peru, which has the potential to render the response to Juntos's incentives more detectable because plausibly more women are at the margin of participation.

[8] In Cambodia, Ferreira, Filmer, and Schady (2009) find that the ineligible siblings of CCT recipients were unaffected by the program.

[9] A discussion of the dynamics of asset holding and their impact on bargaining power goes beyond the labor market focus of this study. In addition, to the author's knowledge, no quasi-experimental study analyzes the impact of asset holdings on the outcomes of interest in this chapter. Nonetheless, like wages (a flow variable), asset holdings (a stock variable) are a key determinant of women's outside options and, hence, their bargaining power within the household. Doss, Grown, and Deere (2008) and Deere, Alvarado and Twyman (2012) provide an overview of the existing evidence on the gender asset holding gaps in LAC (which is unfortunately limited, given the data requirements for such analysis). Doss, Grown, and Deere (2008) document sizable asset-holding gaps between genders by type of asset for a small number of countries for which the data are available (Brazil, Nicaragua, Panama, and Paraguay). However, Deere, Alvarado, and Twyman (2012) caution about the adequacy of the existing data and report that disaggregated data on asset ownership within households suggest that the distribution of property by gender is more equitable than a headship analysis alone would imply.

[10] Bobonis and Castro (2010) was part of the background material prepared for this study.

[11] As an informal check on the consistency of this hypothesis, a comparison of socioeconomic and demographic characteristics of beneficiary and nonbeneficiary households in 2003 and 2006 suggests that important changes occur in their distributions. Over this period, gaps are observed between beneficiary and nonbeneficiary women in age, in their ethnic background and in that of their partner, and in schooling attainment. Moreover, the gap in the proportion of partners who witnessed spousal violence during childhood narrows. The background paper, Bobonis and Castro (2010) also provides evidence that reported levels of emotional violence among beneficiary couples formed subsequent to the start of the program are more than 50 percent lower than those of nonbeneficiary couples. This accords with the hypothesis that those couples more likely to suffer emotional abuse have dissolved and abuse in newly formed couples is less prevalent.

[12] See Baker, Gruber, and Milligan (2008); Fitzpatrick (2010); and Havnes and Mogstad (2009), who consider subsidies or changes in child care provision in Canada, the United States, and Norway, respectively.

[13] Berlinski, Galiani, and McEwan (2008) adopt a regression discontinuity design to overcome the major empirical challenge to identifying the causal effect of preschool attendance on parental labor supply (that is, the nonrandom selection into early education and disentangling whether maternal labor supply responds to the provision of child care services or vice versa). It relies on the plausibly exogenous variation in preschool attendance that is induced when children are born on either side of Argentina's July 1 enrollment cut-off date. Similar results along the intensive margin are found in Gelbach (2002), who makes use of children's quarter of birth as an instrument for the year they are allowed to attend public schools. An alternative strategy has been developed in the context of limited public day-care subsidies, where the behavior of mothers who were eligible for the program with the behavior of those on waiting lists can be compared. For example, Berger and Black (1992), with data from the Kentucky subsidies programs, find a positive effect on hours worked as well as on the quality of the day care used.

[14] An exception to the expected negative relationship between labor force participation and the cost of child care is found in Attanasio and Vera-Hernández (2009), who study Hogares Comunitarios, a large child care and food nutrition program in Colombia. In their analysis of the production function of nutritional status, they consider the program as one of its inputs, as well as female labor supply and food intake. Although it is not their ultimate object of interest, they establish in first stage regressions that distance to the nearest Hogares Comunitarios facility and median child care fees are highly predictive of both day-care use and maternal labor supply (participation, more so than hours worked). But these relationships are counterintuitively of the wrong sign: their first-stage estimates imply a positive relationship between measures of access to child care (both price and distance to nearest facility) and child care use and LFP and intensity.

[15] However, demographic composition is likely endogenous and determined by the same unobserved household (or women's) characteristics that determine employment, compromising the identification of causal effects.

[16] Carvalho and others (2010), a background paper for this study, documents the effect of subsidized child care on female economic participation.

[17] This instrumental-variables estimate is statistically different from zero at the 5 percent level.

[18] The 16 percentage point preprogram difference is obtained via instrumental-variables estimation. That is, it "corrects" for the noncompliance by many control children.

[19] Some of the results for the subpopulation of women who did not work before the program should be interpreted with some caution. In fact, 42 percent of women in the treatment group reported working at least once in the second semester of 2007, while only 35 percent of women in the control group reported doing so. A possible explanation is that many subjects interviewed may have realized that the survey was related to the day-care program and therefore misrepresented what really happened before the program. For instance, mothers in the control group may have believed that if they responded that they had never worked because of lack of access to day care, they would be more likely to gain acceptance into the treatment group.

[20] See Cunha and Heckman (2007), Heckman (2007), and Vegas and Santibáñez (2010) for reviews in developed and developing countries.

[21] These findings are consistent with the gender identity hypothesis of Akerlof and Kranton (2000).

[22] This section features the results of Bosch and Maloney (2011), a background paper for this study on the 1995 part-time labor reform in Argentina.

[23] Bosch and Maloney (2011) restrict their analysis to women between 20 and 40 years of age who are either household heads or spouses. Unfortunately, they cannot perfectly identify part-time contracts in their data since the nature of the contract is not revealed. They rely instead on the total number of hours worked during a week, considering in particular that a woman is a part-time worker if she claims to work less than 30 hours during the interview week.

[24] A significant 3.4 percentage point decrease also occurs in the probability of married women with children being in informal self-employment, relative to married women without children. This may be because the sector is an entry point into the labor force for young workers, perhaps before marrying and child bearing. Alternatively, to the extent that women are working as "salaried" informal workers in family microenterprises, other household considerations (such as child care responsibilities) could be expected to hinder substitutions out of this category.

References

Aizer, Anna. 2010. "The Gender Wage Gap and Domestic Violence." *American Economic Review* 100 (4): 1847–59.

Akerlof, George A., and Rachel E. Kranton. 2000. "Economics and Identity." *Quarterly Journal of Economics* 105 (3): 715–53.

Angeles, Gustavo, Paola Gadsden, Sebastian Galiani, Paul Gertler, Andrea Herrera, Patricia Kariger, and Enrique Seira. 2012. *The Impact of Daycare on Maternal Labour Supply and Child Development in Mexico.* New Delhi: International Initiative for Impact Evaluation.

Angelucci, Manuela. 2008. "Love on the Rocks: Domestic Violence and Alcohol Abuse in Rural Mexico." *B.E. Journal of Economic Analysis and Policy* 8 (1): article 43.

Atal, Juan Pablo, Hugo Ñopo, and Natalia Winder. 2009. "New Century, Old Disparities: Gender and Ethnic Wage Gaps in Latin America." IDB Working Paper 109, Inter-American Development Bank, Washington, DC.

Attanasio, Orazio, and Valérie Lechêne. 2010a. "Efficient Responses to Targeted Cash Transfers." Background paper for this report, World Bank, Washington, DC.

———. 2010b. "Conditional Cash Transfers, Women, and the Demand for Food." IFS Working Paper W10/17, Institute for Fiscal Studies, London.

Attanasio, Orazio, and Marcos Vera-Hernández. 2009. "Childcare Provision, Its Use, and Nutritional Outcomes: Crowding Out and Impacts of a Community Nursery Programme." Working paper, University College, London.

Baker, Michael, Jonathan Gruber, and Kevin Milligan. 2008. "Universal Child Care, Maternal Labor Supply, and Family Well-Being." *Journal of Political Economy* 116 (4): 709–45.

Barrera-Osorio, Felipe, Marianne Bertrand, Leigh L. Linden, and Francisco Perez-Calle. 2011. "Improving the Design of Conditional Transfer Programs: Evidence from a Randomized Education Experiment in Colombia." *American Economic Journal: Applied Economics* 3 (2): 167–95.

Becker, Gary S. 1974. "A Theory of Social Interactions." *Journal of Political Economy* 82 (6): 1063–94.

———. 1991. *A Treatise on the Family.* Enlarged Edition. Cambridge, MA: Harvard University Press.

Berger, Mark C., and Dan A. Black. 1992. "Child Care Subsidies, Quality of Care, and the Labor Supply of Low-Income, Single Mothers." *Review of Economics and Statistics* 74 (4): 635–42.

Berlinski, Samuel, Sebastian Galiani, and Patrick McEwan. 2008. "Preschool and Maternal Labor Market Outcomes: Evidence from a Regression Discontinuity Design." IFS Working Paper W09/05, Institute for Fiscal Studies, London.

Bertrand, Marianne. 2011. "New Perspectives on Gender." In *Handbook of Labor Economics*, volume 4B, edited by Orley Ashenfelter and David Card, 1543–90. Amsterdam: North-Holland/Elsevier.

Bertrand, Marianne, Claudia Goldin, and Lawrence F. Katz. 2010. "Dynamics of the Gender Gap for Young Professionals in the Financial and Corporate Sectors." *American Economic Journal: Applied Economics* 2 (3): 228–55.

Blank, Rebecca M. 1989. "The Role of Part-Time Work in Women's Labor Market Choices over Time." *American Economic Review Papers and Proceedings* 79 (2): 295–99.

Blau, David, and Janet Currie. 2006. "Preschool, Day Care, and After-School Care: Who's Minding the Kids?" In *Handbook of the Economics of Education*, vol. 2, edited by Eric Hanushek and Finis Welch, 1163–278. Amsterdam: North-Holland.

Blundell, Richard, Pierre-André Chiappori, and Costas Meghir. 2005. "Collective Labor Supply with Children." *Journal of Political Economy* 113 (6): 1277–306.

Bobonis, Gustavo J., and Roberto Castro. 2010. "The Role of Conditional Transfers in Reducing Spousal Abuse in Mexico: Short-Term vs. Long-Term Effects." Background paper for this report, World Bank, Washington, DC.

Bobonis, Gustavo J., Melissa González-Brenes, and Roberto Castro. 2013. "Public Transfers and Domestic Violence: The Roles of Private Information and Spousal Control." *American Economic Journal: Economic Policy* 5 (1): 179–205.

Boeri, Tito, Daniela Del Boca, and Christopher Pissarides. 2005. *Women at Work: An Economic Perspective*. Oxford, U.K.: Oxford University Press.

Booth, Alison L., and Jan C. van Ours. 2008. "Job Satisfaction and Family Happiness: The Part-Time Work Puzzle." *Economic Journal* 118 (526): 77–99.

———. 2009. "Hours of Work and Gender Identity: Does Part-Time Work Make the Family Happier?" *Economica* 76 (301): 176–96.

———. 2010. "Part-Time Jobs: What Women Want?" IZA Discussion Paper 4686, Institute for the Study of Labor, Bonn, Germany.

Bordón, Paola. 2006. "El efecto de los jardines infantiles en la oferta laboral femenina: Análisis del caso chileno." Thesis, Centro de Economía Aplicada, Universidad de Chile.

Bosch, Mariano, and William F. Maloney. 2011. "Women on the Move: Female Labor Market Dynamics in the Developing World." Background paper for this report, World Bank, Washington, DC.

Bourguignon, François, Martin Browning, Pierre-André Chiappori, and Valerie Lechêne. 1993. "Intra Household Allocation of Consumption: A Model and Some Evidence from French Data." *Annales d'Economie et de Statistique* 29: 137–56.

Bravo, David, Dante Contreras, and Esteban Puentes. 2012. "Female Labor Supply and Child Care Supply in Chile." Serie Documentos de Trabajo 370, Departmento de Economía, Universidad de Chile, Santiago. http://www.econ.uchile.cl/uploads/publicacion/93fc99073cf6830a16930b8 5e473c49df8b0d854.pdf.

Browning, Martin, François Bourguignon, Pierre-André Chiappori, and Valerie Lechêne. 1994. "Income and Outcomes: A Structural Model of Intrahousehold Allocation." *Journal of Political Economy* 102 (6): 1067–96.

Bruschini, Cristina, and Maria Rosa Lombardi. 2003. "Mulheres e homens no mercado de trabalho brasileiro: Um retrato dos anos 1990." In *As novas fronteiras da desigualdade: homens e mulheres no mercado de trabalho*, edited by Margaret Maruani and Helena Hirata, 323–61. São Paulo, Brazil: Senac.

Camacho, Adriana, and Catherine Rodríguez. 2012. "Who's the Boss at Home after Receiving Conditional Cash Transfers?" Working paper, Economics Department, Universidad de los Andes, Bogotá. https://www.aeaweb.org/aea/2012conference/program/retrieve.php?pdfid =32Contact.

Carvalho, Mirela, Trine Lunde, Pedro Olinto, and Ricardo Paes de Barros. 2010. "Impact of Free Childcare on Female Labor Force Participation: Evidence from Low-Income Neighborhoods in Rio de Janeiro." Background paper for this report, World Bank, Washington, DC.

Cascio, Elizabeth U. 2009. "Maternal Labor Supply and the Introduction of Kindergartens into American Public Schools." *Journal of Human Resources* 44 (1): 140–70.

CEDLAS (Centro de Estudios Distributivos, Laborales y Sociales) and World Bank. 2014. SEDLAC: Socio-Economic Database for Latin America and the Caribbean. http://sedlac.econo .unlp.edu.ar/eng/.

Chioda, Laura. 2011. "Who Gains What from Education? Regression Discontinuity Evidence from Colombia." Background paper for this report, World Bank, Washington, DC.

———. 2014. "How Family Formation Has Shaped Labor Force Participation in LAC." Background paper for this report, World Bank, Washington, DC.

Chioda, Laura, and Gabriel Demombynes. 2014. "The Rise of Female Labor Force Participation Rate in LAC, 1960–2000." Background paper for this report, World Bank, Washington, DC.

Connelly, Rachel, Deborah DeGraff, and Deborah Levison. 1996. "Women's Employment and Child Care in Brazil." *Economic Development and Cultural Change* 44 (3): 619–56.

Contreras, Dante, and Gonzalo Plaza. 2010. "Cultural Factors in Women's Labor Force Participation in Chile." *Feminist Economics* 16 (2): 27–46.

Croson, Rachel, and Uri Gneezy. 2009. "Gender Differences in Preferences." *Journal of Economic Literature* 47 (2): 448–74.

Cunha, Flavio, and James J. Heckman. 2007. "The Technology of Skill Formation." *American Economic Review* 97 (2): 31–47.

Deere, Carmen Diana, Gina E. Alvarado, and Jennifer Twyman. 2012. "Gender Inequality in Asset Ownership in Latin America: Female Owners vs. Household Heads." *Development and Change* 43 (2): 505–30.

Deutsch, Ruthanne. 1998. "How Early Childhood Interventions Can Reduce Inequality: An Overview of Recent Findings." Working Paper POV-105, Poverty and Inequality Advisory Unit, Inter-American Development Bank, Washington, DC.

Dolado, Juan J., Carlos García-Serrano, and Juan F. Jimeno. 2002. "Drawing Lessons from the Boom of Temporary Jobs in Spain." *Economic Journal* 112 (480): F270–95.

Doss, Cheryl, Caren Grown, and Carmen Diana Deere. 2008. "Gender and Asset Ownership: A Guide to Collecting Individual-Level Data." Policy Research Working Paper 4704, World Bank, Washington, DC.

Duflo, Esther. 2000. "Child Health and Household Resources in South Africa: Evidence from the Old Age Pension Program." *American Economic Review* 90 (2): 393–98.

———. 2003. "Grandmothers and Granddaughters: Old-Age Pensions and Intrahousehold Allocation in South Africa." *World Bank Economic Review* 17 (1): 1–25.

Duflo, Esther, and Christopher Udry. 2004. "Intrahousehold Resource Allocation in Côte d'Ivoire: Social Norms, Separate Accounts, and Consumption Choices." NBER Working Paper 10498, National Bureau of Economic Research, Cambridge, MA.

Edmonds, Eric V. 2005. "Does Child Labor Decline with Improving Economic Status?" *Journal of Human Resources* 40 (1): 77–99.

Farber, Henry S. 1999. "Mobility and Stability: The Dynamics of Job Change in Labor Markets." In *Handbook of Labor Economics*, vol. 3B, edited by Orley Ashenfelter and David Card, 2439–83. Amsterdam: Elsevier/North-Holland.

Fernández, Raquel, Alessandra Fogli, and Claudia Olivetti. 2002. "Marrying Your Mom: Preference Transmission and Women's Labor and Education Choices." NBER Working Paper 9234, National Bureau of Economic Research, Cambridge, MA.

———. 2004. "Preference Formation and the Rise of Women's Labor Force Participation: Evidence from WWII." NBER Working Paper 10589, National Bureau of Economic Research, Cambridge, MA.

Ferreira, Francisco H. G., Deon Filmer, and Norbert Schady. 2009. "Own and Sibling Effects of Conditional Cash Transfer Programs: Theory and Evidence from Cambodia." Policy Research Working Paper 5001, World Bank, Washington, DC.

Fitzpatrick, Maria Donovan. 2010. "Preschoolers Enrolled and Mothers at Work? The Effects of Universal Prekindergarten." *Journal of Labor Economics* 28 (1): 51–85.

Fogli, Alessandra, and Raquel Fernández. 2009. "Culture: An Empirical Investigation of Beliefs, Work, and Fertility." *American Economic Journal: Macroeconomics* 1 (1): 146–77.

Fogli, Alessandra, and Laura Veldkamp. 2011. "Nature or Nurture? Learning and the Geography of Female Labor Force Participation." *Econometrica* 79 (4): 1103–38.

Fortin, Nicole M. 2005. "Gender Role Attitudes and the Labour-Market Outcomes of Women across OECD Countries." *Oxford Review of Economic Policy* 21 (3): 416–38.

Gelbach, Jonah B. 2002. "Public Schooling for Young Children and Maternal Labor Supply." *American Economic Review* 92 (1): 307–22.

Gelles, Richard. 1976. "Abused Wives: Why Do They Stay?" *Journal of Marriage and the Family* 38 (4): 659–68.

Gertler, Paul J., Sebastián Martinez, and Marta Rubio-Codina. 2006. "Investing Cash Transfers to Raise Long Term Living Standards." Policy Research Working Paper 3994, World Bank, Washington, DC.

Hallman, Kelly, Agnes R. Quisumbing, Marie T. Ruel, and Benedicte de la Briere. 2005. "Mothers' Work and Child Care: Findings from the Urban Slums of Guatemala City." *Economic Development and Cultural Change* 53 (4): 855–85.

Havnes, Tarjei, and Magne Mogstad. 2009. "No Child Left Behind: Universal Child Care and Children's Long-Run Outcomes." Discussion Paper 582, Statistics Norway, Oslo.

Heckman, James J. 2007. "The Economics, Technology, and Neuroscience of Human Capability Formation." *Proceedings of the National Academy of Sciences of the United States of America* 104 (33): 13250–55.

Leibowitz, Arleen, Jacob Alex Klerman, and Linda J. Waite. 1992. "Employment of New Mothers and Child Care Choice: Differences by Child Age." *Journal of Human Resources* 27 (1): 112–33.

Leibowitz, Arleen, Linda J. Waite, and Christina Witsberger. 1988. "Child Care for Preschoolers: Differences by Child Age." *Demography* 25 (2): 205–20.

López Bóo, Florencia, Lucia Madrigal, and Carmen Pagés. 2009. "Part-Time Work, Gender and Job Satisfaction: Evidence from a Developing Country." Working Paper 4604, Inter-American Development Bank, Washington, DC.

Lundberg, Shelly J., and Robert A. Pollak. 1993. "Separate Spheres Bargaining and the Marriage Market." *Journal of Political Economy* 101 (6): 988–1010.

Lundberg, Shelly J., Robert A. Pollak, and Terence J. Wales. 1997. "Do Husbands and Wives Pool Their Resources? Evidence from the United Kingdom Child Benefit." *Journal of Human Resources* 32 (3): 463–80.

Maluccio, John A., and Rafael Flores. 2005. "Impact Evaluation of a Conditional Cash Transfer Program: The Nicaraguan Red de Protección Social." Research Report 141, International Food Policy Research Institute, Washington, DC.

Manser, Marilyn, and Murray Brown. 1980. "Marriage and Household Decision-Making: A Bargaining Analysis." *International Economic Review* 21 (1): 31–44.

McElroy, Marjorie B., and Mary Jean Horney. 1981. "Nash-Bargained Household Decisions: Toward a Generalization of the Theory of Demand." *International Economic Review* 22 (2): 333–49.

Medrano, Patricia. 2009. "Public Day Care and Female Labor Force Participation: Evidence from Chile." Working Paper 306, Department of Economics, Universidad de Chile, Santiago.

Miller, Carole F. 1997. "Structural Changes in the Probability of Part-Time Employment Participation of Married Women." *Bulletin of Economic Research* 49 (4): 257–73.

Nicodemo, Catia, and Robert Waldmann. 2009. "Child-Care and Participation in the Labor Market for Married Women in Mediterranean Countries." IZA Discussion Paper 3983, Institute for the Study of Labor, Bonn, Germany.

O'Reilly, Jacqueline, and Silke Bothfeld. 2002. "What Happens after Working Part Time? Integration, Maintenance or Exclusionary Transitions in Britain and Western Germany." *Cambridge Journal of Economics* 26 (4): 409–39.

Oster, Emily. 2007. "HIV and Sexual Behavior Change: Why Not Africa?" NBER Working Paper 13049, National Bureau of Economic Research, Cambridge, MA.

Parker, Susan W., and Emmanuel Skoufias. 2000. "The Impact of PROGRESA on Work, Leisure, and Time Allocation, Final Report." International Food Policy Research Institute, Washington, DC.

Perova, Elizaveta, and Renos Vakis. 2009. "Welfare Impacts of the 'Juntos' Program in Peru: Evidence from a Non-experimental Evaluation." World Bank, Washington, DC. http://www .juntos.gob.pe/modulos/mod_legal/archivos/Evaluacion_Cuasi-Experimental1.pdf.

———. 2011. "The Longer the Better: Duration and Program Impacts of Juntos in Peru." Research report, World Bank, Washington, DC.

Pissarides, Christopher, Pietro Garibaldi, Claudia Olivetti, Barbara Petrongolo, and Etienne Wasmer 2005. "Women in the Labour Force: How Well Is Europe Doing?" In *Women at Work: An Economic Perspective*, edited by Tito Boeri, Daniela Del Boca, and Christopher Pissarides, 7–104. Oxford, U.K.: Oxford University Press.

Pollak, Robert A. 2005. "Bargaining Power in Marriage: Earnings, Wage Rates, and Household Production." NBER Working Paper 11239, National Bureau of Economic Research, Cambridge, MA.

Quisumbing, Agnes R., Kelly Hallman, and Marie T. Ruel. 2007. "Maquiladoras and Market Mamas: Women's Work and Childcare in Guatemala City and Accra." *Journal of Development Studies* 43 (3): 420–55.

Salas, Carlos, and Marcia Leite. 2007. "Segregación sectorial por género: Una comparación Brasil-México." *Brazilian Journal of Latin American Studies* 2 (7): 241–59.

Samuelson, Paul A. 1956. "Social Indifference Curves." *Quarterly Journal of Economics* 70 (1): 1–22.

Schady, Norbert R., and José Rosero. 2008. "Are Cash Transfers Made to Women Spent Like Other Sources of Income?" *Economics Letters* 101 (3): 246–48.

Sedlacek, Guilherme Luis, and Eleonora Cruz Santos. 1991. "A mulher cônjuge no mercado de trabalho como estratégia de geração de renda familiar." *Pesquisa e Planejamento Econômico* 21 (3): 449–70.

Sinha, Nistha, and José Montes. 2010. "Impact of Conditional Cash Transfer Programs on Women's Labor Supply: Evidence from Peru's Juntos Program." Background paper for this report, World Bank, Washington, DC.

Skoufias, Emmanuel, and Vincenzo Di Maro. 2008. "Conditional Cash Transfers, Adult Work Incentives, and Poverty." *Journal of Development Studies* 44 (7): 935–60.

Soares, Sergei. 2002. "Female Labor Force Participation in Brazil: 1977–2001." IPEA Working Paper 923, Institute of Applied Economic Research, Brasília.

Thomas, Duncan. 1990. "Intra-household Resource Allocation: An Inferential Approach." *Journal of Human Resources* 25 (4): 635–64.

Udry, Christopher. 1996. "Gender, Agricultural Production, and the Theory of the Household." *Journal of Political Economy* 104 (5): 1010–46.

van Dijk, Liset, and Jacques J. Siegers. 1996. "The Division of Child Care among Mothers, Fathers, and Nonparental Care Providers in Dutch Two-Parent Families." *Journal of Marriage and Family* 58 (4): 1018–28.

Vegas, Emiliana, and Lucrecia Santibáñez. 2010. *The Promise of Early Childhood Development in Latin America and the Caribbean*. Washington, DC: World Bank.

7
Concluding Remarks

Introduction

Latin America and the Caribbean (LAC) has experienced remarkable achievements in terms of gender parity in several key areas, including health, fertility, maternal mortality, and education. Over recent decades, girls have even been outperforming boys on a number of education indicators. A significant portion of these achievements is owing to girls' increased attainment at the higher levels of education. In fact, they are today more likely than boys to be enrolled in secondary and tertiary school and also more likely to complete both. The female share of the total population has risen in tandem with both female and male life expectancy at birth, the gender gap of which has widened in favor of women. Fertility rates in Latin America have dropped dramatically over the past 50 years, converging to those of high-income countries of the Organisation for Economic Co-operation and Development (OECD).

Over the past five decades, LAC has also witnessed unprecedented growth in female labor force participation (LFP), with nearly 80 million additional women entering the labor force since 1970. Female LFP has risen faster in LAC over the past three decades than in any other region, rising from roughly 36 percent in 1980 to more than 53 percent in 2014. In most LAC countries, the rate of female LFP has at least doubled since the 1960s, and it has tripled in Brazil. Improvements in human capital investments, changes in the structure of the family, and changes in the degree to which the market rewards them account for a large fraction of the observed trends. The expanded professional engagement of women has translated into higher political participation, with the share of parliamentary seats held by women in LAC in line with OECD figures.

New challenges for women and policy makers

In light of the region's remarkable achievements over the past five decades, concluding that the gains in access mechanically translate into gains in labor market outcomes and that welfare can unequivocally be inferred from these trends may be tempting. The findings in this study caution against such simplistic views and urge a deeper understanding of women's decision-making processes to improve the design and efficacy of policy.

The relationship between economic development and female economic participation is neither linear nor monotone. The interplay of several microeconomic factors gives rise to one of the most robust empirical regularities in the literature linking female LFP and economic development. In addition, in LAC female participation initially declines with development then rises again and draws different subgroups of women into the labor force in a heterogeneous fashion. This report provides insight on the complex interplay between economic development and female economic participation. Single women enter the labor force at earlier stages than their married counterparts, with their behavior mimicking that of men; married women and mothers then follow in degrees that vary with their characteristics, including their level of education, cohort, and family structure.

The relationship between female participation and economic development is made more complex by the acknowledgment that individuals are part of larger economic units—families. Whatever the reasons for family formation—be it a Beckerian motive to take advantage of complementarities in consumption and economies of scale in the provision of household public goods or a desire to achieve a sense of belonging that enhances intrinsic values and meets the aspirations of social relatedness (Maslow 1943)—intrahousehold dynamics play a central role in determining welfare and in the efficiency and equity of outcomes. At the core of the recognition that household interactions play a mediating role in outcomes is the implicit assumption that men and women, while equal in rights, differ along several important dimensions beyond the obvious physical comparative advantages in fertility.

For these reasons, divergences of opinion, preferences, and comparative advantages are negotiated within the household to reach decisions regarding the division of labor, child care responsibilities, home versus market production, and the like. In some cases, intrahousehold interactions can yield efficient specialization among spouses, such that both spouses do not have identical degrees of engagement in the labor force. In other instances, the interaction may lead to inefficient allocations of resources, destructive outcomes, or both, as in the extreme case of domestic violence, making a case for policy interventions on equity and efficiency grounds.

The evidence and analysis in the report tie the historical process of female economic integration and widening choice sets to a fundamental change in paradigm in women's decision making (Goldin 2006). This paradigmatic transformation includes a shift in the horizon over which women's human capital investments yield returns and, consequently, in their attachment to the labor market. It also includes a contemporaneous shift in women's perceptions whereby they consider their work a fundamental part of their identity, which is related to the distinction between jobs and careers.

These complex transformations widen women's opportunities and aspirations and pose new tensions and challenges for women, which, paradoxically, have been made possible by five decades of steady gains. Understanding the nature and sources of tension for women trying to balance work and family is thus crucial for policy.

However, women's ability to balance their new identities with traditional responsibilities is not without its challenges. Whether with regard to child care choices, part-time employment opportunities, or sectoral allocations, an unmet demand for flexibility consistently emerges among women who are married and women who have children.

Transition patterns between the formal and informal sectors were found to be consistent with their being voluntary and driven by family structure. Women's responses to Argentina's legalization of part-time work in 1995 are also consistent with this view. A large fraction of married women with children rapidly transitioned to formal employment from their previous positions in the informal sector, without any appreciable effect on aggregate female LFP. This behavior reveals a preference for formal—yet flexible—forms of employment among married mothers, suggesting that, before 1995 the demand for flexible arrangements was met by the informal sector, in which women with children were overrepresented, but that formal sector options, in which social security protections are granted, were preferred.

A similar form of substitution is encountered in the response to the introduction of universal child care. A robust finding across virtually all the studies considered (in LAC and OECD economies) is that the effect of universal child care provision on use is sizable: eligibility for public child care provision invariably results in high take-up rates. The significant demand for formal child care services appears to result largely from crowding-out of existing arrangements whereby working mothers who relied on informal child care arrangements before their eligibility—for instance, through agreements with extended-family members—chose the public option.

Satisfying the previously unmet demand for formal child care appears to improve the quality of participation in the labor market for some women, with the increase in quality occurring along the intensive margin of participation (that is, how many hours worked) or sorting into higher-productivity jobs.

The welfare gains from lifting constraints on women and families such as those discussed here are potentially large even though, in both instances, the intervention drew no new women into the labor force. Instead, the behavioral responses come from more subtle forms of substitution exclusively among mothers who would have worked in the absence of the intervention (in the case of free child care provision, the response also involved increased hours worked). Formality is thus highly valued, while the provision of subsidized child care has the potential to increase mother's quality of life by lifting concerns about child care and the quality of their participation in the labor market.

Although not discussed formally in this report, maternal leave policies have in recent years received considerable attention as an instrument for easing constraints on households and enhancing the quality of working women's lives. Part of the interest in these policies is related not only to their high take-up rates, which signal workers' high valuations for this type of benefit and their potential to mitigate the incidence of "mother's guilt," but also to their important benefits for children's cognitive and non-cognitive development in the medium and long runs (see, for example, Carneiro, Løken, and Salvanes 2015). The latter observations are of particular interest in light of potential trade-offs surrounding female LFP discussed in the literature, stressing that, in some cases, the additional income made available to women by being in the labor force may not compensate for the reduction in time investments in their children. More broadly, the welfare consequences of these policies may not be limited to the short run. Interventions that alleviate the burden on working mothers and facilitate balancing work and life can afford parents the possibility of higher-quality parenting and enable them to be present at critical periods of their children's development. With research showing that nurturing children early is beneficial to child development and yields long-term rewards in the form of improved health, human capital, and productivity (Carneiro, Cunha, and Heckman 2003), policies that help reconcile work and parenthood can generate social returns in the long run.

This report has uncovered and highlighted strong parallels between the experiences of women in the region and those in the United States. Specifically, the evolution of LFP of single and married women in LAC mimicked very closely that of American women, only at a 30-year lag. If the analogy to the U.S. experience is extended, the history of American women's experiences could provide a glimpse into the future for LAC, a future that may come sooner than 30 years, given the region's current pace.

Despite the extraordinary progress of U.S. women over recent decades, measures of subjective well-being indicate that women's happiness has declined both in absolute terms and relative to men. In the 1970s, women reported higher subjective well-being than men; the relative declines in female happiness have eroded and reversed a gender gap in happiness that has been linked to the expanding roles and identities of women (Stevenson and Wolfers 2009). Similar trends are found across different measures of subjective well-being, demographic groups, and industrial countries. The literature has also drawn attention to another form of trade-off, this time operating across generations. Maternal employment may be associated with lower child health and cognitive outcomes, suggesting the possibility that the additional income may not compensate for the reduction in time investments in children, particularly during the early and critical stages of human development. For instance, Bernal (2008) documents that having a full-time working mother who uses child care during one of the first five years after childbirth is associated with a 1.8 percent reduction in child test scores. In turn, Morrill (2011) documents that the probability of an overnight hospitalization, an asthma episode, or an injury or poisoning rises by 200 percent with full-time working mothers.

As a possible reflection of some of these tensions, after a century of remarkable gains in economic engagement, female LFP leveled off in the United States in the late 1990s despite continued advances in educational attainment. Given that the LFP of college-educated women had almost reached parity with men's in the mid-1990s, the slight retreat was particularly disappointing for the women's movement. The phenomenon was characterized in the popular press as "opting out" (Belkin 2003; Story 2005; Wallis 2004), wherein changing attitudes may have included backlash from the workplace that made it difficult for women to reconcile their dual identities as "homemaker" and "career woman." Among the professional and managerial ranks, where higher incomes afforded them a wide range of choices, women became more reluctant to juggle their roles as executives and mothers, and more willing to forgo paychecks and prestige in favor of time with their families (Wallis 2004). Conceivably, a similar phenomenon may occur in LAC in the coming decades.

This and other evidence reviewed in the report illustrate a new set of challenges for women made possible by the five decades of achievements and identify new needs for policy intervention to address the delicate and complicated issues of navigating women's expanded set of opportunities.

A new menu of gender policies and a new focus

Today, the complex environment requires women to balance different roles, identities, and aspirations. Jobs, careers, and family place competing demands on women's time and attention, more so than at any other time, and pose new challenges for them and for policy makers. Gender policy in LAC is at a crucial juncture that calls for an expansion of the policy perspective.

This need is in large part the product of success, for substantial progress—amply documented in this study—toward achieving gender parity in key dimensions relating to human dignity has occurred, particularly access to basic services (for example, health, education) and fundamental human rights. These achievements are welcome, because they implicate universal principles that should apply to all humans, independently of sex, race, religion, and so on.[1]

Nevertheless, the policy goal of gender parity with respect to basic rights and services has not been fully or uniformly reached across the region. Much room for improvement remains, particularly where chronic poverty is intertwined with precarious access and where certain institutional arrangements and social norms breed systematic barriers for women. But the improvements in the circumstances of women in LAC over the past decades are undeniable and call for a reassessment and expansion of the policy focus.

The first generation of gender policies in LAC tended to set quantitative objectives for gender parity—focusing not only on equal access (such as to health, education, and judicial services) but also on equality in certain outcomes (such as equal pay for comparable experiences and skills, or equal participation in the labor force, in electoral ballots, or in congressional seats). This focus is appropriate to the extent that societies are trapped in inefficient and inequitable equilibria characterized by discrimination and abuse of women. In such a context, quantitative gender parity targets to monitor achievements can help societies break free from an unfair status quo.

But as the standing of women improves and their opportunities and choices widen—as is happening in LAC—new issues, tensions, and challenges arise. They point to the need for a second generation of gender policies, one that would still encompass certain (more focused) quantitative targets for gender parity but that would also go well beyond them.

The evidence and analysis presented in this study indicate that women in LAC confront competing demands for their time and energy as they, on the one hand, join the labor force and increasingly see employment as part of a career (rather than a simple source of income) and, on the other hand, seek self-realization through marriage, motherhood, and family. These complexities have to be brought to the center stage of policy design.

Of course, no one-size-fits-all policy agenda is well suited to these changing gender realities. Reform agendas have to be adapted to the context of individual countries. But the evidence examined in this study suggests at least three key directions for the new generation of policies.

> The highest equality is equity.
> —*Victor Hugo*

First and foremost is the need to revise gender policy's *goals and expectations*. This follows naturally from the recognition that the equalization across genders of access to basic services and fundamental human rights does not translate mechanically or monotonically into the equalization of outcomes, such as the extent and modality of female economic participation. Nor are outcomes a perfect reflection of well-being.

The ascribed role of preferences, household relationships, institutions, and social mores as mediating factors invites a change in policy perspective from gender parity (which is akin to gender blindness) to *gender consciousness*. In turn, gender consciousness entails an emphasis on equity over equality. Although equality implies sameness and, by definition, ignores differences, equity recognizes differences and engages them to facilitate the realization of each person's potential to the fullest extent possible—to which gender consciousness aspires.

The emphasis on equity sets the stage for policies that expand women's freedom, namely the freedom to choose one's identity and to exercise that choice without facing discrimination or disadvantage. The capability of a person to choose, do, and be can be seen as an essential determinant of well-being. These principles are at the heart of Amartya Sen's notion of development as the process of enhancing freedoms, and of an approach to development that:

...concentrates on the capabilities of people to do things—and the freedom to live lives—that they have reason to value.

—*Amartya Sen*

Second, acknowledging that men and women differ in substantive ways and that their differences are mediated through interactions within the household has important policy implications and yields an *expanded menu of policies* to address gender issues. These new policies have the potential not only to affect equity of allocations within the household, but also to increase effectiveness of policy instruments and ultimately elevate the discussion regarding their welfare implications. With the notable exception of conditional cash transfers, which are designed on the presumption that money in the hands of women is spent differently, household interactions are seldom exploited in the design of policy. The unexploited richness of (gender) policy instruments represents a missed opportunity that needs correction by embedding in policy design certain insights on household dynamics.

As discussed in this report, in some cases, intrahousehold interactions can yield efficient allocations of resources, with both spouses gaining from cooperation. In such instances, policy interventions would be justified only on equity grounds. In noncooperative households, in turn, inefficient or destructive outcomes may arise, as in the extreme instance of domestic violence, thus justifying policy interventions on both equity and efficiency grounds. This discussion emphasizes the value of understanding the types of conditions that affect bargaining positions within the household and that have the potential to curb abusive and nonconsensual behaviors.

Whether directed at women by design or not, any government intervention that influences women's control over fertility, their ability to choose a spouse with certain characteristics, and their realized and potential labor market outcomes can affect the bargaining positions of women within the household and thus the final allocation of resources. Bargaining positions of spouses and their subsequent interactions are not only affected by each spouse's direct control over resources (income, time, or otherwise), but also by their prospects outside the union, should they leave it. Credible exit options raise the incentives for nonconflictual, respectful behavior within existing unions. These policies can thus contribute to reducing the risk of abusive relationships as well as to widening the scope for self-realization of women within the household. Hence, the expanded menu of policies could extend to reforms that include the provision of social insurance, the legal definition of informal unions (for example, unmarried cohabitation) and their corresponding parental obligations, the introduction of antidiscrimination laws, any regulation that directly or indirectly affects sectors or occupations dominated by one gender, the modernization of divorce laws, and the enhancement of property rights and even criminal laws.

> Balancing work and family is one of the country's major challenges. The government wants to change labor laws that have companies help bear the cost of day care, making women more expensive to hire.
> — *Carolina Schmidt, Chile's Minister of National Women's Service,*
> *telephone interview*

Third, this study documents women's need for greater freedom to choose their identities, which manifests itself as an *unmet demand for flexibility*. This puts a premium on policies that help women find an equilibrium among competing demands. Women's ability to balance their new identities with traditional responsibilities is full of challenges. Whether with regard to child care choices or part-time employment opportunities, an unmet demand for flexibility consistently emerges among women who are married or who have children or both. Unfortunately, formal labor market institutions are still woefully insensitive to these realities. Although some, albeit still limited, progress has been made in LAC in terms of regulations concerning maternity leave and the provision of child care services, for instance, formal labor contracts remain unduly rigid compared to women's needs. In the short run, these rigidities do not appear to prevent women from entering the labor force, but all too often married women in LAC resort to informal employment and trade basic labor protections and career advancement for the job flexibility that facilitates balancing family responsibilities.

Legislation that acknowledges the pressures of motherhood and of the day-to-day demands on households' time, more generally, can generate important social returns by enabling women to fulfill their identities as mothers and workers, raising the quality of their economic participation and thereby increasing their well-being as well as that of the entire household.

Indeed, the welfare consequences of the previously mentioned policies may not be limited to the short run. Interventions that alleviate the burden on working mothers and facilitate balancing work and life can afford parents the possibility of higher-quality parenting. Providing flexible alternatives that do not compromise working mothers' career objectives may attenuate the stress exerted by such trade-offs, which have been implicated in the recent emergence of a gap in subjective well-being that favors men in certain industrialized countries. Furthermore, invoking such institutions to foster a healthy equilibrium between work and family can mitigate some of the intergenerational costs that might arise from maternal employment in the event that children's health and development benefit from time spent with their mothers.

Hence, a key policy message from this study concerns the need to revisit labor market institutions and regulations from the gender-conscious perspective that focuses on welfare-enhancing flexibility. Any policy aimed at addressing the new set of issues facing women has to wrestle with (and ideally take advantage of) the fact that women's outcomes in the labor market—including whether or not to work; if working, how much to work; and how to combine work and family—are the result of unobservable household negotiations that depend to a large extent on individual preferences over work and family. Two women who are outside the labor market may have very different reasons for that status that a gender-conscious policy should detect. One may have simply decided to invest more time and energy in her children while taking advantage of her spouse's income. The other may prefer to work in a job but be stymied by the lack of flexible contracts in the formal labor market from fulfilling her desired roles in both motherhood and the professional realm. Labor market outcomes alone are not always informative about welfare, because they distinguish only imperfectly between unhindered decisions and institutional barriers (such as discrimination, rigidity in the labor market, social norms, and the like). In this context, policy can play a role by guaranteeing an environment that is devoid of discrimination and provide a richer menu of options in the labor market that recognizes the trade-offs that women face (as their choices widen) in the pursuit of self-actualization.

Conclusion

In its approach and in the evidence provided, this regional study has endeavored to draw attention to the importance of intrahousehold decision making in shaping gender outcomes. In addition to traditional inputs such as education and income, a household's choices are shaped by social norms, preferences, and expectations, as well as by the manner in which its members interact with one another. The remarkable gains achieved to date by women and girls in LAC on basic indicators such as education, health, and fertility suggest a role for a "second generation" gender agenda, which requires deeper insight into the ways in which household members interact, reach decisions, and allocate resources, as well as of the forces that influence them.

Refocusing attention on the household requires the use (and possibly the development) of analytical tools that can distinguish outcomes arising from unconstrained choices from those restrained by barriers or discrimination toward certain members, whether from social forces or from within the household. The analysis in the report stresses the importance of following individuals over the life cycle to better understand how life events shape the various margins of participation (extensive and intensive) and how preferences and constraints evolve as individuals progress through the various stages of their lives. The lack of available panel data motivated a synthetic cohort approach, which, although it can provide insight, does not allow us to uncover differences in behavior within cohort. Nor does it lend itself to exploring the richness of intergenerational links in participation or shed light on the interplay between norms, experience, and preferences. Finally, by acknowledging that outcomes are incomplete and sometimes misleading indicators of welfare, a challenge is to identify or incorporate a measure of welfare in analyses that focus on multidimensional trade-offs that do not necessarily arise from a simple earnings-maximizing objective.

Progress on this research agenda is made all the more pressing because the intrahousehold perspective can significantly enrich the set of instruments in policy makers' portfolios to affect the welfare of households—and of women in particular. Furthermore, recognition of household interactions may help increase the efficiency and efficacy of policies, precisely by exploiting the manner in which household members interact, for instance, by enhancing women's outside options. Finally, this perspective provides a framework for understanding the different constraints and work-life trade-offs that different household members face. Acknowledging these in policy design will require trading the principle of gender blindness for that of gender awareness, whereby policy recognizes the distinct demands and constraints faced by women relative to men, for instance by adopting labor market policies that alleviate the increasing burdens of balancing motherhood and work.

Of course, given the heterogeneity in gains across countries in LAC, this new agenda should not overshadow or detract from continued efforts to improve human capital and fertility outcomes in those countries that lag the region. These efforts may nonetheless also benefit from the household perspective to the extent that it illuminates new and effective policies that eliminate barriers and distortions. Similarly, despite the noteworthy achievements, the new agenda should not lose sight of the importance of policies intended to eradicate toxic environments, such as discriminatory labor markets or households in which choices are dictated by acts or threats of physical or emotional violence.

Note

[1] Documenting the effect of first-generation policies is beyond the scope of the study. The decline in fertility rates as well as the closing of a number of education gaps is indirectly documented and discussed in this study (and references provided) because of their role in explaining the increasing presence of women in the labor force. Overall, some consensus exists on the lack of rigorous causal evidence on their effects. For instance, the evidence on electoral quotas is in its infancy and provides ambiguous conclusions. For a discussion of the history and role of political quotas in developing countries, see Pande and Ford (2011) and World Bank (2011).

References

Belkin, Lisa. 2003. "The Opt-Out Revolution." *New York Times Magazine*, October 26.

Bernal, Raquel. 2008. "The Effect of Maternal Employment and Child Care on Children's Cognitive Development." *International Economic Review* 49 (4): 1173–209.

Carneiro, Pedro, Flavio Cunha, and James Heckman. 2003. "Interpreting the Evidence of Family Influence on Child Development." Research report supported by National Institute for Child

Health and Development NICHD R01-34598-03. http://athens.uchicago.edu/jenni/klmcarn /FILES/minnesota/paper.pdf.

Carneiro, Pedro, Katrine V. Løken, and Kjell G. Salvanes. 2015. "A Flying Start? Maternity Leave Benefits and Long-Run Outcomes of Children." *Journal of Political Economy* 123 (2): 365–412.

Goldin, Claudia. 2006. "Quiet Revolution That Transformed Women's Employment, Education, and Family." *American Economic Review Papers and Proceedings* 96 (2): 1–21.

Maslow, Abraham H. 1943. "Theory of Human Motivation." *Psychological Review* 50 (4): 370–96.

Morrill, Melinda Sandler. 2011. "The Effects of Maternal Employment on the Health of School-Age Children." *Journal of Health Economics* 30 (2): 240–57.

Pande, Rohini, and Deanna Ford. 2011. "Gender Quotas and Female Leadership: A Review." Background paper for the *World Development Report 2012*, World Bank, Washington, DC.

Sen, Amartya. 1999. *Development as Freedom*. (New York: Knopf).

Stevenson, Betsey, and Justin Wolfers. 2009. "The Paradox of Declining Female Happiness." *American Economic Journal: Economic Policy* 1 (2): 190–225.

Story, Louise. 2005. "Many Women at Elite Colleges Set Career Path to Motherhood." *New York Times*, September 20.

Wallis, Claudia. 2004. "The Case for Staying Home." *Time Magazine*, March 22.

World Bank. 2011. *World Development Report 2012: Gender Equality and Development*. Washington, DC: World Bank.

Appendix: Background Papers

1. "Gender Wage Gaps in LAC." Alejandro Hoyos and Hugo Ñopo, 2010.
2. "The Rise of Female Labor Force Participation Rate in LAC, 1960–2000." Laura Chioda and Gabriel Demombynes, 2010.
3. "How Family Formation Has Shaped Labor Force Participation in LAC." Laura Chioda, 2011.
4. "Who Gains What from Education? Regression Discontinuity Evidence from Colombia." Laura Chioda, 2011b.
5. "Women on the Move: Female Labor Market Dynamics in the Developing World." Mariano Bosch and William Maloney, 2011.
6. "Female Headed Households and Poverty in LAC: What Are We Measuring?" Tami Aritomi, Analia Olgiati, and Maria Beatriz Orlando, 2010.
7. "Factors Influencing Occupational and Sector Choice by Male and Female Workers." Maria Beatriz Orlando and José Montes, 2010.
8. "Impact of Conditional Cash Transfer Programs on Women's Labor Supply: Evidence from Peru's Juntos Program." Nistha Sinha and José Montes, 2010.
9. "The Role of Conditional Cash Transfers in Reducing Spousal Abuse in Mexico: Short-Term vs. Long-Term Effects." Gustavo J. Bobonis and Roberto Castro, 2010.
10. "Impact of Free Childcare on Female Labor Force Participation: Evidence from Low-Income Neighborhoods in Rio de Janeiro." Mirela Carvalho, Trine Lunde, Pedro Olinto, and Ricardo Paes de Barros, 2010.
11. "Efficient Responses to Targeted Cash Transfers." Orazio Attanasio and Valérie Lechêne, 2010.
12. "Linking Labor Market Outcomes and Intra-Household Dynamics." Laura Chioda, Rodrigo García-Verdú, and Ana Maria Muñoz Boudet, 2010.

Index

Boxes, figures, notes, and tables are indicated by *"b," "f," "n,"* and *"t"* respectively.

family formation and its relationship to
 level of education, 108, 109, 109*f*,
 119–28. *See also* family formation and
 household structure
homeownership, 135–36
household production technology, 134*f*,
 135–36
sectoral structure of the economy, 134*f*, 136
single vs. married women and education,
 128–32. *See also* single vs. married
 women
urbanization, 108, 133, 134*f*
developed countries. *See also* OECD countries;
 United States
allocation of resources for child welfare in, 183
changes in sectoral structure of the
 economy in, 136
delays in fertility, effect on marriage in, 121
female labor force participation in, 86
gender of child, effect on parent's allocation
 of resources in, 183
gender wage gaps in, 157–58, 173*n*2
household production technology, effect
 of, 135
part-time jobs, women in, 204
shift in women's view of employment from
 jobs to careers, 108
sick days, men vs. women using in, 170–71
traditional gender models, attitudes on, 7
Di Maro, Vincenzo, 187
discrimination. *See* antidiscrimination laws;
 employment discrimination; gender
 attitudes; gender parity
divorce and dissolution of marriage, 12, 50,
 77*n*9, 185, 191, 192, 224
divorce threat, 11–12, 20, 24*n*10, 185, 192,
 210*n*5, 223
domestic violence, 189–92, 210*n*11, 226
Dominican Republic
gender wage gaps in, 155, 163*f*, 173*n*6
maternal age at first child in, 46–47*f*
parliaments, female representation in, 78*n*13
teen pregnancy rates in, 13*n*2
Doss, Cheryl, 210*n*9
Duflo, Esther, 183

E

earnings, gender differences in. *See* wage gaps
 between genders
East Asia. *See* comparisons of LAC to other
 regions

economic development
gender wage gaps and, 162
poverty reduction, xv, 2–4, 179. *See also*
 conditional cash transfer (CCT) programs
"quiet revolution" in, 107, 141
relationship with female economic
 participation, 3–4, 76, 92–93*b*, 218
GDP per capita, 74–75*f*
Ecuador
Bono de Desarrollo Humano (Human
 Development Voucher), 184
changes in sectoral structure of the
 economy in, 134*f*, 136
education levels of attainment, historical
 trends in, 112
family formation, relationship to female
 labor force participation in, 120
female-headed households in, 50, 51*f*
female labor force participation in, 88–90*f*,
 89, 94
cohort and age profiles, 102, 103*f*
married females, 101*f*
single females, 100*f*
fertility rates in, 2, 45
gender wage gaps in, 155, 163, 163*f*,
 165*f*, 173*n*6
maternal employment levels in, 122, 125
parliaments, female representation in, 2,
 78*n*13
returns to education in, 111–12*f*
cohort differences, 113–16, 114–115*f*
combined with factors of marriage and
 fertility, 123*f*
single vs. married women, 129–30*f*
World Values Survey data from, 53
Edmonds, Eric V., 183
education, 22, 29–37, 110–19
achievement patterns by gender, 33,
 36–37*f*, 37
closing of gender gap, 155, 192–93*b*
compulsory schooling, 192–93*b*
as determinant of trends in female labor
 force participation, 85, 94, 108, 109,
 109*f*, 110–19, 125
decomposition exercise, 137*n*4
diploma or degree completion (sheepskin
 effect), 116
disparities in progress across countries, 33, 37
enrollment rates of girls, 1, 13*n*1, 15,
 77*n*2, 217
primary education, 30, 31*f*, 77*n*3
secondary education, 30, 32*f*

tertiary education, 30, 77n4
wage gaps and, 167
indigenous populations, gender
inequality in, 1
level of attainment, 1, 33, 34–35f,
110, 217
as determinant of female labor force
participation, 112–13
family formation and, 120–28
female-headed households and, 50
of married vs. single women in
workforce, 3
secondary education, 33, 35f
tertiary education, 33, 35f, 77n4, 113,
125–26, 128–31, 130f, 161
wage gaps and, 155–56t, 157, 157f,
159–60t, 159–61, 173–74n7
preschool attendance and parental labor
supply, 211n13
quality of education, 37
returns to, 30, 110–16, 111–12f
cohort differences, 108–9, 111, 113–
16, 114–15f, 123, 124, 128, 133,
135, 137nn6–7
combined with factors of marriage and
fertility, 123f
compulsory education requirements,
193b
convexification of, 173–74n7
single vs. married women, 128–32,
129–30f
social and cultural views of women's role,
effect of education on, 53, 54–55t, 62,
76–77n1
wage premium as disincentive for, 4, 167
egalitarian views, 53, 56–63, 96
business leaders, men vs. women as, 60,
60f, 62, 63
disparities across LAC countries, 62–63
disparities by generation, 62–63
jobs considered to be male prerogative, 56,
57f, 63, 119
political leaders, men vs. women as, 57f,
59, 59f, 61–63
electricity, access to, 135, 138n16
El Salvador
fertility rates in, 2, 13n2, 45
gender wage gaps in, 155, 162, 163, 163f
life expectancy, men vs. women in, 40
parliaments, female representation in,
78n13

employment discrimination, 15, 119, 143, 154,
167, 174n9. *See also* antidiscrimination
laws
employment status, defined, 104n2
EMPSTAT, 104n2
Engel's law, 184
equality of opportunity approach, 24n13
equity vs. equality, 10–11, 222
social equity, progress in, 2–3
Europe and Central Asia. *See* comparisons of
LAC to other regions
European Union
child care in, 201
female-headed households in, 51f
gender wage gaps in, 157
European Values Study, 77n12
Evans, William N., 121–22, 124

family formation and household structure, 49–50,
218. *See also* children in household;
fertility rates, decline in; household
dynamics; single vs. married women
age at first marriage, 47, 48–49f
compensating transfers across household
members, 125
definitions of households, 24–25n3
as determinant of trends in female labor
force participation, 85, 109, 109f,
116–19, 117–18f
education level and, 120–28
female-headed households, 13n3, 50, 51f,
56, 132b
as microsocial factor in determining
economic opportunity for women, 5–6,
15, 16f
withdrawal of women from labor force and,
120. *See also* children in household
Farber, Henry S., 205
farming
transition of economy from agriculture to
manufacturing, 120
wage differentials due to male
overrepresentation in, 174n8
West African households' inefficiency in,
21, 190
Fehr-Duda, Helga, 170
female attitudes
executive positions considered to be male
prerogative, 62

cost of child care related to female labor
participation rate in, 197–98
education in
girls' enrollment rates, 13n1, 30, 37, 167
girls' levels of attainment, 1, 4, 33
primary education enrollment rates,
77n3
gender wage gaps in, 4, 155, 162, 163f,
165f, 167
indigenous populations, gender inequality
in education in, 1
maternal age at first child in, 46–47f
parliaments, female representation in, 78n13
teen pregnancy rates in, 13n2
World Values Survey data from, 53
Guiso, Luigi, 77n10
Guyana parliaments, female representation
in, 78n13

H

Haiti
fertility rates in, 2, 45
life expectancy, men vs. women in, 40
maternal age at first child in, 46–47f
parliaments, female representation in, 2
school enrollment rates of girls vs. boys
in, 13n1
Hallman, Kelly, 198
health, 22, 38–42
birth ratios, male to female, 77n5
gender equality in LAC in, 1–2
improvements in female health care, 2
life expectancy, 38, 39–40, 40–41f,
76–77n1, 217
maternal mortality rates, xv, 2, 40–41,
42–43f
sex imbalance of male to female, 38–39,
38–39f
homeownership, 135–36
Honduras
full-time vs. part-time work in, 206
gender wage gaps in, 155, 163, 163f, 173n6
parliaments, female representation in, 78n13
school enrollment rates of girls vs. boys
in, 13n1
household dynamics, 6, 16, 17, 23, 179–216
asset holdings as factor in, 210n9
bargaining power, 19, 187, 191, 192,
210n9, 223
child care and women's labor supply,
194–202

competing demands on women's time
and economic participation, 192–93,
194, 209
control over resources, effect on female
labor force participation, 6, 7, 186–
89, 223
cooperative bargaining, 19–20, 24n10,
184–85, 223
difficulty in studying, 179–80, 225–26
divorce threat, effect of, 11–12, 20, 24n10,
185, 192, 210n5, 223
domestic violence and, 189–92,
210n11, 226
intrahousehold allocations and bargaining,
6, 20, 21–22, 59, 124, 182–84,
218, 223
leisure, related to increase of resources, 187
noncooperative environment, 21, 138n14,
189, 223
part-time arrangements and economic
participation, 202–3
preferences of husbands vs. wives, 19,
24n8, 124, 218
public policy and, 180, 225
shadow price of home production and, 187
unitary models and income pooling, 17–22,
18f, 24n8, 182–84, 209nn1–2
household production technology, 134f,
135–36
Hoyos, Alejandro, 155, 159, 160, 167, 172,
173n1, 173n5, 174n7
Hubbard, William H. J., 77n4
Hugo, Victor, 10, 222
human capital. *See also* education; health
definition of, 24n2
as microsocial factor in determining
economic opportunity for women,
15, 16f, 17
occupational choice and, 141
human dignity, 6, 9, 221
human rights, 6, 9, 221

I

Ichino, Andrea, 171
identities, women's, 5, 7, 11, 12, 17, 219.
See also career choices
ability to choose, 222–23
level of education as factor, 126
occupation as factor, 108
tension in roles, 8. *See also* work-life
balance

income gap. *See* wage gaps between genders
income pooling in household, 182–84, 209*n*1
   cooperative bargaining and, 185
indigenous populations, gender inequality in
   education of, 1, 33
infant mortality, 76*n*1
infertility shocks, 122–23, 137*n*11
informal sector jobs, 12
   definition of, 142
   overrepresentation of women in, 142,
      199, 224
   transitions between formal and informal
      sectors, 141–51
      evidence across the business cycle,
         147–49
      part-time work in formal sector, 9, 181
      rationing vs. choice reflected in,
         144–47, 145*f*
Integrated Public Use Microdata Series
   (IPUMS), 104*n*2, 104*n*4, 108, 121,
   136, 137*n*10
intergenerational effects, 12, 13*n*4, 77*n*1, 96,
   127, 202, 203, 224, 225. *See also* social
   and cultural norms
International Labour Organization, 143*b*
intrahousehold allocations, 6, 11, 182–84.
   See also household dynamics
Iyigun, Murat, 119

J

Jamaica
   age at birth of first child in, 46
   teleservices industry in, 149
job tenure, effect on wage differentials,
   168–69, 168*t*

K

Kahn, Lawrence M., 153
Katz, Lawrence F., 171
Kaufmann, Katja M., 119

L

labor force participation (LFP), 16–17. *See also*
   female labor force participation; male
   labor force participation
   gender gap in participation, 72–76, 72*f*
labor market reforms, 9, 13, 13*n*4, 224
   part-time work in Argentina, 9, 181,
      206–9, 219

Lai, Lei, 170
Latin America and the Caribbean (LAC).
   See also specific countries
   comparison to other regions. *See*
      comparisons of LAC to other regions
   determinants of female labor force
      participation in, 107–40. *See also*
      determinants of trends in female labor
      force participation
   education trends in, 29–37. *See also*
      education
   family formation in, 49–50. *See also* family
      formation and household structure
   female labor force participation in. *See*
      female labor force participation
   fertility rates in. *See* fertility rates, decline in
   gender wage gaps in, 153–76. *See also* wage
      gaps between genders
   health in, 38–42. *See also* health
   household dynamics in, 179–216. *See also*
      household dynamics
   marital status as factor in. *See* single vs.
      married women
   policy goals of gender parity in, 9–13.
      See also policy goals of gender parity
   social norms in, 50–70. *See also* social and
      cultural norms
   transitional behaviors between formal
      and informal sectors, 142–51. *See also*
      transitional behaviors, men vs. women
Lechêne, Valérie, 184, 210*n*4
legislative action. *See* divorce and dissolution of
   marriage; labor market reforms
life expectancy improvements for women, 2, 38,
   39–40, 40–41*f*, 76–77*n*1, 217
life satisfaction and part-time work, 206
Loewenstein, George F., 170
López Bóo, Florencia, 206
Lundberg, Shelly J., 20, 24*n*10, 183

M

Madrigal, Lucia, 206
male attitudes. *See also* egalitarian views
   jobs considered to be male prerogative,
      56, 57*f*, 119
   negotiation intensity, 170
   overconfidence, 170
   political leaders, men better suited than
      women as, 57*f*, 59
   preferences and risk-taking behavior, 5, 6,
      169–70

4884046